Patterns
FOR Living
FROM THE OLD TESTAMENT

Patterns
FOR Living
FROM THE OLD TESTAMENT

PAUL F. IRELAND

WINEPRESS **WP** PUBLISHING

Unless otherwise noted, all Scriptures are taken from the Holy Bible, New International Version, Copyright © 1973, 1978, 1984 by the International Bible Society. Used by permission of Zondervan Publishing House. The "NIV" and "New International Version" trademarks are registered in the United States Patent and Trademark Office by International Bible Society.

Scripture references marked KJV are taken from the King James Version of the Bible.

ISBN 13: 978-1-57921-880-5
ISBN 10: 1-57921-880-6
Library of Congress Catalog Card Number: 2006932702

Dedication and Acknowledgement

I dedicate this book to my dear deceased wife, Naomi, my son, Timothy, my daughter, Deborah Mills, and her husband, Cory. I also dedicate this book to my three grandchildren, Joshua, Heidi, and John Mills, and also to my mother, Vivien Ireland, who being 104 years of age, continues to participate in a women's Bible class that she started in her own home some years ago. My sister, Ruth, helps with this class.

I also want to express my sincere thanks and appreciation to Nicole Riddle for her patient typing of this book. Thanks, Nicole. I appreciate your help very much, and may God bless you and your family in the years to come.

A special thanks to my wife, Millie, who made this book possible with encouragement for publication.

Table of Contents

I

Introduction

Introduction

We can learn many lessons from the lives of men and women of the Old Testament. These lessons, once learned, can be a great help in living for God from day to day.

We are on firm theological ground when studying the lives of those we read about in the Old Testament. Some were good examples. We are encouraged by these. They gave us good patterns to live by. But some were bad examples. We are warned by these. They gave us bad patterns for living.

Referring to the Old Testament Scriptures, the apostle Paul said, "For everything that was written in the past was written to teach us, so that through endurance and the encouragement of the Scriptures we might have hope" (Romans 15:4).

He also said about some of Israel's experiences, "Now these things occurred as examples to keep us from setting our hearts on evil things as they did" (1 Corinthians 10:6) and "these things happened to them as examples and were written down as warnings for us, on whom the fulfillment of the ages has come" (1 Corinthians 10:11).

Talking about the mistakes of Israel, the writer of the New Testament book of Hebrews calls the believers to learn from their errors, when he says, "Let us, therefore, make every effort to enter that rest, so that no one will fall by following their example of disobedience" (Hebrews 3:6–4:11).

The apostle Paul urges believers to "Join with others in following my example brothers, and take note of those who live according to the pattern we gave you" (Philippians 3:17).

A great part of Paul's methodology in teaching people how to live for God was showing them living patterns in his own life, and urging believers to follow the example of the godly lives of men and women among the churches he had founded.

At all times, our "Supreme Pattern for Living" will be that of God, our Creator and Father, and Jesus Christ our Savior.

But while God our Father and the Son of God our Savior are our "Supreme Patterns" for living, there are many lessons that we can learn by studying the lesser lives of the men and women whose lives we are told about in the Old Testament.

Much practical wisdom will be learned from these human examples we read about in the Old Testament. This wisdom will equip us to be strong and useful in the kingdom of God.

II

Patterns from Adam and Eve to the Exodus

II

Adam and Eve

Genesis 1–3; Romans 5:12–21; 1 Corinthians 15:20–22

*T*he first people whose lives we shall study are Adam and Eve, our first parents.

Before Eve had been created, God put the man Adam that He had created in the Garden of Eden and said to him these words, "You are free to eat from any tree in the garden but you must not eat from the tree of the Knowledge of good and evil for when you eat of it you will surely die" (Gen. 2:16).

Soon after this God made Eve as Adam's helpmate. Satan appeared in the form of a serpent and successfully persuaded her to eat from the forbidden fruit.

She offered some to Adam and he also ate of it.

Together, then, our first human couple disobeyed God and His clear command.

This joint disobedience to God's command was a rebellion against Him. It immediately placed the entire human race on the broad road that leads to destruction (Matt. 7:13–14).

Instead of traveling the road to eternal life and heaven, the human race was now in jeopardy.

The sluice—gates of Hell—were opened wide to receive every human being into its hopeless eternal loss unless God were to provide some way of escape.

St. Paul, referring to what Adam and Eve did, called it sin's entrance into the world; and death through sin. He called it a "trespass" that brought "judgment" and "condemnation" upon all man. It caused death to reign through that one man Adam.

He called what they did "disobedience" that made "many sinners." Sin would reign in death (Rom. 5:12–21).

In another place Adam's deed is described as follows: "For as in Adam all die, so in Christ all will be made alive" (1 Cor. 15:22), i.e. all who by faith receive forgiveness through Christ will live in him.

From the very first day when Adam and Eve rejected God's command not to eat of the forbidden fruit in the garden of Eden, God began to provide a way of escape for all human beings from the death and hell which their disobedience had caused.

Those who would avail themselves of this salvation would receive eternal life and escape from hell.

Those rejecting this gracious offer of salvation would continue on in a life that would end in condemnation and eternal judgment—a place of which Jesus often spoke where there would be "weeping . . . and gnashing of teeth" (Luke 13:28).

He spoke of "the fiery furnace, where there will be weeping and gnashing of teeth." See Matthew 13:42, 50 and Revelation 20:11–15.

What lessons—what warnings do the experiences of Adam and Eve have for people today?

Clearly, it brings to us a solemn warning that a clear direct order from the Lord should not be ignored.

Men everywhere in the world today have been polluted by the sin and death that our first parents' disobedience has caused among us. All men are inheritors of the curse and condemnation that has come from their disobedience.

But now, since we are all sinners and subject to God's wrath, God commands all people everywhere to repent and believe the gospel.

When we do this our sins are forgiven and we receive salvation (Luke 24:47; Acts 2:38–39; Acts 17:30–31).

Obedience to God's prohibition would have been pleasing to Him and would have resulted in blessing to Adam and Eve. Their disobedience to His command brought them into deep, deep trouble, along with all their descendants.

Our *obedience* to God today in all He says to us through the preached gospel will likewise bring blessing to all who hear His voice and obey it.

Our *disobedience* to what He says to us through the preached gospel will result in an eternal curse, an eternal separation from the presence of God—a separation similar in some ways to Adam and Eve's being banished from the Garden of Eden after they disobeyed Him (Gen. 3:23–24).

Such refusal to obey God and the gospel will result in God's refusal to allow people to have any part in the kingdom of God with Abraham, Isaac, and Jacob, the prophets, and with all others who will be in His gracious kingdom.

A final rejection of God's will and the gospel will result in people's being cast out of the kingdom, weeping and gnashing of teeth as they are cast into a fiery furnace prepared for the Devil and his evil angels. See Matthew 13:40–42, 47–50; Luke 13:28–29, and Matthew 25:41.

But obedience to God's instructions by the gospel will bring forgiveness and peace and the righteous will shine like the sun in the kingdom of their Father (Matt. 13:43).

Let the disobedience of Adam and Eve to God serve as a solemn, solemn warning to us and to all men never to follow their example. Rather run far from their example, and from their terrible mistake.

Rather, let us quickly and literally obey the Lord, trust the Lord, and live all our lives in fellowship with Him and enjoy His peace, His favor, both in this earthly life and in the life to come.

CAIN AND ABEL

Genesis 4:1–26; Hebrews 11:4; 1 John 3:11–12

Both Cain and Abel had reached adulthood and were engaged in their respective occupations. Abel kept flocks, being a shepherd-herdsman. Cain was a gardener-farmer, giving emphasis to tilling the soil for raising crops.

For religious purposes, both men brought offerings to the Lord.

Cain brought some of the crops he had raised. Abel brought fat portions from some of the firstborn animals he had raised among his herds.

Abel's offerings were accepted by God with favor. Cain's offerings were not accepted by God with favor.

The apostle John tells us that Cain's actions were evil whereas Abel's actions were righteous.

It is obvious that both brothers had been given prior instructions as to the kind of offering that God had wanted them to bring to Him.

Cain obviously was acting in an attitude of rejection of God's instructions; hence his actions were those in disobedience and unbelief. Abel's actions, on the other hand, were actions done in obedience to God and thus were actions done in faith and obedience.

Because Abel acted in faith and obedience he was commended by God. See Hebrews 11:4.

Cain who should have shown love to his brother did not do it. He, belonging to the Devil, killed his brother because his actions were evil. Instead of loving his brother, he hated him and killed him.

Sin that had entered the newly formed human race through the disobedience of the two parents of these brothers was already beginning to have its devastating effect in the very first family on the earth.

It is clear, even at this early point in the history of the human race, that a means of spiritual salvation was being made known to men by God. Abel was availing himself of it, but Cain was not.

Later descendants of Adam and Eve, aside from Cain and Abel, were all given free and open opportunity to return to God as Abel had done through his correct sacrifice, and as Noah would do later.

All of Noah's contemporaries could have found favor in God's eyes as Noah had found, had they desired and decided to do so.

But they decided against returning to God and as a consequence were destroyed in the flood.

Some clear lessons to be learned from the lives of Cain and Abel are the following:

DON'T FOLLOW CAIN'S EXAMPLE

Cain rejected God's will for his life. It was obvious that both he and his brother had been given clear instructions from the Lord about acceptable sacrifices—sacrifices that would atone for their sins. But Cain rejected these instructions. That was a foolish decision.

After learning that Abel had made a decision different from his—one that pleased God—he was jealous and angry, so angry that he planned his brothers' murder. After carrying out his murderous plan, he only added to his problems. Now he had not only displeased God with his offering, but he was a murderer, with blood on his hands—his brother's blood. Banishment was now his lot, from both his home and God's presence.

ABEL, THE BEST EXAMPLE TO FOLLOW

Abel obeyed the Lord and received God's approval for it. His obedience cost him his life, yet the legacy of his short life is stupendous. *He believed the Lord. He obeyed the Lord* and his soul was saved forever. What Abel did speaks volumes about the way of salvation for every human being. It also speaks thunderously about the wisdom of accepting the way of salvation shown us by the Lord.

Abel left us a marvelous pattern for living.

MEN DURING THE DAYS OF
SETH AND HIS SON ENOSH

Genesis 4:25–26; Judges 4:1–24; 2 Chronicles 14:11–15; Psalm 79:6; Psalm 99:6; Luke 3:38

Men during the days of Seth and his son Enosh began calling on the name of the Lord. It was "Yahweh" the Redeemer God that they were beginning to call upon.

Among the several names in the Old Testament that refer to the God of the Bible, the name "Yahweh" specifically refers to the God who provides redemption for mankind. It refers to God's role as Redeemer and Savior.

Therefore, during this era of mankind's history, many men began to call on the true God as the God of Redemption. They were looking to Him in their prayers and worship as the source of redemption and salvation.

Because of this, in heaven we will meet many of the people of this early era who exercised saving faith in God as Abel did and later on Enosh and Noah and Abram.

Later, when the descendants of Abraham had become a nation and were living in the Promised Land, they at times would depart from the Lord, and neighboring enemy nations would come in and oppress them and often dominate them as a nation.

During such times, when Israel found themselves in trouble, they would cry out to the Lord for deliverance from their oppressors.

This happened when Eglon, the king of Moab, was given power over the Israelites. The Israelites cried out to the Lord, and He gave them a Deliverer—Ehud (Jud. 3:15). Ehud delivered Israel from the power of Eglon.

Again God sent Jaban, the king of Canaan, who oppressed Israel for twenty years.

Israel cried out to the Lord again and this time, the Lord sent Deborah, a female prophetess, and Barak, an army commander. These two led in Israel's deliverance (Jud. 4:1–24).

Much later, king Asa, king of Judah, called to the Lord for help against the mighty army of the Cushites and their leader—General

Zerah. God heard king Asa's cry for help, for he had a much smaller military force than Zerah did. God gave king Asa a great victory over Judah's aggressive enemy that was threatening the entire nation (2 Chron. 14:11–15).

During the plagues and judgment of the extreme last days of this age, many people, although seeing the plagues and judgments coming on the earth as punishment for their wickedness, will refuse to repent of their evil works and call on the Lord for forgiveness. These people will suffer eternal judgment for their sins and refusal to repent and turn to the Lord (Rev. 9:20–21). These people will be living a pattern for death not a pattern for living.

But as these men did, during the days of Seth and his son Enosh, men do well in every age to call on the Lord. To all such persons the promise is given, "Everyone who calls on the name of the Lord will be saved" (Rom. 10:11–13).

When men call on the Lord from the depths of their hearts in faith, God will hear. God will save and God will bless them abundantly.

Did those men in the days of Seth and his son Enosh, do right in calling on the name of the Lord—yes! Emphatically yes! And God, whose hearing is perfect, came to them and blessed them richly according to their faith and obedience.

Of this we can be certain—when men call on the Lord He will make their lives better. Whether men are in jail or out of jail, in trouble or out of trouble, but perhaps bored with life or perplexed as to its purpose or meaning—if men will call on the Lord as those men in Seth's day were doing, they will come to know the Lord and rejoice in Him. I know, for He has done great things for me and for many, many of my friends.

How wonderful it will be when either by suggestion or by persuasion, many of the people of the fifty states and 3,130 county and county equivalents of America, who do not yet know God, will begin to call upon the name of the Lord as the men in the days of Seth began to do.

People calling on the name of the Lord will be saved and blessed with forgiveness and salvation.

Those calling on His name will be heard and answered by the Lord with unspeakable blessings.

The same blessings will come to the people in the other nations of the world, who will likewise call on the Lord as the men did in the days of Seth and his son Enosh.

Did not St. Peter truly say when addressing the Jewish Sanhedrin in Jerusalem, concerning Jesus Christ of Nazareth?

"Salvation is found in no one else, for there is no other name under heaven given to men by which we must be saved" (Acts 4:12).

Truly, eternal salvation is to be found in the name and in the person of Jesus Christ by calling on His name in repentance and faith.

But the men during the days of Seth and his son Enosh were beginning to seek the Lord and found him as their Redeemer-Savior. But they still had an exceedingly long life expectancy ahead of them, for men lived for centuries in that era before death took them away.

During their lifetime they could regularly call upon the Lord for their daily needs and problems. These men left us a marvelous pattern for living. This is our privilege, too.

This calls to mind a passage from the Psalms that was drawn to my attention while I was doing a research paper on the life of D.L. Moody as a personal soul winner, while I was an undergraduate student at Wheaton College, in Wheaton Illinois.

During the research I came across a photograph of one Mr. Moody's marked Bibles. It was a photograph of Psalm 91. He had underlined especially verses 14–16. The suggested theme of his markings, for use as a message, was under the title "Because He hath set His love upon me, therefore . . ." the Lord will do several things for that person.

Mr. Moody marked the six or seven promises and blessings that are made in the passage to the one who sets his love upon God.

One of the several blessings that would come to that person would be that he would receive God's answers when he would call upon him. That would be the privilege of those in Seth's day, too, and it is also the privilege of God's people today.

"He shall call upon me, and I will answer him: I will be with him in trouble; I will deliver him, and honour him" (Ps. 91:15 KJV).

Let's take full advantage of our daily opportunities to call upon the Lord, to bless Him and thank Him for all He does for us. The men of Seth's day have given us a superb pattern for living by what they did.

ENOCH
A MAN WHO WALKED WITH GOD
Genesis 5:21–24; 1 Chronicles 1:3, 33 (Henoch); Luke 3:37; Hebrews 11:5–6; Jude 14

Enoch, for 300 years walked with God. This afforded him extensive opportunities to influence his own family members.

Each generation growing up saw a grandpa who was walking with God. They saw his kindness, his honesty, his compassion and love for God and for those as he was walking in fellowship with God.

Then also, Enoch's friends, neighbors and business associates all saw this stalwart godly man and how he was living.

Enoch clearly set a moral and character standard by which his family, friends and acquaintances could measure their lives.

Like Noah, who lived somewhat later, Enoch walked with God in the midst of a society, many of whom were straying away from God and from godly living.

For 300 years, Enoch's life shown like a beacon light in the society of his day. We are told by the New Testament writer of Hebrews that Enoch, during his lifetime, pleased God, especially during the last 300 years of his total lifetime of 365 years (Heb. 11: 5–6).

When reading the Bible's account of the life of Enoch, the question may have come to you, as it has come to me, Why was it recorded that Enoch walked with God, but only from the time of the birth of his son Methuselah, very likely his first born child, and not prior to his birth?

I was thirty-two years of age. My wife Naomi was pregnant with our first child. When the day for this child to be born finally came, I took Naomi to the hospital in St. Charles, Illinois, near to where we lived.

From about 8:00 P.M. on, Naomi was in the delivery room. I, her husband, sat out in the waiting room, near to the delivery room—praying all through the night for Naomi as she was giving birth.

I did not sleep all night long, but sat praying for my sweetheart as she was trying to give birth to our child.

Finally, at 6:00 A.M. the next morning, the doctor came out of the delivery room and said, "Mr. Ireland, you have a fine healthy son," and he told me his weight!

I was so happy. I wept briefly and told the doctor that my son's name would be Timothy.

At that very point, moreover, the thought came strongly into my mind that *Now I am a father! As my son grows up I need to be an example to him.* Now, being a father made me want to stand a little taller, so to speak, and begin to take more pride and care in my responsibilities in life so I could be a good example before my son.

I had been a Christian believer for several years before Timothy's birth but now my son would be looking to me as his father and as his example. I wanted him to see God in my life.

Perhaps Enoch went through an experience similar to my experience after the birth of his son, Methuselah, for the Bible says, "After he became the father of Methuselah, Enoch walked with God 300 years, and had other sons and daughters" (Gen. 5:22).

Sons look to their fathers, and daughters look to their fathers and their mothers as examples from their earliest years. This was true in the case of young Methuselah, as it is in the case for every young son and daughter growing up in their parents' home.

Enoch had, during his lifetime, earnestly sought God and had a living relationship with Him.

Like king Uzziah, who later ruled over the nation of Judah and had a long and very prosperous reign because he sought the Lord on a regular basis, so Enoch regularly sought God and was richly rewarded for doing so.

One of the greatest rewards that God gave Enoch was to have God miraculously take him up into heaven without his ever having to experience death.

There came a day when his family and friends could not find Enoch. Why? Because God had taken him up instantly into heaven. This astonishing event became known to those who had known him, and it was recorded and reported in the Holy Scriptures.

This experience of Enoch—being taken away by God—was not unlike the experience of the prophet Elijah who also was taken up directly to heaven without experiencing a physical death.

The young prophet-trainees of that time could not find Elijah, although they looked for him for three days (1 Kings 2:1–18).

There will come a day when all the believing saints of these last days, will be taken up to heaven to meet the Lord in the air—this, in a way similar to that which was experienced by both Enoch and Elijah (1 Thess. 4:13–18).

What a tremendous day that will be for God's people. Moreover, all the saints who have lived and died in years past will join those who are living on the earth at that time—a glorious meeting in the air with our Lord. From that time on and into eternity we shall live with the Lord and all the saints in heaven.

We bless you, Lord, for your marvelous love and grace! As it was said of Enoch, may it be said of us, His people, in that day, when we are taken up, "This people walked with God, then they were no more, because God took them away!"

Enoch, in his patient walking with God has given us a marvelous pattern for our daily living.

NOAH'S CONTEMPORARIES

Genesis 6:1–13; 7:17–23; 1 Chronicles 1:4; Isaiah 54:9; Ezekiel 14:14, 20; Hebrews 11:7; 1 Peter 3:20; 2 Peter 2:5

In Genesis 6:2 and v. 4, the phrase "the sons of God" occurs twice and in the same two verses the phrase "the daughters of men" occurs twice.

It is thought by some Bible scholars that the phrase, "the sons of God" refers to the more godly descendants of Seth and those of his generation, who had begun to call on the name of Yahweh, the true God of redemption and salvation. "The daughters of men" is a possible reference to a more humanistic, anti-God line, traced from apostate Cain's family of descendants.

If the above assessments are correct it would mean that a more godly line began to intermarry with an anti-godly, pagan line. As a consequence, the knowledge of the true God would have become replaced with pagan anti-god ideas and practices, especially if the mothers were allowed to dominate the education and raising of the children of such mixed families.

As to the reference to men called "heroes of old, men of renown" one commentator notes that in the Hebrew language the term "giants" in the King James "implies not so much the idea of great stature as of reckless ferocity, impious and daring characters, who spread devastation and carnage far and wide."

We are told that the wickedness of Noah's generation had become great. We are told that "every inclination of the thoughts of the people's heart was only evil all the time" (Gen. 6:5). And the earth "was corrupt in God's sight and was full of violence" (Gen. 6:11). And "the earth is filled with violence because of them" (Gen. 6:13).

Later St. Peter referring to Noah's contemporaries says they were disobedient to God (1 Pet. 3:20), and referring to the ancient world of that time, calls its people "its ungodly people" (2 Pet. 2:5).

God's Spirit was contending with or endeavoring to hinder the excessive sinfulness of mankind during those days, but it was to little avail for Mankind continued his sinful ways, corrupting himself more and more.

Perhaps godly Enoch's life was a restraint in the lives of some against the evil tide of wickedness of his day.

We do know for certain that Noah was a preacher of righteousness in his time, calling the people to repentance and a life of holiness and righteousness. Yet it is obvious that the people rejected his message and call to return to God.

Seeing this growing and massive evil among Noah's contemporaries, God was grieved. Their evil filled God's heart with pain (Gen. 6:6). God was grieved He had even created man now that he had gone into sin and evil, always away from God, not coming toward Him in humility and repentance.

Grief is a "love word"; their sin was filling God's heart with grief and pain. Sin was killing these people as sin always does.

St. Paul said ". . . Sin entered the world through one man, and death through sin . . ." (Rom. 5:12). If not interfered with, sin finally brings death. "The wages of sin is death" (Rom. 5:23). The people had corrupted themselves with wickedness; the earth became filled with violence because of them (Gen. 6:13).

Had their sins been repented of and turned away from and forgiven, they could have lived on as Noah and his family did. But they did not repent or turn away from their sins. As a consequence the entire generation of Noah's day was put to death by a massive flood. Only Noah and his family were spared because Noah had found grace in the eyes of God through a proper repentance and saving faith in Him. This grace was also part of the faith of his wife, his three sons and their wives.

The judgment that was brought upon the civilized world of Noah's time serves as a solemn example and warning to the people of all nations in these last days who decide to live ungodly and wicked lives. Turning away from God, the Bible and His truth will result in doom and eternal loss and in the end, weeping and gnashing of teeth in hell as Jesus and the apostles have forewarned us (Matt. 13:36–43; 47–50; Luke 13:22–30; 2 Thess. 1:8–10; Rev. 20:11–15).

Noah's contemporaries left us a pattern for living that leads to death and eternal loss. Why did this happen? Because they refused to turn from a wicked life to one of holiness and righteousness.

NOAH
A MAN WHO FOUND FAVOR IN THE EYES OF THE LORD
NOAH
A MAN WHOM GOD FOUND[1]
RIGHTEOUS IN HIS GENERATION.

**Genesis 5:28–33; 6:1–9:29; Hebrews 11:7;
1 Peter 3:18; 2 Peter 2:5**

The practical lessons that can be learned from the life of the man Noah are many and they are deep and far-reaching in their importance. Men and women in every generation will do well and become wise when they approach life as Noah did and make wise decisions as he made throughout his long life.

Stated in brief form, the principle lessons we may learn from Noah's life are the following:

He availed himself of the knowledge of the true God in the early part of his career and did what was necessary to come into a saving relationship with Him.

He persevered in maintaining a close spiritual walk with God from the time he first came to know God until the end of his life.

He maintained a living and willing faith in God, first for his own personal life, later in believing God's announcement of a coming judgment, then believing and acting on God's ark-building instructions.

He obeyed God in all he was told to do, first regarding his own personal relationship with God, then in becoming a

---

[1] P. 21 Jameson, Fausset and Brown, *Commentary on the Old and New Testaments.*

preacher of righteousness, then in building the ark and fully obeying the Lord regarding all the preparations that were necessary for the coming flood judgment.

Noah was a good husband, father, father-in-law, preacher, and builder. In all these roles and relationships he carefully maintained his love for God, his faith and obedience to God and his love, care, and protection for his family.

Noah, in spite of the wickedness that had developed during his lifetime, availed himself of the knowledge of the true God—a knowledge that had come down to him from his father Lamech and his other ancestors. Acting on this knowledge, he became a righteous and blameless man of God. He found favor in God's eyes and he clung to the Lord, learning to walk with God as his ancestor Enoch had done (Gen. 6: 8–10).

This is something his contemporaries *did not do*. They all allowed the truth of salvation to slip away from them, disregarding it, and refusing to avail themselves of it.

Noah, being informed and warned by God of a coming worldwide judgment, acted in holy fear and began building an ark at God's command.

He acted in careful obedience to God's instructions in all these preparations for a coming great flood—judgment (Gen. 6:22; 7:5).

Noah's obedience to God in building the ark and in making the preparations, constituted an act of great faith on his part. This combination of faith in God and obedience to God in the world of his time made him an heir of the righteousness that comes by faith (Heb. 11:7; 1 Pet. 3:20).

Noah acted with a combination of godly fear and faith and obedience to God, upon being given a revelation of a future worldwide judgment on the world of his day.

By his acting in such faith and obedience to God as he did, he accomplished the following things:

He saved himself and his family from death.

He condemned the world of his contemporaries that refused to believe the same revelation of the impending judgment—a judgment which Noah clearly warned about in both his preaching and his ark-building preparations.

Noah's life, his preaching and his ark-building, constituted him God's prophet—a prophet through whom God was calling his generation to repentance and faith in Him as the only way to escape judgment.

Noah's preaching had its counterpart in the preaching of Jonah to Nineveh (Jonah 3: 1–10), of John the Baptist to Israel, prior to Jesus' public ministry (Matt. 3: 7–10), and Peter's preaching to Israel after Jesus' public ministry (Acts 2:38–40).

Noah's obedience to God, we must note, had these two unique characteristics:

His obedience to God in his preparations for the flood gave very careful attention to detail; and secondly,

His obedience to God gave very careful attention to completeness. For see the two passages that give report of Noah's obedience:

"Noah did everything *just as* God commanded him."
                                                (Gen. 6:22)

"Noah did *all* that the Lord commanded him"
                                                (Gen. 7:5)

We are not told at what period of Noah's first years of life he became a godly man and began walking in fellowship with God, but it was at some time during the first 500 years of his career. After coming to know the Lord, he remained ready for whatever came to his hand to do.

Peter says he was a preacher, and after he reached 500 years of age, he became the father of three sons. Three sons who would undoubtedly help their father build the ark after they reached their strength of manhood, and three sons who would later have families and make a fresh beginning in re-populating the earth.

After Noah's sons were born, God asked him to become a builder. He was ready to do this building. So in addition to preaching, he became a builder—a preacher and a builder—remaining obedient to God in both endeavors.

He was living a holy and godly life while engaged in both activities.

It appears that he gained few converts from his preaching, but at least he influenced his three sons and three daughters-in-law to follow the Lord. And his wife continued to follow the Lord. There were no signs of disagreement or displeasure with her husband's actions. She, with her husband's support, had raised their three sons, Shem, Ham, and Japheth. These three sons, moreover, had married three young women all of whom were in sympathy with God's call upon Noah's life and were living in cooperation with him.

All seven members of Noah's family continued with the Lord along with their aged leader, Noah.

This made eight members, in total, staying true to the Lord and their God. And this, despite the widespread decadence and wickedness being practiced by all their contemporaries in the society in which they were living.

All eight persons in this family were like light and salt in the midst of a spiritually-dark environment.

Noah possessed a living faith in God but his contemporaries did not possess such a living faith.

Noah's faith and obedience to God condemned the lack of faith on the part of his contemporaries.

But Noah's faith made him an heir of God's righteousness, and enabled him to continue serving God his Lord to the end of his life of 950 years, when he died and went to be with his Lord in His heavenly kingdom.

Ham and his son Canaan

Genesis 9:18–29

Some years after the flood, Noah planted a vineyard. As was usually done, he made some wine from the grapes he had raised in his vineyard.

On one occasion during a time when his son Ham and his wife had a son named Canaan, Noah obviously overindulged on the wine he had made from the grapes in his vineyard. And being intoxicated from the wine, he fell asleep and became disrobed during his sleeping time.

His son Ham discovered his father in this naked sleeping state and should have graciously covered him up. But he did not do this.

Ham's failure to immediately cover his father when he saw him in this condition was a serious mistake on his part. It became for him no small thing. It constituted a serious act of disrespect for his father at that time—a disrespectful act in the eyes of his two brothers and later was seen as such in Noah's eyes as well.

When Noah finally awoke and learned what Ham had done, he spoke a severe curse upon him, a curse which would affect not only Ham and Ham's son Canaan, but all his posterity for generations to come.

What practical lesson does Ham's experience as recorded in Genesis chapter nine have for us today?

It is a warning against showing disrespect for our parents whether it be to either our father or our mother, as in Ham's case, he made a serious breach of respect to his father and that action brought upon him and all his posterity a lot of trouble.

Shem and Japheth in contrast to their brother Ham showed proper and due respect by covering their father's nakedness without viewing it themselves (Gen. 9:23).

Their actions were obviously commended by their father, whereas Ham's actions were not.

Respect for parents is very important and this incident, as reported by Moses in Genesis chapter nine, certainly points to its great importance for all time and for all families in the human race.

Ham and his son Canaan received three curses from his father: Noah said of his son Canaan that he would:

1. Be a servant of servants to his brethren. v 25
2. Be Shem's servant. v 26
3. Be Japheth's servant. v 27

By the manifestation of a little more wisdom, judgment, foresight and plain parental respect, this son of Noah who had come safely through the flood as one of its eight sole survivors, could have avoided this curse that was placed upon him and his posterity.

SHEM AND JAPHETH

Genesis 9:20–29

The actions of both Shem and Japheth in covering their father with a garment as they did, was an act of respect and was certainly appreciated by Noah, their father, when he learned what they had done.

The actions of both Shem and Japheth, therefore, in this regard are a praiseworthy example for all sons in every family, for all time. Not only was Noah obviously pleased with what they had done, but God is pleased when sons and daughters show due respect to their parents as these two adult sons did to their father, Noah.

All three of these sons of Noah were perhaps about one hundred years old at the time of the incident.

Noah, their father, was over six-hundred years of age.

Noah's prophecy gave two blessings to Shem. Noah said:

1. "Blessed be the Lord God of Shem" (Gen. 9:26).
2. "He (the Lord) shall dwell in the tents of Shem" (Gen. 9:26).

Noah's prophecy gave one blessing to Japheth. Namely, "God shall enlarge Japheth" (Gen. 9:27).

The blessings given to Shem are of particular significance, especially the one that said, "May Japheth live in the tents of Shem." The preferred subject for the sentence is "He" rather than "Japheth," referring to God Himself, living in the tents of Shem.

James E. Smith, in his book on messianic prophecy in the Old Testament, says of this passage, "it is altogether proper that the God of Shem should be depicted dwelling in the tents of Shem. God is the portion of the Shemites; they were those entrusted with preserving the knowledge of the true God in primeval times."[2]

From this prophecy given by Noah at this time we see a combination of curses and blessings. Curses were placed on Ham and his descendants. Blessings were placed upon Shem and Japheth.

The blessing given to Noah's firstborn son, Shem, is of particular importance because it is constituted the second of two messianic prophecies that appear in the book of Genesis and in the entire Old Testament.

The first prophecy informed the human race that the Messiah-Savior would come from the seed of woman (Gen. 3:15)—a human deliverer would crush the head of Satan.

The second messianic prophecy is the one we see in Genesis chapter nine, where we are told that the Messiah-Savior would come through the race of Shem, through his chosen part of the human race (Gen. 9:23).

Yahweh, our Redeemer God, had not abandoned the human race that was now lost in sin and eternal death.

From the day of man's fall, God gave us hope of a future Savior.

This hope of a future Savior was kept alive for the suffering human race with periodic repetitions of this promise. Each time with more details given, as to how and where this Redeemer-Savior would be brought forth into the world—a world of people that needed him so badly.

The hopes of the coming Savior were kept alive and men of God made note of these renewed predictions as they came forth.

This prediction given through Noah when he was over six-hundred years old, was one of many gracious predictions that were given in the book of Genesis and in the Old Testament, a prediction involving

---

[2]P. 46, James E. Smith, in *The Promised Messiah*.

his firstborn son Shem and his future descendants—Abraham and the Jewish race.

Finally, after many years of predictions, after many years of waiting, and after many years of expectations, the promised Savior came and was first wrapped in swaddling clothes and laid in a manger.

Later he sat in Mary's lap.

Perhaps Mary rocked her precious Savior-Son to sleep on many a night during his infancy.

After many years this son of Mary and Son of God grew to manhood, had a public ministry, then gave His life as a sacrifice so people everywhere, upon hearing of His sacrifice and the gospel, would by believing, have a chance to be remade and to receive eternal life and live in fellowship with God in His kingdom forever.

ABRAM AND SARAI

Genesis 11:27–25:11; 26:5; Acts 7:2–3;
Romans 4:1–25; Galatians 3:1–20; Hebrews 6:13–20; 11:8–19

Abram's ancestral line, from the time of the flood, began with Shem, one of the three sons of Noah. His ancestors included men whose names were Arphaxad, Shelah, Eber, Peleg, Reu, Serug, Nahor, and finally Terah who was his father.

Abram was one of three sons of Terah, of which Abram was the firstborn. Abram's two brothers were Nahor and Haran.

Abram lived a long and relatively quiet life, yet a life filled with important events, events that involved communication with God and the founding of a unique nation. That nation was the nation of Israel.

Because of the uniqueness of Abram's call and the way in which he responded to the many promises and instructions which God gave him, his life has given Christian believers many practical lessons in how to live a successful life for God and others.

Israel as a nation was a nation to which the knowledge of the true God was entrusted. This knowledge of the true God was later to be shared with the other nations of the world.

Fortunately, Abram responded to God's dealings with him, in nearly every case, as God had hoped that he would.

The true God, the creator of the heavens and the earth, spoke to Abram and appeared to him several times.

The first reported appearance of God to Abram was while he was living in Mesopotamia, the Ur of the Chaldeans. God said to him there, "Leave your country and your people . . . and go to the land I will show you" (Acts 7:2–3).

How did Abram respond to the instructions given to him by God? He "obeyed and went, even though he did not know where he was going" (Heb. 11:8).

At the time of this appearance of the Lord to Abram, while he was living in Mesopotamia, along with the instructions about leaving his homeland, God also gave him some solemn promises. God said to Abram,

"I will make you into a great nation and I will bless you;

I will make your name great, and you will be a blessing.

I will bless those who bless you,

and whoever curses you I will curse;

and all peoples on earth will be blessed through you" (Gen. 12:2–3).

Certainly this was a great, and comprehensive and far-reaching promise to give to this man Abram.

With this set of promises settled in his mind and heart, Abram continued his journey down into the land God was leading him into, the land of Canaan. Abram was seventy-five years of age when he left Haran, to journey southwest into Canaan. With him came Sarai his wife, Lot, his nephew, and all the possessions he had accumulated while living in Haran.

Upon arriving in Canaan, the land to which God had led him, the Lord appeared to him and said, "To your offspring I will give this land" (Gen 12:7).

Abram upon hearing the message from the Lord, built an altar to the Lord, his God (Gen. 12:7).

This act of obedience, on Abram's part, at the outset of what was to become a long walk with God, was also a giant step of faith for him. Abram's lifetime journey became many giant steps of faith for him. But God was directing his footsteps, first west, and then south, to the land God had in mind for him.

This journey for Abram, then, leaving his family and his growing-up environment, was his first successful walk with God, a walk involving obedience to God's instructions and faith in God's guidance as to the direction in which he should go.

From this point on in Abram's life there would be many other instructions from his Lord, with further opportunities to respond with faith and obedience. At the age of seventy-five years, he had 100 years more to live for his Lord, for Abram lived to the age of 175 years (Gen. 25:7).

Soon after arriving in Canaan a famine began to afflict the land. So Abram moved his family and possessions down into Egypt. There he planned to remain until the famine in Canaan was passed. Then he planned to return again to Canaan.

While in Egypt, Abram told Pharaoh that Sarai, his wife, was his sister. This was only a half-truth, for in reality Sarai was Abram's half sister, she with Abram having the same father but not the same mother. Abram had feared that the Egyptians would kill him and take his beautiful wife Sarai, to be another wife for Pharaoh; therefore, he told everyone there that she was his sister, believing that knowing this, there would be less likelihood that Abram's life would be endangered.

But Pharaoh, later learning that Sarai was indeed Abram's wife, rebuked Abram and told him to leave Egypt with his wife and all his possessions. For Pharaoh had taken Sarai to be his wife and for this God had afflicted pharaoh and his entire household with serious diseases (Gen. 12:14–20).

Upon returning to Canaan, Abram soon showed himself a peace-maker. This occurred when quarrels began to arise among the herds-men of Lot and Abram. The flocks of both men had grown so great in number that there was conflict over the land space. So Abram suggested that he and Lot separate themselves. Given a choice of lands, Lot chose a very fertile land area and moved into it along with his flocks and herds. Lot himself moved ever closer to the twin cities of Sodom and Gomorrah. Finally he moved into Sodom itself and became part of its community (Gen. 13:1–9).

Meanwhile God repeated His previous promise to Abram, this time with more detail, that all the land Abram was walking on would become his and his descendants', also that his descendants would become very numerous.

This promise, being repeated, comforted Abram regarding Lot's choice of the better land (Gen. 13:1–17).

Abram now built a third altar to the Lord, among the great trees of Mamre (Gen. 13:18).

Next in Abram's life, he initiates courageous leadership in rescuing Lot and his family with a small rescuing force of his own of 318 men and the assistance of two or more friends, Aner, Eshcol, and Manore.

Lot had been captured amidst a conflict among nearby kings in the land of Canaan and taken several miles in a northerly direction where he was held captive with his family and all his possessions.

Abram rescued Lot, along with all his family and possessions and brought him back again to safety. God had given Abram a remarkable military victory over a much larger force, a force that was routed and pursued to defeat and powerlessness (Gen. 14:14–16).

Abram now paid tithes to the Lord of all the spoils that his men had acquired in their military victory. These tithes were given as an act of worship and, therefore, to the Lord who had given him success in his rescue attempt of Lot and his family (Gen. 14:17–24).

Soon after Lot's rescue the Lord spoke to Abram in a vision saying,

> "Do not be afraid, Abram,
> I am your shield,
> Your very great reward"
>
> (Gen. 15:1)

Then the Lord told Abram that from his own body he would have a son who would become his heir. Through this heir Abram would have an innumerable offspring during the generations that would follow.

Abram believed this promise, a promise that was confirmed to him by the Lord's personal oath.

Regarding this promise now given to Abram, it was said, "Abram believed the Lord, and he credited it to him as righteousness" (Gen. 15:16). See Genesis 15:1–21; 17:1–27; Romans 4:1–25; Galatians 3:6–20, and Hebrews 6:13–20.

When Abram had reached the age of ninety-nine years, God appeared to him again. He said at the outset, "I am God Almighty (El-Shaddai); walk before me and be blameless. I will confirm my covenant between me and you and will greatly increase your numbers."

God then said Abram would become the father of many nations. Then Abram's name was changed to Abraham, meaning "father of many." Also at this time Sarai's name was changed to Sarah, meaning "princess."

God now repeated and reaffirmed His precious promises to Abraham. Abraham would indeed have an innumerable offspring and many nations would come from him. Also all the land of Canaan would be the everlasting possession of Abraham's descendants.

God, moreover, at this time gave Abraham the rite of circumcision, as a sign of His everlasting covenant made with him and with all of his descendants.

God instructed Abraham to circumcise himself and all the males in his household at this time.

Abraham, upon receiving these instructions, moved immediately to obey them. The promptness of Abraham's obedience to God regarding circumcision in his household is outstanding in this chapter (17:23–27). Obedience, and extra prompt obedience, is beginning to appear as a hallmark of Abraham's character. It is similar to that of Noah, whose obedience gave attention to detail and completeness. See Genesis 6:22; 7:5. But Abraham's promptness and eager willingness to obey God's commands, when given, is becoming very obvious as the narrative of his life and career unfolds. He is learning that the pathway of prompt obedience and faith in God's word and commands is the pathway of blessing and favor with Him. He is following that pathway with regularity.

The next extra-significant experience in Abraham's life was the appearance of the Lord to him. The Lord Himself appeared along with two angels. These three individuals appeared as three ordinary men, but in actuality, one of these was the Lord Himself and the other two were angels from heaven, accompanying the Lord.

Abraham hurried to meet these three, bowed and extended an invitation to them to sit down for a rest under a shade tree and offered to have their feet washed and that they accept something to eat from his household.

These three visitors accepted Abraham's offer of hospitality. A meal was brought for them.

Then they had a message for Abraham and his wife Sarah. The Lord said He would return again in about nine months and that Sarah would about that time give birth to a son. Abraham believed this report, but Sarah had doubts about the prediction. But just as the Lord said, in approximately nine months, Sarah had become pregnant and was prepared to give birth to her son Isaac

At the time of Isaac's birth, his mother was ninety years of age and Abraham, his father, was 100 years of age. God had wrought a birth-miracle for this old couple. They named the child "Isaac," which means "laughter" (Gen. 21:1–7).

One of the most solemn events in Abraham's life had to have been his witnessing the judgment of God upon the cities of Sodom and Gomorrah.

Abraham had pleaded with God to spare the city of Sodom if the minimum of ten righteous persons could be found there. But as it soon was discovered, there were fewer than ten righteous persons living in the city. Therefore, God proceeded to destroy the city of Sodom, Gomorrah and all those living in the entire plain (Gen. 19:23–25).

But Abraham's nephew Lot, Lot's wife and their two daughters were rescued before the destruction of these cities was accomplished. Lot's wife, however, lost her life because she disobeyed the angels' direct order to not look back to Sodom as the city was being destroyed. She was turned into a pillar of salt as she was leaving the city with her family. That left only Lot and his two daughters who escaped God's destructive judgment on these wicked cities.

Abraham, therefore, like his ancestor Noah, saw firsthand, the devastating effects of sin and wickedness in human beings and the severity of God's hatred of sin and the severity of God's judgment upon sinful living when it is not repented of before the Lord.

That which happened to Noah's contemporaries and the inhabitants of Sodom and Gomorrah was recorded and reported in the Scriptures as a warning and example to people of all generations who elect to live ungodly lives. Also the rescue of Noah and Lot, with their families, illustrates God's ability to rescue the godly of all ages who live righteous lives, notwithstanding the evil lives of those among whom they are living (2 Pet. 2:5–9).

To both Pharaoh, king of Egypt and to Abimelech, king of Gerar, Abraham told them that Sarah, his wife, was his sister. These reports by Abraham were only half-truths, and although Abraham's motives were to protect himself from being killed, this social practice was somewhat questionable in its results and may have become an obstruction in his testimony for God to these two leaders.

But other than before these two leaders, it becomes quite clear that Abraham's intention throughout his career was to leave a clear testimony to the true living God whom he served. Perhaps even to Pharaoh and then to Abimelech, whose household was prayed for by Abraham, certainly to the king of Sodom and to the Hittites and others in Canaan, and certainly before his entire household and his servants, the godly man, Abraham, sought to conduct all his affairs with justice. He was conscious that he was representing the true God, maker of heaven and earth, before many who were worshipers of idols (Gen. 12:14–20; Gen. 14:17–24; Gen. 20:1–18; Gen. 23:1–20).

ABRAHAM AND ISHMAEL

Abraham was eighty-six years of age when Ishmael was born to Hagar, Sarah's maidservant. But Ishmael was not the son of promise through whom the Jewish nation was to come. As we shall learn later on in this book, Hagar symbolized Mt. Sinai and Ishmael symbolized a natural-born son of Abram, whereas Isaac, who was to be born later, was to symbolize believers who are born of the spirit and are sons of promise.

Abraham was told by the Lord that Isaac, not Ishmael, was to be the heir to the covenant promises that God had made to Abram, whose name now was changed to Abraham. Abraham had wished that Ishmael might live under these covenant blessings, but it was not to be. God comforted Abraham, telling him that He would bless Ishmael and make him into another great nation.

Later, after Isaac was born and weaned, both Ishmael and Hagar his mother had to be sent away from Abraham and Sarah's household.

Both the Lord and Abraham worked together, in love, as Hagar and Ishmael were sent away to live elsewhere, separated from Abraham's household. God spoke audibly to Hagar from heaven while she was in the desert of Beersheba, assuring her that her son would become a great nation. God then opened her eyes and she saw a well of water, from which she soon gave her son a drink. Then "God was with the boy as he grew up. He lived in the desert and became an archer." Later his mother got a wife for him from Egypt (Gen. 16:1–5; 17:15–27; 21:1–21).

Both Abraham and the Lord, therefore, looked out fully for the future welfare of Hagar and her son, and Abraham's son, Ishmael.

ABRAHAM TESTED

Genesis 22:1–9; Hebrews 11:17–19

Abraham continued his walk with God after the birth and weaning of Isaac, and also after the separation of Hagar and Ishmael from his household.

After Isaac had grown up several years, God tested Abraham with his greatest test yet, a test of his faith and obedience. Would Abraham pass this test or fail to pass it? The test?

God instructed Abraham to offer up his son on a certain mountain, Mt. Moriah.

Instantly, Abraham moved into action, intending to obey God implicitly in offering up Isaac.

Abraham knew it was the Lord who had spoken to him, and so he moved to obey what God told him to do. God had said, "Abraham," Abraham replied, "Here I am."

Now God gave Abraham specific orders what to do and in the general region where to do it. God later would tell Abraham on which specific mountain in the Moriah region he was to sacrifice his son Isaac.

Not late but early the next morning, after God had told Abraham what to do, Abraham moved to carry out God's orders given to him. This was a test and so far so good. Abraham understood and accepted what he had heard and was obeying promptly his Lord's orders given to him.

After a three-day journey, Abraham, with his son, the wood, the fire and the knife, placed a bound Isaac atop the wood, and upon the altar Abraham had erected.

He moved to kill his son when the Angel of God stopped him (Gen. 22:12; 16–19).

Abraham reasoned that God would raise Isaac from the dead if necessary so his promise to build a nation through Isaac would become a reality (Gen. 22:1–19; Heb. 11:17–19).

Abraham had passed God's test with flying colors.

His faith and obedience had demonstrated beyond a shadow of a doubt that he feared God and was determined to please Him.

So God reaffirmed, even expanded His covenant promises to him.

Because Abraham obeyed the Lord, doing what the Lord had told him to do, he passed the test the Lord gave him. He proved his faith in God's promise that an innumerable nation would come through Isaac his son. He believed God's promises would be kept without fail.

Abraham's obedience at this time pleased God immensely and positioned Abraham in a relationship with God so secure, that God reaffirmed to him all His previous promises concerning a coming great nation.

This nation would see victory over all its enemies and there would be worldwide blessing among all the nations through Abraham's seed—Jesus, the Savior.

All of this was assured to him in the strongest possible terms and by an oath given by God Himself. And all this because Abraham had obeyed God and had not withheld his son in a refused obedience.

Abraham's obedience at this time was an action of faith on his part. His mind-set through the entire test of several days was faith in God and obedience to God who had given to him the order (Gen. 22:15–18; Gal. 3:15–18; Heb. 16:13–20; Heb. 11:17–19).

ABRAHAM LOSES HIS BELOVED WIFE

Sarah, at the age of 127, died. Abraham, a man of God, after mourning and weeping at her death, purchased a field and a cave as a burial site for her. So this field with trees and a cave at the end of it became Abraham's possession.

Ephron, a Hittite, sold it to Abraham in the presence of leading Hittites in the vicinity. Abraham held a respectable place as a prince among all these Hittite men, meeting at the city gates near Machpelah and Mamre (Gen. 23).

ABRAHAM FINDS A WIFE FOR ISAAC

Abraham had now grown old. God had blessed him in every way. He now moved to obtain a wife for Isaac, sending Eliezer, the servant in charge of all Abraham's possessions to get a wife for his son Isaac.

Eliezer returned from Paddan-Aran with a beautiful virgin named Rebekah, who became Isaac's wife. Isaac loved her (Gen. 24:1–67).

ABRAHAM'S FINAL DAYS

After Sarah's death, Abraham marries again, this time to Keturah. He was 137 years of age at the time of Sarah's death and sometime after her death, Abraham remarries. By Keturah he has six more sons: Zemran, Jokohan, Medan, Midean, Ishbok, and Shuah.

Finally, nearing his one-hundred-and-seventy-fifth year of life, Abraham gave all his possessions to Isaac, but he gave generous gifts to all his other seven sons and sent them to eastern lands, away from the promised land of Canaan.

Abraham died at one hundred and seventy-five and was buried alongside his wife by Isaac and Ishmael (Gen. 25:1–11).

SUMMARY OF LESSONS TO BE LEARNED
FROM ABRAHAM'S LIFE

As a young man Abram came to know about the true God. It is not known how he first learned about Him who is the Creator of the heavens and the earth. Perhaps through a friend who knew God or perhaps God revealed Himself to him personally, but from some source he learned about the true God. Also, he learned that this God was loving, intelligent, and compassionate, and that He was pure and wise, and that He should be obeyed if directions or an order was given by Him.

For Abraham to obey God, to believe instructions and promises that God gave him, to acknowledge Him in all the relationships with the people he came to know during his lifetime, all these became the basic attitudes of his life.

Some outstanding examples of his obedience to God are these:

He left his home in Mesopotamia when God told him to depart to go to a land that he knew nothing about. He came first to Haran, Syria. Then after his father died he came south into present-day Israel. There he lived for the remaining years of his life, finally dying at 175 years of age (Gen. 12:1–3; Acts 7:2–3).

When ninety-nine years of age, when told to adopt the sign of circumcision for himself and his entire household, he obeyed immediately, circumcising all the males in his household (Gen. 17:1–27).

When Isaac was a teenager, most likely, Abraham obeyed immediately to sacrifice him, because he knew God had spoken this commandment to him. "Early the next morning he got up and saddled his donkey" (Gen. 22:3). He made these preparations and took Isaac and some servants with him to carry out the order the Lord had given him the day before. The Lord prevented Abraham from killing his son, but had God not stopped him, Abraham was intent upon completing this act of obedience to God. This was a supreme test of his faith in God, and he passed the test.

He was convinced God would raise him from the dead if he had been killed, for he believed God's promises that an entire nation was to come into being through Isaac's offspring (Gen. 22:12, 16–19).

He practiced a general obedience to all God's laws and statutes throughout his life (Gen. 26:5).

Some examples of Abraham's faith in God:

He believed he would become the father of a great nation and that all peoples on earth would be blessed through him (Gen. 12:1–3).

His offspring would be given Canaan (Gen. 12:7–8; 13:14–18).

He believed and received a solemnized reaffirmation of God's covenant with him concerning an offspring and a worldwide blessing, a promise confirmed by God's oath (Gen. 15:1–21).

He received a change of name, "Abraham" meaning he would be a father of many nations (Gen. 17:4–8).

He paid tithes to the Lord, showing his love and respect to Him (Gen. 14:14–20).

He showed hospitality to angels and to the Lord (Gen. 18:1–8).

He interceded for Sodom, showing concern for any righteous souls living within the city (Gen. 18:16–33).

He endeavored to give a clear testimony of the true God to everyone he met and had contact with (Gen. 12:14–20; 14:17–24; 20:1–18; 23:1–20).

He looked out for both Hagar and Ishmael's welfare, along with the Lord (Gen. 16:1–15; 17:15–27; 21:1–21).

He was a peacemaker concerning the dispute between his shepherds and the shepherd's of his nephew, Lot (Gen. 13:1–9).

He was a war maker when an appropriate time came for war. This time came for him when Lot and his family had been captured and taken away by warring neighboring kings. Abraham armed his servants and went to war in rescuing Lot and all his family. He knew there was a time to fight and a time when not to fight (Gen. 14:1–24).

At Sarah's death, he honored her with a special burial, burying her only after mourning and weeping for her (Gen. 23).

After Sarah's death, with health and strength remaining in his body, Abraham married again and had six sons. The name of his new wife was Keturah.

He finally died at the age of one hundred and seventy five. His sons Isaac and Ishmael buried him (Gen. 25:1–11).

Sarai, whose name was later changed to Sarah, meaning "princess" (Gen. 17:15), was Abraham's half sister (Gen. 20:11–13). Sarah was a beautiful and godly woman, ten years younger than her husband.

She not only possessed an outward natural physical beauty, but an inward beauty of character, "the unfading beauty of a gentle and quiet spirit, which is of great worth in God's sight" (1 Pet. 3:1–6). She was submissive to her husband Abraham and obeyed him, even calling him master.

In Holy Scripture, Sarah, as to the manner of her life and character, is given as a superb example of the holy women of the past, the patterns of whose life which, when followed by godly women of all ages, will bring great delight and honor to their Lord.

SODOM AND GOMORRAH

Genesis 13:10–13; 14:1–24; 18:16–33; 19:1–29;
2 Peter 2:6–9; Proverbs 13:5–6, 9.

That which happened to the cities of Sodom and Gomorrah and the reasons for it is to serve as a solemn warning to all men of all ages who would live an ungodly life.

Sin and wicked living is hateful to God and such sinful godless living will finally be punished with the severe judgment of God. God is holy and righteous and sinful; wicked living by human beings will be punished by God in a way similar to the punishment that came on the cities of Sodom and Gomorrah (2 Pet. 2:4–9; Matt. 13:24–50; Luke 13:1–5; 22–30; 1 Thess. 1:10; 5:1–11; Rev. 6:12–17).

After Abram and his nephew Lot separated, Lot moved into the fertile valley surrounding Sodom and Gomorrah. Lot himself ultimately moved into the city of Sodom itself.

Prior to the destruction of Sodom and Gomorrah, the land nearby was well-watered, like the land of Eden and fertile Egypt (Gen. 13:10).

But the men in Sodom "were sinning greatly against the Lord" (Gen. 13:13). Their sin had become "grievous" so much so that the Lord Himself came down to see for Himself if it was as bad as the cry that had come up to heaven had been indicating (Gen. 18:20–21).

The Lord began to inform Abraham of His plan to destroy those living in the twin-cities of Sodom and Gomorrah.

Soon, Abraham, in face to face conference with the Lord, negotiated with Him. Finally, the Lord promised He would not destroy the city of Sodom, where Lot and his family were living, if the Lord could find ten people there who were righteous. But the Lord was unable to find ten such righteous people within the city, so He planned to destroy the city.

The two angels who had accompanied the Lord were able to assist Lot, his wife, and Lot's two daughters—four people only, to hasten out of the city.

As they were barely outside the city and finally entered into a small neighboring town called, Zoar, God rained down burning sulfur on the cities of Sodom and Gomorrah and upon all the vegetation in the valley.

The warning cry of the angels to Lot and his family was, "Flee for your lives. Don't look back, and don't stop anywhere in the plain! Flee to the mountains or you will be swept away!" (Gen. 19:17). They were told to flee, flee, flee from the coming judgment.

As soon as Lot and his family were safely outside the city, God rained down burning sulfur. All in these two cities were destroyed. Lot's wife, turning around to look at what was happening, was turned into a pillar of salt (Gen. 19:26).

Our Lord Jesus referred to what happened to Lot's wife as a warning to those who would attempt to return to salvage anything they might leave behind. This at the time when the Lord returns to establish His kingdom. As Lot and his two daughters who walked straight out of Sodom without looking back one time, so Christian believers are to remain prepared for the Lord's return, putting to death the self-life and living a life holy and devoted to the Lord and His service (Luke 17:30–37).

The warning given to Lot and his family to flee from the city of Sodom is reminiscent of the warning given by John the Baptist in the form of a question to the Pharisees when they were coming to his baptism. John said, "Who warned you to flee from the wrath to come?" (Matt. 3:8). The Lord would warn everyone to come to the Lord today, when the opportunity for salvation is at hand, so everyone may stay prepared for the day of the Lord's return and for the day of

God's judgment—a time when every person will give an answer for what he or she has done in their lives.

The entire passage of St. Peter (2 Peter 2:4–9) is a solemn warning, summary passage, pointing out not only the warning of future judgment of the ungodly, as that of Sodom and Gomorrah, but several other judgments which God meted out upon ungodly people in Noah's day and upon wicked angels prior to Noah's day. Peter makes mention of a still future judgment that will come upon the ungodly at a future time (2 Pet. 2:4–9).

God is also able to rescue the righteous from His judgments as He did Noah and his family and Lot and his family.

ISAAC

Genesis 15:1–6; 17:15–22; 21:1–13; 22:1–19; 24:1–67; 25: 1–28: 9; Exodus 3:5–6; Matthew 22:29:23; Galatians 4:21–31

St. Paul called Isaac a child of promise as true believers in Christ are today. Gal. 4:25. Isaac was the son God had promised would be born and from him God's chosen people, the Jews, would be descended. When God promised Abram that he would have numerous descendants, it was through Isaac, a promised son, to whom He was referring. It was not Ishmael but through Isaac that God's chosen people would come.

Both Abraham and Sarah needed a miraculous assistance from the Holy Spirit of God to bear a son, this because of their advanced ages. Abraham was 100 and Sarah was ninety years of age.

After Isaac's birth, Sarah, his mother, lived thirty-seven more years. Abraham, his father, lived seventy-five more years, to the age of 175.

Approximately three years after Sarah died, Abraham sent his servant to procure a wife for his Isaac.

He returned with a beautiful virgin girl named Rebekah. Rebekah became Isaac's wife when he was about forty years of age. But following their marriage they had no children until twenty years had passed. Isaac prayed to the Lord and Rebekah became pregnant with twin boys (Gen. 25:19–21). When these boys were born, Esau came out first, and then Jacob.

The Lord said to Rebekah prior to the birth of these two boys,

"Two nations are in your womb, and two peoples from within you will be separated; one people will be stronger than the other, and the older will serve the younger."
(Gen. 25:23)

These boys grew to adulthood and Isaac their father had become aged with failing eyesight. Isaac thinking he would soon experience death, asked his hunter son Esau to go out and catch and prepare a favorite venison meal for him. After this meal, Isaac planned to bestow his greatest family blessing on Esau, his firstborn.

But Rebekah, learning of Isaac's plan, yet knowing that God had told her earlier that Jacob, the younger son, would be served by the older son, and that God's special favor was to be with Jacob and not with Esau, made a move to interfere with her husband's blessing on Esau's life. She disguised Jacob as her son Esau and as a consequence, Isaac's greater blessing was placed on Jacob rather than on Esau.

It seems to me that Rebekah's manipulation of the blessing of the father at this time, although perhaps flawed as to her methodology, was at its base an act of faith on her part. For she was acting on the basis of revealed prophetic knowledge which God had made known to her even prior to the time of the twin boys' birth.

Moreover, it would also appear that Jacob, like his mother, had a greater sensitivity to spiritual values than was possessed by his brother Esau. Why do I say this? Because Jacob perceived a higher value in the birthright of the family than did Esau. And Jacob desired to have the birthright and did obtain it from a sworn promise from his brother Esau.

Esau clearly devalued this birthright and sold it for a single meal of stew and bread.

The writer of the book of Hebrews assessing Esau's action and decision at this time said, "See that no one is godless like Esau, who for a single meal sold his inheritance right as the oldest son. Afterward, as you know, when he wanted to inherit this blessing, he was rejected. He could bring about no change of mind though he sought the blessing with tears" (Heb. 12:16–17).

Esau's action in this incident clearly despised the spiritual dimension of this family blessing, whereas his brother Jacob highly valued it.

This is not to say that in the case of Jacob's methodology in obtaining his brother's birthright and Rebekah's methodology in obtaining the greater blessing for her son Jacob there were not present some elements of spiritual immaturity. Yet despite this immaturity, there were present elements of true faith and a commendable spiritual sensitivity.

Notwithstanding the fact that Isaac had blessed Jacob, having been deceived into thinking he was blessing Esau, his firstborn, he performed the blessing by faith. Later when the real Esau returned from his hunting mission, Isaac blessed him also, but with a blessing inferior to that which he had promised in the presence of the Lord on his son Jacob. Both these blessings were in regard to the future careers of his two sons (Heb. 11:20; Gen. 27:1–40).

Earlier, when Isaac was a teenager, God told Abraham to sacrifice his son on an altar, but he was stopped before the sacrifice was actually made.

Isaac was yielded to his father's will and cooperative throughout, not resisting his father, Abraham (Gen. 22:1–19).

Later, after Sarah's death, Isaac married Rebekah, a beautiful virgin girl. He loved and cared for her (Gen. 24:1–67).

Isaac and his half-brother, Ishmael, buried their father Abraham when he died at age 175 (Gen. 25:5–11).

All of Abraham's possessions were inherited by Isaac (Gen. 25:5–11).

After the birth of the twin boys, Isaac moved south into Gerar, the land of the Philistines, this because of a famine in Canaan. But God told Isaac not to go to Egypt but to remain where he was and He would bless him. Isaac obeyed God and God blessed him a hundredfold because of his obedience to the Lord.

Later, when the Philistines began to take the wells which Isaac's servants had dug, Isaac did not fight back in retaliation but only moved to a new location and his servants dug new wells. This well thieving continued for some time until finally everybody had all the wells which were needed. Isaac showed himself of man of peace and

God blessed him immensely for it. He became recognized as the true prince that he was in the same way his father had become recognized among the Hittites and others living in Canaan (Gen. 36:1–33).

Isaac, at Rebekah's urging sent Jacob away to Laban's people where Jacob remained for twenty years. In Paddan Aram, he found refuge from his brother's wrath and raised a family of twelve sons and a daughter, Dinah (Gen. 28:1–5).

Isaac finally died in Mamre, in Kirath arba, i.e. Hebron, where his father Abraham had stayed.

Isaac died at 180 years of age and was buried by Jacob and Esau in peace (Gen. 35:27–29).

Isaac was "old and full of years." He breathed his last and was gathered to his people.

He had fulfilled God's purpose for his life.

He had worshiped and served the God of his father Abraham and the God that his son Jacob would later serve so long and so faithfully.

So now, forever after, the living God and creator of the heavens and the Earth would be called the God of these threefold patriarchal men as "the God of Abraham, Isaac, and Jacob."

The life spans of Abraham, Isaac and Jacob overlapped, but the total life span of all three men totaled 232 years i.e. within the total span of 232 years, one of these three great men of God was living, beginning with Abraham and ending with Jacob.

The three men lived 175 years (Abraham) 180 years (Isaac) and 147 years (Jacob). Together a long-term witness and testimony to the true God, the Creator of the heavens and earth and later the God of the entire nation of Israel (Ex. 3:5–6; Matt. 22:29–33).

SUMMARY OF LESSONS TO BE LEARNED FROM ISAAC'S LIFE

He loved his wife

After Isaac's mother, Sarah, died, and he was of marriageable age, his father, Abraham, procured a wife for him from among his own family members.

Rebekah was a beautiful young virgin.

She and Isaac were married and the Bible said of him, "So she became his wife, and he loved her" (Gen. 24:67).

Isaac loved his beautiful young wife and cared for her. But they had no children for twenty years. During the twenty-year period, Isaac faithfully prayed for Rebekah because she was barren. "Isaac prayed to the Lord on behalf of his wife, because she was barren. The Lord answered his prayer and his wife became pregnant" (Gen. 25:21).

So Isaac was a prayerful and believing husband who loved his wife, a man who prayed and persevered in prayer until an answer was given to him by the Lord.

Isaac was an obedient man. To illustrate this:

During a famine in Canaan, he was told by the Lord to remain there and not to go down into Egypt as his father had done during a previous famine in Canaan. God told Isaac, "Stay in this land for a while, and I will be with you and will bless you." Isaac listened to the Lord; Isaac believed the Lord, and Isaac obeyed the Lord. He remained in Canaan, despite the famine there and God kept His promise and blessed Isaac immensely. "Isaac planted crops in that land and the same year reaped a hundredfold, because the Lord blessed him. The man became rich, and his wealth continued to grow until he became very wealthy. He had so many flocks and herds and servants that the Philistines envied him" (Gen. 26: 12–14).

But his immense wealth brought some problems with the Philistines. Because of their jealousy they began filling up Isaac's water wells that his father's men had dug previously. So Isaac, instead of fighting over the wells, moved on to new wells that he re-opened again, wells that had been stopped up also by the Philistines after Abraham had died. Isaac's men dug further wells also over which the Philistines disputed, saying the wells were theirs. Each time a dispute arose over the possession of wells, Isaac would move on and dig another one. He did this rather than fight with the Philistines. He knew there was enough water for everyone and it was unnecessary to dispute and fight about water rights.

This attitude of Isaac marked him.

Isaac was a man of peace.

He had been and still was being blessed by the Lord and he moved on to dig new wells, until everyone had enough water for their flocks (Gen. 26:12–25).

Isaac was a man of faith

He blessed his two sons, Jacob and Esau, regarding their futures by this faith. He laid hands on both of them and pronounced blessings appropriate to them both (Gen. 27:1–40; Heb. 11:20).

He honored his father Abraham with an honorable burial. He and his half-brother Ishmael buried their father "in the cave of Machpelah near Mamre, in the field of Ephron son of Zohar the Hittite" (Gen. 25:9).

"Isaac lived a hundred and eighty years, then he breathed his last and died and was gathered to his people, old and full of years. And his sons Esau and Jacob buried him" (Gen. 35:28–29).

Isaac lived a long and fruitful life, doing God's will for his unique life and leaving all of us as tremendous example of godly and holy living.

Forever after, the God of the Bible, for both Jews and non-Jews, has been known as, "the God of Abraham, the God of Isaac, and the God of Jacob."

ESAU AND JACOB
ESAU

**Genesis 25:21–34; 26:34–35; 27:1–45; 28:6–9;
32:1–32; 33:1–16; 36:1–43; Romans 9:10–16;
Hebrews 11:20; 12:14–17; Malachi 1:1–5**

JACOB
Genesis 25:19–49; 33; Hebrews 11:21

Esau and Jacob were the twin sons of Isaac and Rebekah. There had been a period of twenty years' wait, from the time of Isaac and Rebekah's marriage until the twin boys were born. Because of Rebekah's barrenness during the long period, Isaac had prayed perseveringly to the Lord and the Lord answered his prayer and his wife became pregnant.

Prior to these infants' birth, they jostled one another in their mother's womb. The mother, wondering why this was happening to her, went to the Lord with her inquiry as to why this jostling was happening. The Lord answered her with this explanation:

> The Lord said, "Two nations are in your womb, and two peoples from within you will be separated; one people will be stronger than the other and the older will serve the younger."
>
> (Gen. 25:23)

These infants turned out to be two boys. The first one to come out was red all over and hairy. So they later named this boy "Esau," which means "hairy" or "Edom," which means "red."

Esau's brother came out second, with his little hand grasping his brother's heel, so they named this boy "Jacob" which means "he grasps the heel." So later when these young growing boys were running around playing in their neighborhood they would likely have been known as the American equivalent of "Harry" or "Red" (Esau), and "heel-grasper" (Jacob).

Esau and Jacob grew up together in the happy household of Isaac and Rebekah. Isaac was sixty years of age when his twin sons were born (Gen. 25:26).

Esau grew up and loved the outdoors and became a skillful hunter, like his ancestor and partial relative, Ishmael, who became an archer after he reached adulthood (Gen. 21:20).

Jacob, his brother, on the other hand, was of a quieter nature. He enjoyed staying around his family home, among the tents. Isaac, who had a taste for wild game, loved Esau who would frequently bring some of his wild game for his father to enjoy. But Rebekah had a special love for the quieter boy, Jacob.

One day Esau came in from hunting and he was famished for something to eat. His brother Jacob had some stew cooking, so Esau, being famished, asked if he could have some of the stew. Jacob said yes, but "First sell me your birthright." At this point, under the duress of his extreme physical hunger, Esau made a bad decision, a serious decision, a decision that had long-term consequences with it. Esau did agree at this time to sell his right as the firstborn son of his parents, in exchange for a single meal of Jacob's stew along with some bread and something to drink.

The "birthright of the firstborn" obviously carried with it more than material and property dimensions. It had a spiritual dimension with it as well. Moses in reporting the incident involving Jacob and Esau, reports it as follows, "So Esau despised his birthright" (Gen. 25:34c).

The New Testament writer of the book of Hebrews describes Esau's actions in this incident as follows, "See that no one is sexually immoral, or is godless like Esau, who for a single meal sold his inheritance rights as the oldest son.

"Afterward, as you know, when he wanted to inherit this blessing, he was rejected. He could bring about no change of mind, though he sought the blessing with tears" (Heb. 12:15–17).

Esau's decision at this time was not an incidental decision but a determinative one. It revealed his lack of sensitivity to spiritual things. But on the part of his brother it plainly revealed that Jacob not only did not despise the birthright of the firstborn, but fervently desired it for himself along with all the spiritual privileges and obligations that were included with it.

Jacob was not afraid to shoulder all the responsibilities along with the privileges that went along with the full right of the firstborn in a patriarchal family at that time.

Jacob was happy to have procured for himself these rights, although his methodology in obtaining them perhaps manifested some spiritual immaturity on his part, a spiritual immaturity which in later years he most likely would have outgrown.

A second incident related to the birthright incident was that which happened later when Jacob and his mother, Rebekah, worked together to deceive Isaac in his granting a superior blessing to Jacob rather to Esau. This superior blessing would have been given to Esau had it not been for the intervention and planning of Rebekah and the willing compliance of her younger son Jacob.

Rebekah, the mother, had never forgotten the message the Lord had given to her before her twin sons were born. That message from the Lord had indicated that the older son would serve the younger. She always knew that there was a special and distinctive call on the life of her son Jacob. It was obviously with this knowledge in mind that she moved to interfere with Isaac's plan to bless Esau with the greatest blessing which he planned to bestow.

Her methodology, like the circumstances attending Jacob's methodology in obtaining the initial birthright, may appear to some to be somewhat unethical, yet at the base of her motivation in doing what she did was a faith in God's revelation to her about the future destinies of her two sons. Her actions were being influenced by God's revelation to her. She had a sensitivity to spiritual things and to the overriding purposes of God for the lives of her two sons.

Along with Rebekah's actions, insofar as they were at their base motivated by faith in God's revelation to her, were Isaac's actions and faith also, for we are told in Hebrews that "By faith Isaac blessed Jacob and Esau in regard to their future." His blessings, first on Jacob, then Esau, were pronounced by faith and hence were true prophecies regarding their respective futures (Heb. 11:20).

After Jacob had received the greater blessing from his father Isaac, and this being deceitfully done by Rebekah and Jacob, Esau returned from his hunting trip and discovered what had been done. Esau received a blessing, too, but it was a blessing greatly inferior to the one that had been given to his brother Jacob. He was angry with his brother and secretly planned to kill him after his father died.

Rebekah, learning of Esau's plan, moved to have Jacob leave his home and travel to his uncle's homestead at Paddon Aram, Syria. Here he remained for twenty years. He married two women and two concubines and at the end of twenty years, Jacob with these four women, had produced a large family of twelve sons and one daughter. These twelve sons became the heads of the later twelve tribes of Israel.

God's plan for Jacob, the younger of the twin boys of Isaac and Rebekah, was now well underway.

God had planned that Jacob would marry and that his twelve sons would become the joint founders of a special nation, called Israel. Each of Israel's twelve tribes would bear the name of one of Jacob's twelve sons for all time to come.

Through the mature years of Jacob's life as he progressed in age and maturity, he had successive experiences with God. Through these experiences there was a gradual deepening of his spiritual life. It seems that he never resisted or fought against God's leading in his life but was open to know God in a deeper way. Some of these experiences with God were the following:

He had a God-given dream at Bethel. While traveling on his journey to Uncle Laban's homestead, while sleeping one night, he had a dream in which he saw a stairway resting on the earth with its top reaching to heaven. Angels were ascending and descending on this stairway. Above the stairway stood the Lord who spoke to Jacob, telling him that He was the God of his father Abraham and of his father Isaac.

God promised, moreover, that he would be with Jacob and would watch over him wherever he went and someday would bring him back to his original homeland again. God said also to Jacob, "I will not leave you until I have done what I have promised you" (Gen. 28:10–15).

When Jacob awoke from his sleep he realized that God, the Creator of the heavens and Earth and the God of his forefathers, had visited him. He set up the stone upon which he had rested his head during the night and poured oil on top of it as a memorial.

Then Jacob made a vow that if indeed God would watch over him and supply all his needs in the years to come and then bring him back again safely to his father's land, then God would indeed be his God.

The stone he had set up would be God's house and Jacob would give God a tenth of everything He would give him.

This dream and meeting with God was a crucial experience for Jacob at the time of the serious beginning of his career for the Lord and the laying of the foundations of the nation of Israel.

Also, in the course of the growth of Jacob's family, some of his wives would often pray for God's assistance, especially regarding the opening of their wombs to pregnancy.

We read of Leah, "God listened to Leah, and she became pregnant and bore Jacob a fifth son" (Gen. 30:17) and of Rachel, "Then God remembered Rachel; He listened to her and opened her womb." Joseph later was conceived and born (Gen. 30:22–24).

Later God told Jacob through an angel in a dream how he could multiply his flocks and later God told Jacob to leave Paddan Aram and return to his father's land.

Jacob in all these experiences was being guided by the Lord and instructed so as to fulfill God's highest purposes for his life and career. See Genesis 31:1–3; 10–13.

Later, when Jacob was traveling on his return to Canaan with his flocks, servants, and all his family, he knew that he was in danger of being attacked by his brother Esau who was in the vicinity with four hundred armed men.

So Jacob, after taking initial safety measures, being finally alone, wrestled with God's angel throughout the night. He wanted God to bless him. Jacob would not allow the angel of the Lord to leave him until he was blessed.

The angel finally touched Jacob's hip joint so that the hip joint was wrenched as he continued to wrestle with the angel.

Finally the angel blessed Jacob, after Jacob had struggled with God and with men and had overcome (Gen. 32:22–32).

Here Jacob had seen God face to face and yet his life was spared.

From that day forward wherever Jacob walked, it was a walk with a limp, but he walked as a man with a new name, "Israel," which means "he struggles with God" (Gen. 32:28).

Jacob from that day forward would have a new power both with men and with God.

Thus, as the years passed, Jacob was becoming a stronger and stronger man of God. Any carnality in his character was gradually being rooted out and replaced with holiness and godly character.

Jacob continued growing in spiritual stature.

After his wrestling with the Lord he experienced a peaceful meeting with his brother Esau.

Now, he continued his journey returning to Canaan the land of his fathers. Here he lived for many years until he with all his people moved down to Egypt because of the widespread famine in Canaan.

After his move into Egypt he lived seventeen more years, finally dying at the age of one hundred and forty-seven.

Forever after during the years of Israel's national history, the God of Israel, among the Jewish people, was to be known as the God of the three leading patriarchs, "the God of Abraham, the God of Isaac, and the God of Jacob" (Ex. 3:6).

After Jacob and his family returned to Canaan after living in Paddan Aram for twenty years, he was called upon to live through some very difficult years.

This was due to Jacob's ten brothers selling their brother Joseph into Egypt and their lying to their father about what had truly happened to him. Jacob for twenty-three years or so believed his son Joseph was dead.

Only later during the worldwide famine did he learn that Joseph was still alive.

How happy he must have been and what a soul relief, and surprise it must have been to him when he learned that Joseph was not only still alive but that God had promoted him to a position of rulership over the great nation of Egypt.

Certainly it was only the grace and mercy of his God and the God of his fathers that sustained Jacob and enabled him to fulfill the calling of God during his long and difficult life and career.

Meanwhile Esau and his descendants were becoming a great and numerous nation, called the Edomites.

Esau had married two Hittite women and a wife who was a daughter of Ishmael.

An entire chapter in Genesis is devoted to reporting about the development of the Edomites, Esau's descendants.

Names of his sons and the rulers and kings of Edomites are listed in this chapter.

The Edomites were all moved away from Canaan and lived in the hill country of Seir, south of Canaan.

Esau's destiny and career was undoubtedly changed, from what it most likely would have been, by his foolish attitude toward the right he had as the firstborn son in his family.

Instead of cherishing his birthrights, he despised them and sold them to his younger brother, Jacob.

Involved with these birthrights were undoubtedly an heirship and family trusteeship to all the pertinent promises that God had made to Abraham and Isaac and trusteeship to all the covenants that God had made with Abraham and Isaac and were to be passed on to the next generation. That trustee would have been Esau since he was indeed the natural firstborn son of Isaac and Rebekah. But Esau forfeited his right to these honors and privileges. Instead they became the property of his brother Jacob.

Decisions have consequences and this decision of Esau to despise his birthright had severe and long-range consequences for him and his descendants.

Had he not despised his birthright, but rather cherished and used it wisely, men may well have referred to the God of the Bible as "the God of Abraham, Isaac, and Esau," rather than "the God of Abraham, Isaac and Jacob."

PRACTICAL LESSONS TO BE LEARNED FROM THE LIVES OF ESAU AND JACOB

What are some of the practical lessons we may learn from the lives of the twin boys, Jacob and Esau?

Do not be like the man Esau, Esau, who pushed aside and despised the holy heritage that was his.

If your parents, or some friend or friends, have given you a copy of God's Word, the Bible, then do not push it aside or neglect it or despise it.

Or if your parents, or some friend or friends, have summarized for you the message of the Bible, the message of a loving God, a suffering and dying Christ, and the gospel and how one may avail oneself of Christ's blessings through repentance and faith, one certainly will be wise to avail oneself of those blessings as soon as he is able to do so.

Be like the man Jacob, who not only did not despise the birthright of the firstborn, but earnestly desired to have it for himself.

For us today, it means that one in this day and age should seek all God's plan and purpose for his or her life, and commit oneself fully to God's service. This person will do well to allow God to prepare him and lead him into a place of responsible and useful service in the advancing of His kingdom, wherever and into whatever areas that service may be.

That was the path Jacob chose and God mightily blessed him, allowing him and his sons to establish an entire nation, the chosen nation of Israel. What an honor was bestowed on Jacob!

Through Israel have come immeasurable spiritual blessings upon all the other nations of the world as well as great blessings on the people of Israel themselves.

JOSEPH

Genesis 30:22–50:26; Exodus 1:1–8; 13:19; Numbers 1:10, 32; 1 Chronicles 5:2; Psalm 105:17; Ezekiel 47:13, 37; Acts 7:11–16; Hebrews 11:22

His Birth—

God heard and listened to Rachel's prayer for children. He "remembered Rachel" and enabled her to become pregnant. When the child was born she declared that, "God has taken away my disgrace." It was a son and she named him "Joseph" which means, "May he add," meaning for her "May the Lord add to me another son" (Gen. 30:22–24).

Rachel now had one son and she wanted another son besides Joseph. Later this desire of Rachel's was also fulfilled, and she had another child, Joseph's brother, Benjamin.

But at Benjamin's birth she had great difficulty and it took her life. Rachel died during the birth of this second child. And her husband buried her on the way to Ephrath. i.e. Bethlehem. Over her tomb Jacob set up a pillar to mark the grave.

His dreams—

Joseph was a seventeen-year-old young man, tending the family's flock with his brothers, the sons of Bilhah and Zilpah. He brought a bad report to his father about the activities of his brothers. This angered his brothers along with the fact that Jacob loved Joseph more than his other sons; this further angered his brothers, causing them to be jealous.

Compounding his brother's jealousy was Jacob's making Joseph a special coat for him, a coat of many colors.

Jacob's had a special love for Joseph because he had been born in his old age.

All this show of favoritism for Joseph on Jacob's part caused a serious hatred by his brothers.

Moreover, about this time Joseph had two dreams. The first dream was of grain sheaves out in the field. Joseph's sheaf rose up and the other eleven sheaves of his brothers gathered around Joseph's sheaf and bowed down to it. This dream caused the brothers' hatred for Joseph to increase even more.

In Joseph's second dream, the sun and moon and eleven stars were all bowing to Joseph.

This second dream again only increased the hatred of Joseph's brothers toward him.

So on a later occasion when Jacob had sent Joseph to find out about the welfare of his brothers and the flocks, Joseph's brothers took him and put him into a dry cistern well, intending to later kill him because of their rabid hatred for him.

While Joseph's brothers were eating their lunch a group of traveling Ishmaelite traders came by and one of Joseph's brothers suggested that they sell Joseph as a slave rather than kill him. The others agreed to this plan.

So Joseph was sold to these traveling merchants and taken to Egypt.

In Egypt Joseph was bought by an official of Pharaoh, named Potiphar.

Joseph's brothers now lied to their father, saying it appeared that a wild animal had killed Joseph, but they themselves had killed a goat and covered Joseph's robe with its blood, they then showed this blood spattered coat to Jacob, suggesting that perhaps an animal had indeed killed Joseph.

Jacob, believing his sons' story, fell into prostrated grief for the tragic "death" of his son Joseph (Gen. 37).

Joseph in Egypt—

His first stop in Egypt was to be sold into the hands of Potiphar, a government official in Pharaoh's administration. Potiphar was captain of the king's guard.

But from the very beginning, the Lord was with Joseph and Joseph prospered while living and serving in the household of Potiphar.

Because the Lord was with Joseph he prospered as anyone today will prosper when the Lord is with that one.

Joseph obviously was regularly seeking the Lord and as with king Uzziah at a much later time, one of the kings of Judah, we are told that "as long as he sought the Lord he prospered" (2 Chron. 26:5).

Potiphar began to see that the Lord was with Joseph and soon made him his attendant and then placed him in charge of all his household—all his servants and all his fields and property.

Now God blessed Potiphar and all he possessed because of Joseph's presence in his household.

All went well both in his household and in his fields.

But Joseph because he was young, well-built and handsome, Potiphar's wife soon took notice of him and said, "Come to bed with me."

But Joseph refused this lady's solicitation, being a godly young man.

This lady persisted, day after day, in her attempts to seduce Joseph. Joseph not only refused her solicitations but refused even to be near the woman. He feared and loved God and said to the woman, inasmuch as my master has shown such a great and full trust in me as he has, "How then could I do such a wicked thing and sin against God?" (Gen. 39:9).

Joseph firmly refused all her invitations to go to bed with her. He remained true to the Lord during this entire episode.

But finally in her frustration, Potiphar's wife accused Joseph to her husband, saying he had tried to rape her. As circumstantial proof of this, she showed to her husband a cloke, belonging to Joseph, which Joseph had left behind in one of his attempts to flee from her grasp.

Potiphar, believing his wife's false accusation, had Joseph put in jail.

Here, Joseph, framed as he was, stayed for many years.

Joseph in Prison—

Notwithstanding Joseph's being sent to prison on a false charge, he did not show bitterness or rancor.

Rather, from the first, the Lord was with him in the prison, showing him kindness. The Lord gave him favor in the eyes of the prison warden.

Soon the warden placed Joseph in charge of all the other prisoners. Joseph's care for the prisoners was so unique and complete that the warden paid no attention to anything under Joseph's care, "because the Lord was with Joseph and gave him success in whatever he did" (Gen. 39:23).

Again, because the Lord was with Joseph here in prison as he had been with him on his previous first stop in Egypt, in Potiphar's household, Joseph was given great favor and success in everything he did here, too.

The question we may well ask ourselves is this: "May I or we as ordinary Christian believers today even expect to have the Lord with us to bless us in all we do as Joseph experienced in his early years in Egypt as a young man?"

Joseph was being prepared to fulfill a special role on behalf of the future of his own people, Israel, the chosen people of God.

Israel would emigrate to Egypt and remain there for many years, growing into a numerous people and would become the Israel of history. Ultimately they would occupy the promised land of Canaan.

The answer to the above question will require some careful and contemplative thought to be sure.

1. To be sure, the focus of God's presence and attention is going to be particularly and uniquely on the life of the man with a special call on his life, a call to a special ministry for God and for His people, a call like that of Moses, Samuel, or David or one of the prophets or later the apostles of the New Testament.

Yet, who of us knows the deep importance of an ordinary Christian life lived for God and the eternal influence we may have on our family members and among the friends and acquaintances that our life may influence as we pass through our earthly years?

The Lord gives a general message to all His followers, a message that can be appropriated by anyone in any age, when he says, "The eyes of the Lord range throughout the earth to strengthen those whose hearts are fully committed to him" (2 Chron. 16:9).

Also, the conditional promises given to all Christian believers in a passage such as Psalm 1:1–3, certainly are available and applicable to all of us. The promise of Psalm 1:3c is, "whatever he does prospers," if we abide faithfully and obediently in His word.

And the multitude of promises given to us in the second chapter of the book of the Proverbs are available too if we seek God's wisdom and knowledge so as to obey and trust our Lord with all our hearts and with all our lives (Prov. 2:1–22).

While in prison Joseph, with God's help, interpreted the dreams of two of Pharaoh's servants, a cupbearer and a baker. These interpretations came faithfully to pass.

Pharaoh's dreams—

Later Pharaoh had some dreams. One of the two servants of Pharaoh, who had been in jail with Joseph, told Pharaoh that a prison-acquaintance of his had interpreted his dream when he was in prison.

Pharaoh immediately sent for Joseph. Joseph then with God's help, interpreted Pharaoh's dreams.

Being able to do this caused Pharaoh to appoint Joseph as second man in authority over the nation of Egypt.

Immediately, then, the young prisoner, Joseph, was elevated to a position of great power and authority in the important and great nation of Egypt.

Joseph would begin administering Egypt through seven years first, of great agricultural prosperity. Then he led Egypt through seven years of worldwide famine.

God's eternal purposes were being worked out for His people Israel. He was directing world affairs so His people could become established finally in their own land, the land of Canaan.

Through Israel, God was arranging circumstances and raising up a chosen nation through which He could provide a message of salvation and redemption for the peoples of the entire world. Joseph was fitting into God's plan and contributing his chosen part in it.

The Lord was with Joseph from his earliest years until his last years. He was one-hundred-ten years of age when he finally died and was gathered to his people.

Finally, Joseph's brothers came to Egypt for grain during this severe period of famine.

In the course of time they discovered that Joseph was alive and in power in Egypt.

Later, Jacob and all his people moved down to Egypt where they remained 430 years, becoming a great and numerous people.

Joseph and Pharaoh arranged for Jacob and his people to live in an ample and fertile part of Egypt.

They helped them to become properly settled in their new environment and land. Here they prospered and grew to become a great people.

PRACTICAL LESSONS TO BE LEARNED
FROM JOSEPH'S LIFE

What are some of the practical lessons we may learn from the life of Joseph?

We are not told in Scripture how fully Joseph's dreams as a teenage young man, may have influenced his early life. Yet after being forcibly separated from his family and taken into Egyptian slavery, he seems to have been submissive to his new circumstances and he tended to serious business as a servant in Potiphar's household.

The Lord was with Joseph from the beginning of his sojourn in Egypt.

He fulfilled his daily duties with excellence, and because the Lord was with him, he was given favor in Potiphar's eyes—and so prospered greatly.

As I mentioned previously, God gave Potiphar prosperity in all things for Joseph's sake.

Thus Joseph was satisfied to serve with the Lord's assistance by his side.

This is the way we all may prosper i.e. by daily trusting Christ and serving Him each day with the Lord's assistance by our side, as well.

Joseph remained true to the Lord although strongly tempted with sexual sin by an evil woman, Potiphar's wife. He has left us a shining example by his purity, despite of and in the face of, a strong temptation to impurity.

Joseph remained faithful to the Lord during his time in prison. Because the Lord was with him he was given favor in the eyes of the jailor. He served the Lord as a trusted prisoner and prison supervisor until the day of his discharge.

Joseph's faithfulness to the Lord and his integrity during his preparatory years in Egypt serves as an excellent example to all Christian believers today.

Also, his faithfulness and godly life during his many later years of service in the Egyptian government is an example to all Christian believers today who have a call to work in government service in any country at any level, be it an elective or appointive office.

Joseph was not afraid to accept positions of responsibility when they were offered to him. This was seen to be true at the first when he was in Potiphar's household, then also when he was placed in prison, where he was asked to be in charge of the entire prison population.

Lastly, when called by Pharaoh, the king of Egypt, he was offered the number-two position in rulership over the entire nation of Egypt. He accepted this position and served with distinction there for many years.

Joseph depended upon the Lord's presence and help for success in whatever position of responsibility he was placed. First, again, in Potiphar's household, secondly, during his time in the prison, lastly, while he was a long-term ruler in Egypt, he had the Lord with him to ensure his success.

From Joseph's earliest years he acknowledged the lordship of God in his life. He was willing to fit into God's overall plan and calling of God on his life. And in the carrying out of the divine plan he depended upon the presence and assistance of God throughout the whole of his life. At his life's end he could look back and see that he had fulfilled God's plan and purpose for his life.

Joseph was a faithful and good representative for the Lord in his time as in later years other men were faithful servants for the Lord in government service—men such as Mordecai, Daniel, and Daniel's three friends Shadrach, Meshach, and Abednego (Dan. 1–3).

As Joseph moved into his high position of authority in Egypt he had the spiritual maturity and insight to see that God was working out His purpose in his life. This all was in accordance with the dreams that God had given him in his early years.

Despite the hateful mood, motives and actions of his brothers in selling him as a slave into Egypt, Joseph later said to his brothers that,

> "God sent me ahead of you to preserve for you a remnant on earth and to save your lives by a great deliverance.

> So then, it was not you who sent me here, but God. He made me a father to Pharaoh, lord of his entire household and ruler of all Egypt" (Gen. 45:7–8).

Joseph's earliest twelve-to-thirteen years in Egypt not only gave him opportunity to become faithful as a servant and a lead servant, and as a prisoner and a lead prisoner, but these years gave him the occasion to learn of the Egyptian language and people and culture and grow up into maturity in preparation for his ultimate position as a national ruler over the entire nation of Egypt.

These twelve-to-thirteen years of preparation, during his late teen years and during his twenties, prepared him to assume high authority at the age of thirty.

JOSEPH'S BROTHERS
Genesis 29:31–30:1–24; 35:16–18

Joseph had eleven brothers and one sister, Dinah. The name of his brothers were Reuben, Simeon, Levi, Judah, Dan, Naphtali, Gad, Asher, Issachar, Zebulun, and Benjamin (Gen. 29:31–30:1–4; Gen. 35:16–18).

Joseph's youngest brother, Benjamin, it seems, was not part of the hatred that his other ten brothers had for him.

But because of Jacob's special love for Joseph and due to his showing his favoritism by making a beautiful robe for him, Joseph's ten brothers developed a hatred for him.

The reason for this was due to the apparent meaning of the two dreams. Both dreams indicated that the ten brothers would bow down someday to Joseph. Moreover, in the second dream that not only the ten brothers, but Joseph's parents also would someday bow down to Joseph in a social and political posture.

Both of these dreams of Joseph were God-given prophetic dreams, but Joseph's brothers could not accept their possible meaning at that time.

Jacob, however, kept the possible meaning of his son's dreams in the back of his mind, he being more experienced and more spiritual than were his ten sons.

The ten brothers, now impelled by their extreme hatred for Joseph, sold him as a slave to some passing merchants, who took him down to Egypt. There Joseph served for several years as a servant-slave, and then spent several years in prison for an accused crime he had not committed.

Joseph's brothers did not see him again for approximately twenty-two or twenty-three years, when a worldwide famine caused them to visit Egypt to obtain food.

Finally these ten men were reconciled to Joseph when they learned that Joseph was not only still alive but was the ruler in Egypt.

Joseph's brothers had committed this crime against him, intending it for evil, but God overruled it so as to accomplish His higher purposes for the nation He was in the process of founding, the future great and key nation of Israel—this nation He was bringing into existence through which He would provide salvation and redemption for the whole world.

So despite the malicious act which these ten brothers had brought to pass against one of their own family members, God used them, together with Benjamin and Joseph himself—twelve sons of the one man Jacob, to bring into existence a nation called Israel, a great and well populated nation made up of twelve separate tribes united into a single people and nation.

God had promised to Abraham, Isaac and Jacob that their descendants would become a great nation and this promise would ultimately be fulfilled.

They became a great and numerous nation and later occupied the land God had promised to give them, the land of Canaan. This land was to be their land forever, a land occupied by the people of Israel, consisting of the twelve tribes, each tribe bearing the name of one of the twelve sons of Jacob.

What are some of the practical lessons to be learned from the story of the twelve sons of Jacob, but especially from the story of the ten sons who sold their brother into slavery?

In spite of the sins of His chosen servants, God is still able to accomplish His overall purposes through them.

God founded a nation through these twelve sons of Jacob notwithstanding the serious crime ten of these men committed in the process.

Moreover, the twelve separate tribes shall bear the names of each of the twelve sons of Jacob, during their entire earthly history and this shall continue into eternity. See Revelation 7:4–8; 21:12.

This ability of God to still use men who committed serious sins prior to their call was also seen in the case of Moses and later in the life of St. Paul and in the lives of many others as well.

It reminds me of the words of the gospel hymn, "His blood can make the vilest sinner clean," and the example of John Newton, the writer of the widely known song, "Amazing Grace," whose author was a vile sinner prior to his conversion to Christ.

In spite of our sins and in spite of the blackness of our hearts, a spiritual blackness produced by our sins, Jesus, by His blood, is able to wash us whiter than snow.

Did not the Lord say through the prophet?

> "Come now, let us reason together,
> Though your sins are like scarlet,
> They shall be as white as snow;
> Though they are red as crimson,
> They shall be as wool."
>
> (Isa. 1:18)

Over and over again God's dealings with the men and women in the days of the Old Testament and in the days of the New Testament as well, demonstrated His great love and mercy toward sinners and His desire to forgive them and restore them to fellowship with Himself.

God's willingness to forgive sins was certainly shown in His dealings with Joseph's ten brothers and it was shown also in the heart attitude of their brother Joseph as well, against whom the ten had sinned with such treachery.

Joseph forgave his brothers and wept much during the period of reconciliation with them, forgiving them for what they had done (Gen. 42:21–24; 45:1–15).

He even said that God had used them to send him to Egypt to fulfill God's purposes for them all.

Despite the hateful mood, motives, and actions of Joseph's brothers in selling him as a slave into Egypt, Joseph later said to his brothers that,

> "God sent me ahead of you to preserve for you a remnant
> on earth and to save your lives by a great deliverance.

So then, it was not you who sent me here, but God. He made me a father to Pharaoh, lord of his entire household and ruler of all Egypt."

(Gen. 45:7–8)

Hebrew Midwives

Exodus 1

After the Israelites moved into Egypt they became fruitful and multiplied. The land where they were living soon became full of Israelites (Ex. 1:7).

These Israelites did what God had earlier instructed Adam and Eve to do, "Be fruitful and increase in number . . ." (Gen. 1:28).

And these Israelites did what God had later instructed Noah and his three sons to do, following the flood. God said to them, "Be fruitful and increase in number and fill the earth" (Gen. 9:1).

For Israel to now become strong and numerous would be to their advantage and be pleasing to the Lord.

Pharaoh, an Egyptian King who had not known Joseph, fearing that the multiplying Israelites would join a future Egyptian enemy, placed the Israelites under slavery.

Then he ordered some Hebrew midwives to kill the Israelite boys as soon as they were born. But the midwives, fearing God more than the king's murderous order, refused to kill the newly-born Israelite boys.

Their actions so pleased the Lord that He gave the midwives families of their own.

Meanwhile the Israelite population continued to grow, but Pharaoh put in place another strategy intended to solve his problem of an increasing Israelite population growth.

He now instructed all his people as follows, "Every boy that is born you must throw into the river, but let every girl live" (Ex. 1:22).

What practical lesson can we learn from the response of the Hebrew midwives to the order of the king of Egypt? Some of the lesson and lessons are these:

There are times when certain laws and orders issued by government officials are so clearly in conflict with God's higher law that God-fearing people are justified in disobeying such laws and orders.

The actions of the midwives is a case in point. The actions of Daniel and his three friends is another case illustrating the principle (Dan. 3:1–30; 6:1–28).

The actions of the twelve apostles after Pentecost, choosing to obey God rather than the prohibitive orders of the Jewish Sanhedrin, is yet another case, illustrating this principle (Acts 4:1–22; 5:17–42).

When the obedience issues are clearly seen, as was the case with the Hebrew midwives, it is more pleasing to the Lord to obey His holy law than it is to obey an evilly conceived man-made law—a man-made law that will require a transgression of God's law.

Public, civic laws are to be obeyed as long as they are in harmony with divine law and authority.

When public, civic laws depart from their harmony with divine law, they are not to be obeyed by public citizens.

God's laws have always provided the foundational principles for all of the laws and legislation of the nations of history. The closer is the harmony between the laws of the nations and the laws of God, our Creator, the greater is the fairness and justice of these national, humanly-formulated laws.

God's laws have always been supreme. Humanly-formulated laws are excellent when they reflect and coincide with God's laws.

Whenever humanly-formulated laws depart from God's laws, they work havoc in civil society, causing unrighteousness rather than righteousness, a curse instead of a blessing.

Did the actions of the Hebrew midwives and the reasons for their actions have any bearing upon the issue of child abortion in America today?

Clearly, the answer is "Yes!"

When American women allow themselves to become pregnant and then decide they do not want to allow the living human infant to be born and grow up into a mature human being, they consult with and cooperate with an abortion doctor and his associates. Plans are then made to end the unborn infant's life, killing the infant within the pregnant woman's womb.

In effect, the pregnant American women in cooperation with the abortion clinic people are doing what the Hebrew midwives would have been doing if they had gone along with the Egyptian King's orders to kill all the Hebrew boys at birth.

But the pregnant women and the abortionists are going beyond even that which the king of Egypt desired.

The women and abortionists are killing not only the baby boys, but also the baby girls along with the baby boys.

The Hebrew midwives feared God too much to carry out the king's order. For them to obey the king's order would have meant incurring the wrath of a Holy God by flying in the face of His law which prohibits the murder of another human being.

But the actions of the American pregnant women and the abortionists in killing their young is a horrible violation of God's holy law against murder. Their actions show an utter disregard of anything even approaching the reverent fear of God that was a deterrent for the Hebrew midwives.

God was so pleased with the actions of the Hebrew midwives that He showed them kindness and rewarded them by giving them families of their own.

In contrast, we can say boldly that God is not pleased with the actions of the pregnant American women and the abortionists—killing baby boys *and* girls—nor do their actions deserve God's kindness nor a reward of any kind, but rather severe, severe punishment and divine judgment because of the evil being committed against beings created in God's own image.

Had the midwives heeded the king's evil order they would have been disregarding the fear of God.

But the pregnant American women and their cooperating abortionists *are* clearly disregarding the fear of the Lord in killing the thousands upon thousands of the soon to be born American babies, while still in their mother's wombs.

As to the question: Are the yet unborn infants, while still in their mother's womb's fully human beings or not?

It does not take a rocket scientist to give an intelligent and true answer to this question.

Even a student who has finished the eighth grade of an American grammar school or a student who has graduated from high school knows how to give an intelligent and true answer to the above-posed question.

Yes, the unborn infants are complete human beings. They are merely in the formative beginning stages of their human life span.

Time and care would allow each infant to reach his or her mature adult state.

For ages without end when brothers or sisters in a family have asked their pregnant mother why her tummy is so big, has not that mother often answered by saying something like this? "Your little baby brother or sister is inside. Someday we will see him or her after the baby has come out into the world."

This mother is speaking of the infant human being who will be given a name and hopefully will one day grow to be a fully mature human being, a man or a woman who will become a part of human society.

The massive killing of thousands and millions of unborn infants in their mother's wombs in the "enlightened" and "civilized" society called America is a travesty of justice of massive proportions.

It is in the same class as the Nazis' murder of six million Hebrews during the Second World War.

Men and women in America, who fear God, let us continue to speak out and act until the curse of abortion is swept from our land.

Let the same fear of God that motivated the Hebrew mid-wives in Egypt, motivate the God-fearing men and women in America to continue to pray, speak, and act until child-abortion killing is removed from American society.

MOSES' PARENTS

Exodus 2:1–10; Hebrews 11:23

Their names were Amram and Jochebed (Num. 26:59).

It was during an era of Israel's early history. The Israelites were a rapidly growing people living in Egypt at the time.

The king of Egypt, under whose political jurisdiction the Israelites were living, out of fear of Israel's growing population, had issued a strict edict to all of his people, including the Jews as follows, "Every boy that is born you must throw into the river, but let every girl live" (Ex. 1:22).

Because of this nationwide edict it was a very risky and dangerous time for any Israeli couple to marry and have children. This risk was certainly acute if the Israeli couple had sons born in their family. Any infant girls were allowed to live, but that was not the case with any infant sons.

All infant sons, born during this era, were to be killed by drowning in the Nile River.

It was during this dangerous era that the future parents of the boy Moses were married.

These two young people, both members of the tribe of Levi, were married, and before long a son was born to them.

These two parents Amram and Jochebed already had at least two other children. They had Moses' older sister, Miriam, and an older son, Aaron.

We do not know how Moses' older brother had escaped the danger of the kings edict to kill all the Hebrew boys, but in some providential way, he, too, had been kept out of reach of this wicked plan of Egypt's king. Miriam of course was in no danger, because she was a girl.

But the infant Moses was certainly in danger.

Would this little Jewish boy survive and grow up through his childhood years and finally become a mature adult, or would his young life be snuffed out by drowning in the river of Egypt?

That was the question! What would be the answer to this question at this time?

The answer to the above question lay within the minds and hearts of the baby's parents and beyond that in the mind and heart of God, little Moses' creator.

First of all, when this child's parents looked at their newly-born son, they "saw he was no ordinary child" (Heb. 11:23).

The mother, we are told, saw that he was "a fine child" (Ex. 2:2).

Perhaps by a God-given intuition, they both saw an unexplainable destiny, when they looked into the countenance of their sleeping infant son as he lay in his crib.

Whatever were their perceptions and the reasons for these perceptions, this young couple decided that whatever else happened among their Jewish friends and neighbors, this little newly-born son of theirs was not going to be put to death by them. In no way, would that happen!

So the mother, with the father's compliance, hid the baby away, caring for him secretly and in private.

This mother did for baby Moses that which a much later God-fearing woman named Jehosheba, did for young Joash, who would ultimately be crowned king of Judah. Jehosheba protected and raised Joash for six years, hidden from the eyes of a wicked queen-ruler of Judah named Athaliah (2 Chron. 22:10–12).

Moses' mother hid her son for three months. But when this hidden-child process became too risky she changed her tactic.

She, like Noah, built a small ark-basket using papyrus, and like Noah, coated it with tar and pitch so as to make it leak proof. Then she placed her baby in this small ark-boat, placing a light cover over its top.

Then she put her son in the Nile River, the place where the king of Egypt had intended as a place of death for all the Jewish baby boys.

But thanks to the providentially given wisdom of this mother, Jochebed, the Nile River became the place from which the child was rescued and his life saved from a watery grave.

Moses' parents, like the earlier Hebrew midwives, did not fear the king's wicked edict, and in taking steps to save their infant sons life, they defied this edict, and rightly so. The efforts of these parents like the earlier efforts of the Hebrew midwives were immensely blessed by God. God certainly was pleased by what these parents had done. To work further with these parents, God providentially acted, doing an amazing thing for both them and for the young child who later would be named "Moses."

Pharaoh's own daughter, while river bathing, discovered the child in the floating papyrus basket and ultimately the rescued child became her own son, cared for at first by the child's own mother, unbeknown to Pharaoh's daughter. Then later, the young child was taken into the full care of Pharaoh's daughter.

She named the child "Moses" meaning, "I drew him out of the water" (Ex. 2:10).

She proceeded to raise up Moses to adult maturity with all the benefits and privileges of a full Egyptian education and enculturation.

The providential hand of God was certainly at work in the lives of Moses' parents. God gave them wisdom and a healthy fear of God and faithfulness in raising their other children, Aaron and Miriam, while their extra special son, Moses, was being providentially raised up and trained in the midst of Egyptian culture and education.

The God of Israel had a special task ahead for the man Moses, a task made known to him when he reached his eightieth year of life.

PRACTICAL LESSONS TO BE LEARNED FROM MOSES' PARENTS

Lesson no. 1

Moses' parents, like the Hebrew midwives, feared God more than an evil and unjust edict by the king of Egypt.

God worked with these parents, as a sign of approval of their actions in refusing to kill their son, by providing a providential saving of little Moses' life. He also arranged for an education and training he would need for his future work. God was preparing a leader who one day would free his enslaved people.

Lesson no. 2

May there come into being a resurgence, in the United States of America, those who value human life and fear God enough to cease aborting unborn infants in their mother's wombs. The killing of four-thousand infants each day is a travesty of justice and shame in our so-called civilized and enlightened American society.

The killing of thousands of our unborn boys *and* girls in America is every bit as tragic and wicked as was Pharaoh's order to kill all the Hebrew boys in his era.

MOSES

Exodus 2:1–Deuteronomy 34; Psalm 90; Acts 7:17–38; Hebrews 3:1–6; Hebrews 11:24–28

Moses was born during a period of Hebrew history when the Hebrews were suffering extreme oppression and forced hard labor under the Egyptians. Yet because of Israel's continual population growth and the Egyptian king's fear of this, attempts were being made to curtail Israel's population growth by means of killing Israel's boys at birth.

Many Israeli parents complied with the Egyptian king's decree and killed their sons (Acts 7:19).

But young Moses' life was providentially saved from a watery grave in the Nile River by wise parents and the providential hand of God on his life. His two parents refused to kill their son as so many of their Hebrew friends were being forced to do. Moses' parents were like the God-fearing Hebrew midwives who likewise did not fear the king's earlier edict and had refused to kill Hebrew baby boys.

Moses lived for one-hundred-and-twenty years and then he died.

One-hundred-and-twenty years is certainly a long lifespan when compared with the average lifespan of those of us who are living in the twenty-first century. Moses was healthy and strong and possessed good eyesight even to the day of his death.

Moses' life is easily divided up into three sections of forty years each. And inasmuch as our purpose in this book is to note the practical lessons to be learned from the lives of the men and women in the Old Testament, I will approach the life of Moses as follows:

I.   Practical lessons to be learned from the life of Moses from his first forty years—life in Egypt.
II. Practical lessons to be learned from the life of Moses from his second forty years—Life in Midian.
III. Practical lessons to be learned from the life of Moses from his third forty years—Life in the desert with Israel.

III

Patterns from the Exodus to the Judges

III

Practical lessons to be learned from Moses' first forty years—Life in Egypt.

$\mathcal{T}$ he first forty years of Moses' life were spent in Egyptian schools, in Egyptian society and Egyptian activities and life.

He was not living during this forty-year period with his fellow Israelites, but separate from them.

He made many important decisions prior to the age of forty. Stephen in his sermon-speech that he gave prior to his martyrdom said this about Moses' accomplishments in his early years: "Moses was educated in all the wisdom of the Egyptians and was powerful in speech and action" (Acts 7:22).

From this we can conclude that:

1. Moses studied diligently and responded well to the teaching of his tutors and professors in the Egyptian schools.
   He undoubtedly became acquainted with Egyptian history and world history, philosophy, and other subjects that were taught to willing and intelligent students in Egyptian schools at that time.

2. He learned to speak and write well in the Egyptian language. He became widely read in all important subjects having to do with government, government administration, and public law.
He was trained not only scholastically but in the practical aspects of public service, perhaps with practical experience in governmental administrations and in the military as well.

I. Practical lessons to be learned from Moses' first forty years—Life in Egypt

These years were Moses' time of providential preparation for the years to come.

If we today, like Moses, will take full advantage of our educational opportunities in grade school, in high school and college, if such opportunities are afforded to us, along with involvement in diligent practical experience, we, like Moses, will at least be partly prepared to fulfill God's call on our lives.

The diligent study and practical experience by Moses would do much to prepare him for the work God would later call him to do as Israel's leader and ruler.

During the first forty years of Moses' life he was immersed totally in Egyptian life and culture. But after this relatively young man had attained full maturity and had grown up, he began to make a series of critical decisions that changed the entire course of his life. What were some of these decisions that the now mature man Moses made at this time of his life? Speaking of this important series of decisions, the writer of Hebrews said that they were all decisions that Moses made "by faith" (Heb. 11:24–27).

1. First, he refused to be known any longer as the son of Pharaoh's daughter. Certainly this decision was not because of a lack of gratitude to Pharaoh's daughter for all she had done for him. His reasons are to be found elsewhere.
2. Secondly, he chose to identify himself with his afflicted people. He chose to leave behind him the comforts of the riches and pleasures of Egypt.
3. Thirdly, he left Egypt not fearing the king's wrath.

This series of three great decisions changed the course of his life. They put him over on the side of God and His will and out of the stream of the world and an anti-God life for Moses.

Moses saw that there was a better road to travel than the one he was on. So he turned off the one and onto the better road that he saw. The better road moved him closer to God and to loving God. It would bring him more hardship, but it led to a far superior destination—an eternal reward in heaven. The other road he had been traveling was leading through scenes of beautiful luxuries and pleasures and glory, but these were only temporary and its destiny was deplorable and without God's blessing.

Moses took the long, far-reaching view of the road choices before him. That was the road for Moses and he turned onto it and remained on it to the end of his life. The next forty years in Midian was only a first-stage result of his decision to identify himself with his people and God's plan for the rest of his life.

No more Egypt and a self-pleasing life, but God's better way was Moses' wise choice at this juncture of his long life.

In Moses' fortieth year Moses was to pay a visit out among his oppressed, slave-driven, fellow Hebrews.

His decision was to visit them, something he had never done in this way before. During this visit, he killed an Egyptian who was mistreating a Hebrew.

Moses thought that his people would accept him as their champion-leader and allow him to lead them out from under their oppressive slavery and into freedom.

That had been Moses' hope and thinking, leading up to the first visit out among his people. But his people did not recognize him as God's providential leader at that time, although ultimately he was their man to accomplish that very goal.

Moses' timing was off, although innately, it is clear that he had an inner sense, although an immature sense of God's call on his life.

Moses was not fully ready to become Israel's leader. God was not yet ready to put His Israelite deliverance plan into effect. And this because even the people of Israel, themselves, although enslaved and suffering, were not fully ready for their deliverance.

Israel's deliverance from their bondage was still up ahead—forty more years ahead.

At that time, and not until that time, would Moses be ready, God would be ready, and the people of Israel would be fully ready for their deliverance from their oppressors.

Moses concluded, in his thinking about his future, that for him to be required to suffer, mistreatment after identifying himself with his suffering Hebrew people, would be far better in the long run, than it would be if he remained among the pleasures, riches, and luxuries of Egypt.

He made a value judgment during this time.

On an imaginary balancing scale he placed on one side the short-term pleasures of sin and the treasures of Egypt, on the other side of his scale he placed the mistreatment and disgrace, for the sake of Christ, he would suffer with his people, but also the reward he would receive from God at the end of his earthly life. This would be a reward which would be his, not for five or six decades, but a reward that would be his forever in God's future kingdom.

Moses' thoughts and reasoning at this time were very similar, in kind, to those of the apostle Paul when he was comparing the temporary troubles which the saints are often called upon to suffer during our Christian walk, to the eternal glory that shall be ours for having gone through them. See these words:

> "For our light affliction, which is but for a moment, worketh for us a far more exceeding and eternal weight of glory; while we look not at the things which are seen, but at the things which are not seen: for the things which are seen are temporal; but the things which are not seen are eternal."
>
> (2 Cor. 4:17–18, KJV)

For a Christian believer to identify himself with Christ and his redeemed people and find and do God's will for his life, serving God's people and the unsaved world around him, such persons will often suffer affliction and hardships and oftentimes persecutions.

But these difficulties will be compensated for by an eternal reward similar to that which Moses saw up ahead in his eternal future.

Moses made a wise decision in identifying with his suffering people—for eternal reward, while leaving behind him a luxurious Egyptian life, "to enjoy the pleasures of sin."

Christian believers today also make a wise decision when identifying with God's blood—bought people for eternal reward, while leaving behind them a luxurious earthly life bereft of fellowship with Christ and his people, "to enjoy the pleasures of sin" (Heb. 11:24–26).

II. PRACTICAL LESSONS TO BE LEARNED FROM MOSES' SECOND FORTY YEARS—LIFE IN MIDIAN

Moses left Egypt, not fearing the king's anger (Heb. 11:27).

It would appear from the account in Ex. 2:15 that Moses' flight from Egypt was indeed to escape the anger of Pharaoh who was trying to kill him. But to the writer of the book of Hebrews, the deep-down and inner-heart motives and attitudes of Moses at this time in his life were more fully revealed.

This was a turning-point time for Moses. This was a radical change in the overall direction of his life at this time. He was thinking and making decisions that were in line with God's overall calling upon his life and career. Yet he was feeling his way, as a man walking through a dark room with his hands held out in front of him, as he looks for the door and a better lighted way leading to his intended destination.

He made some mistakes at this time, killing a man and having to flee and live in a foreign land miles away from Egypt.

He fled southeast to a country called Midian, but his flight from Egypt to Midian at this time sealed in a practical way his decision to leave a self-indulgent, worldly life and come over on the side of God and His will and plan for his life.

At forty years of age he had not yet learned how to find and follow God's perfect leading for his life. But he was seriously searching to find God's leading.

His present attempt to find and fulfill God's call on his life reminds one of Rebekah and Jacob's attempt to find and fulfill God's purpose and call on Jacob's life. Also it reminds one of Abram and Sarah's attempt to help God fulfill His promise of a son-heir, by bringing Hagar into the picture.

These were all attempts being made by those who loved God and desired to fulfill God's plan in their lives, but whose endeavors were characterized by a mixture of several ingredients: much genuine faith, but also large amounts of unsanctified, carnal human effort.

Rebekah and Jacob would fulfill a prenatal prophecy by means of deception.

Abraham and Sarah would fulfill God's promise of a son through natural conception rather than through a son "born by the power of the Spirit" (Gal. 4:29).

Moses would fulfill a perceived call upon his life to become Israel's national leader and deliverer, but this perceived call was not yet from God. It was premature and a humanly-conceived perception only.

Hence, Moses made a grave mistake and bad decision at his first attempt at national leadership and spilled a man's blood needlessly and certainly to his regret and humiliation.

Moses' experience was similar in some ways to that of Saul, who was later called Paul, who aided and approved of the murder of many saints in a later era, yet who later became a holy apostle and preacher of the gospel when he finally learned of God's true purpose for his life.

But most of these decisions and actions of Moses in his fortieth year were decisions and actions of faith—that does not mean guesswork, but decisions and actions based upon God-given perceptions of the future.

His refusal to be any longer called the son Pharaoh's daughter, his decision to identify himself with his fellow Israelites, and his decision to leave Egypt—all these decisions were decisions based on faith.

Moses' decisions were like the decisions of Abraham to leave Mesopotamia and go to Canaan, and like the decision of Noah to build an ark for his family.

God told all these men to do these various things and they all acted in faith and obedience, based upon God's revelation to them. See Hebrews 11.

There are decisions and actions of faith we also make as Christian believers. We make these decisions after waiting upon God in prayer and in connection with our claiming scriptural promises of guidance for our lives.

God does guide us throughout our lives and gives us clear leading if we wait patiently upon Him for His guidance. See Psalm 25:9–10, 12; Psalm 37:5; Proverbs 3:56, and James 1:5–6.

Noah, Abraham, Isaac, Jacob, and even Moses had no Bible as we have today, yet they were able to find the Lord's guidance for their lives.

God has always led His people along if they would wait upon Him for His guidance with a sincere desire for it and a ready willingness to follow it when it was revealed to them.

Moses had forty years of school and practical experience. Then he had forty years of outdoor shepherding and ranch experience. This second forty years of activity in the out-of-doors undoubtedly blessed his general health.

During this second forty-year period he had abundant time for thought and reflection.

He had married and so become a husband, and in time a father of two sons. He had become a shepherd.

But finally when Moses reached the age of eighty, God would give him a new task to lead His Hebrew people out of slavery and form them into a nation under God.

This was to be Moses' new God-assigned task, given to him at eighty years of age. This task occupied him for the next forty years until, at the age of one hundred twenty, he died.

III. Practical lessons to be learned from Moses' third forty years—Life in the desert with Israel

Moses' call and commission
Exodus 3–4

During the forty-year period during which Moses lived in Midian, the king of Egypt died and the bondage of the Israelites grew more severe. The cry of the Israelites came up to God more and more clearly. God remembered the covenant He had made with Israel's forefathers; now God grew more and more concerned about their condition.

God one day appeared to Moses in a burning bush on the backside of the desert near Horeb. He told Moses that His concern for Israel's oppression had reached a point where He now wanted Moses to return to Egypt and bring the people of Israel out from under the bondage they were suffering and into a land of freedom, milk and honey, the land He had promised to their forefathers.

God was indeed calling and sending Moses to lead Israel out of Egyptian bondage.

To assure him that God was indeed sending him, God gave him sign number one—that sign was that Israel would worship God on the very mountain, Mt. Horeb, that was in Moses' view at the time God was appearing to him from the bush.

While Moses was standing before the Lord with sandals removed, God identified Himself, telling Moses that He was, "I am." God's name is, "I am who I am" (Ex. 3:14).

God then began to give Moses instructions in preparation for his first meeting with the elders of Israel, then later with Pharaoh, the king of Egypt.

These early instructions were a general summary statement of what Moses would encounter as he began his moves to see his people released from their position of bondage in Egypt.

Further preparations were made for Moses when God gave him three signs which he should use to overcome unbelief should it be encountered, first among the Jewish elders, then later as he dealt with Pharaoh.

The three signs were these:

1. Moses' rod would become a serpent when thrown on the ground. It would return to a rod when it was retrieved.
2. Moses' hand became leprous and diseased when thrust into his cloak. It would become normal again when thrust back into his cloak a second time.
3. Water from the Nile would become blood when poured on the ground.

God would faithfully empower Moses and Aaron to perform these three signs whenever they were needed (Ex. 4:1–9).

God gave Moses his own brother, Aaron, as his partner, Aaron, who could speak well.

But God assured Moses that He would enable both Moses and his brother to speak well and that He would teach them both what to say as the need arose (Ex. 4:10–17).

MOSES RETURNS TO EGYPT

Exodus 4:18ff

Moses had now received directions for his life from the Lord. It was that he should return to Egypt.

God had said to him, "So now go, I am sending you to Pharaoh, to bring my people the Israelites out of Egypt" (Ex. 3:10) and, "Now go, I will help you speak and will teach you what to say" (Ex. 4:12). And after Moses asked his father-in-law Jethro's, permission to go to Egypt, Jethro said, "Go and I wish you well" (Ex. 4:18).

So now, Moses had clear direction from the Lord as to where he was to go and as to what he was to do.

He had a brother partner. He had signs he could perform. He had the assurance of the Lord's presence with him as he went.

He now left with his wife and his sons on donkeys. And soon Aaron would join him.

The circumstances back in Egypt had been prepared for Moses with the death of those who had wanted to kill him. The people of Israel were ready. Moses was prepared and ready. Now he had been well instructed as to his assignment.

He was retold to use the signs God had given him to do. During the long forty years wait in Midian, these necessary changes made Moses' return possible.

If some of those who are reading these lines have a call on their lives to do a special work for God but the circumstances do not yet seem favorable to begin the work, as we wait faithfully and patiently upon the Lord, finally the circumstances will become favorable, as they did for Moses.

God will be ready; you will be ready, and the people and their circumstances will be ready for you to begin your ministry. God will go with you and bless your efforts abundantly as He did with Moses and Aaron.

At an overnight stopping place the Lord would have killed Moses because he had not circumcised one of his two sons. Zipporah went ahead and performed this rite of circumcision for their son, a sign that was an important sign of God's covenant with the Israelites.

Following Zipporah's act, all was well. God's anger with Moses was abated.

Meanwhile, God had told Aaron to go to meet Moses. The two met near Mt. Horeb where they kissed and greeted one another.

Moses briefed Aaron concerning their mission, their instructions and the planned use of the miraculous signs in the near future.

Moses and Aaron continued on toward Egypt and Zipporah and their two sons returned to Midian.

Moses and Aaron soon arrived in Egypt and after gathering the elders together, they told them of their mission, and performed the signs before them.

After the elders had heard Aaron and seen the signs, they were glad for the Lord's concern for them.

They thus bowed down and worshiped.

MOSES AND AARON MEET PHARAOH

Exodus 5:1–23

Pharaoh emphatically rejected the request to allow Israel to leave temporarily to worship in the desert.

Instead, the king increased the work pressure on the Israelites by removing the straw supply of those making bricks, but still requiring the same brick production quotas.

This action by Pharaoh, which intensified the pressure upon the Israelites, is blamed on Moses and Aaron.

So Moses goes to the Lord with his complaint and trouble. He was learning early in his new assignment to go to the Lord whenever any troubles arose.

This practice became a regular pattern with him throughout the coming months and years of leadership of the people of Israel.

This is practical lesson number one that we can learn from the third forty-year period of Moses' life.

This is a pattern-practice that we, as God's people today, will do well to adopt as our pattern-practice whenever we encounter difficulties in our daily lives and work assignments for the Lord.

Moses talking to the Lord said, "O Lord, why have you brought trouble upon this people? Is this why you sent me? Ever since I went to Pharaoh to speak in your name, he has brought trouble upon this people, and you have not rescued your people at all" (Ex. 5:22–23).

But Moses had previously been told by the Lord that Pharaoh would not let His people leave immediately. More force and pressure from the Lord would need to be applied. Finally, the king would give in, and allow their departure from Egypt.

Moses had been forewarned about this during his instruction time while he was still in Midian on the backside of the desert (Ex. 3:18–20).

In response to Moses' going to the Lord in prayer, the Lord reassured him again in plain simple words that His hand of power would indeed accomplish Israel's freedom.

Their present bondage and oppression and suffering would soon be behind them. They would be a freed people (Ex. 6:1).

Then God told Moses that as the God "I am," He was making himself known to both Moses and the Israelites. This revelation about God was new to Moses and to the Israelites. This name of God and its significance had not been disclosed to Abraham, Isaac, and Jacob.

By the name "El Shaddai" God had been known to the patriarchs. But now by "I am," the Almighty, God was to become known to Israel.

This God of great power now continued speaking to Moses. He gave five great "I will" statements to him to pass on to the Israelites (Ex. 6:6–8):

1. "I will bring you out from under the yoke of the Egyptians." v. 6a
2. "I will free you from being slaves . . ." v. 6b
3. "I will take you as my own people and . . ." v. 7a
4. "I will be your God." v. 7b
5. "I will bring you to the land . . ." v. 8

Moses repeated this message to the Israelites, but due to their discouragement and bondage, they would not listen to him (Ex. 6:9).

God now told Moses to go again and tell Pharaoh to let the Israelites to be freed from their bondage, but Moses was reluctant to do this, saying, if the Israelites would not listen to him, how would Pharaoh listen to him?

God responded to this reluctance with a direct command given to both Moses and Aaron to bring the Israelites out of Egypt (Ex. 6:13). A "direct command" from the Supreme Commander of heaven and earth was a very serious act on God's part. Both Moses and Aaron got the message. But God assured these two men that after God had laid His hand on Egypt the Israelites would finally be released from Egyptian bondage (Ex. 7:4).

As it was with Moses and Aaron so it will be with those who are reading these lines, namely, whatever task God assigns for us to do, with the task He will provide the enabling until the task is fully accomplished as He would have it.

THE COMMISSION OF MOSES AND AARON.

1. *Only with God's help* could these two men succeed in freeing Israel from Egypt's control. God worked with these two men to finally procure the release and freedom of His enslaved people.
2. *Continued strict obedience* to God's instructions throughout their task in Egypt would enable the Lord to remain by their side, directing the bringing and the removal of each of the ten plagues, so they would have the most desired effect on Pharaoh and the Egyptian people.
3. This strict and careful obedience to God was combined with *a constant faith in God's promise and power.*

These two men maintained a daily dependence upon God and a constant fellowship with Him so as to hear His voice giving daily directions as they proceeded. They were two prophets hearing God's voice each day.

The original signs were all brought before Pharaoh and the ten plagues into all Egypt (Ex. 7–11).

Finally, after the death of Egypt's firstborn, of people and animals, Pharaoh let the people of Israel go free.

The Israelites plundered the Egyptians, taking gold and silver articles and clothing and dough for bread without yeast.

On the tenth day of Israel's first month, the Israelites held their first Passover, a feast of lamb or goat, with bread without yeast. It was eaten with haste, they leaving Egypt at the conclusion of the feast.

The Lord passed over all of the Israeli households where lamb's blood had been sprinkled over the door entryways.

The Passover feast was to be observed throughout Israel's future history as a permanent national feast.

April the sixth, of the month the Jews call Abib, is the day when the Jewish people still to this day, observe their national Passover.

The display of God's power during the ten plagues was to be a testimony to the might and power of the true God, the God of Israel.

Pharaoh and all Egypt saw this power as well as the other nations of the world of that time.

And ever since in world history, the occurrence of the plagues in Egypt has become known.

These miraculous divine interventions in Egypt and the later opening of the Red Sea and other miracles in the wilderness, together with the miracles in connection with the occupation of Canaan under Joshua were all manifestations of God's great miracle-working power. They were power manifestations for Israel and other nations to see. These manifestations of the power of the True God were seen in contrast to the weaker satanic power and the "no power" of the false idols of the other nations.

Moses had previously told the Hebrews to ask the Egyptians for gold and silver articles and clothing. Meanwhile the Lord caused the Israelites to be viewed with favor by the Egyptians. So God was constantly working along with Moses to bring about success and attend to his efforts in this regard.

Much plunder was received from the Egyptians for use by the Israelites. These articles and clothing and dough for bread would be needed later in their journey.

God brought Israel out with a great and powerful hand. The Passover feast would be a perpetual reminder of this.

God gave specific instructions to Moses and Israel as to the route they were to take in leaving Egypt.

Such specific instructions as to their movements were given not only at the start of their journey but throughout the many years to come until Israel reached the Promised Land.

They took a route, camping near the Red Sea, where God would receive glory as Pharaoh pursued the Israelites across the Red Sea.

Also the shorter route to the Promised Land was not taken, God knowing that His people were not yet ready for warfare. He believed they would change their minds and return to Egypt if they faced such warfare.

With a strong east wind, God divided and dried up the bed of the sea so the Israelites could walk through to safety on the opposite shore.

A hard-hearted king of Egypt, following with his chariots and army, perished as the waters were returned over them.

The Israelites, seeing all of this, feared the Lord and believed in the Lord and in Moses his servant (Ex. 14).

During the crisis of the Red Sea crossing, Moses remained a stalwart and courageous and believing leader and servant of God. He reassured the people that God would take them safely through their place of danger to safety.

Moreover, God would rid them of the threat of Pharaoh and his army.

Moses stood as a pillar of faith and confidence in behalf of God's people.

The hard-blowing warm east wind sent by the Lord, divided the Red Sea waters and caused the sea bottom to be dry land—no muck or mud, but dry land for the Israelites to walk through on to the other side.

When our Lord undertakes a task He does it right and completely. We praise your great name, our great Lord and King.

Moses with the Israelites from the Red Sea to the Promised Land

Moses was faithful and obedient in doing signs and wonders before the elders and Pharaoh.

"He led the Israelites out of Egypt and did wonders and miraculous signs in Egypt, at the Red Sea and for forty years in the desert" (Acts 7:36).

Moses was faithful as God's servant in God's house, establishing Israel in God's law, God's sacrificial system, and His worship and service (Heb. 3:2–5).

After leaving the Red Sea area, Israel came on the third day to the desert of Shur and Marah, but they had no water except some water that was undrinkable due to its bitterness so Moses "Cried out to the Lord" and the Lord showed him a certain piece of wood which he threw into the bitter water. The bitter water immediately became sweet and drinkable (Ex. 15:22–27).

Moses had learned early to call out to the Lord when he and his people had a need.

This is a practice which believing Christians will do well to learn early, as Moses had learned, and practice throughout our earthly journey. God always supplied Israel's need when Moses cried out to the Lord. He will do the same for us if we follow Moses' practice.

MASSEH AND MERIBAH

At Masseh and Meribah Moses continued his custom of crying out to the Lord when Israel encountered a need—this time water was needed again.

Moses called. God answered with an immediate solution to the problem. Moses, with God and the elders standing close nearby, struck the rock and water came forth for all Israel (Ex. 17:1–7).

THE AMALEKITES

During Israel's first military engagement, that with the Amalekites, Israel's victory was undoubtedly a clear lesson and example to Joshua, Israel, and Moses and his associates, Aaron and Hur, a lesson about the vital importance of a continued obedience and faith in the Lord, so that His blessing and success would remain with Israel. Moses was seeing this blessing by the Lord. Now his young assistant, Joshua, was seeing it, along with his older associates, Aaron, and Hur, and somewhere in the crowd a believing Caleb was seeing and rejoicing in this victory along with the others of faith and purity of heart (Ex. 17:8–16).

Jethro visits Moses

Exodus 18

Jethro, Moses' father-in-law, sent word to Moses when Moses and Israel were camped near Mt. Horeb that he was coming with Moses' wife and his two sons for a meeting and visit.

Jethro met Moses and rejoiced upon hearing all that God had done for Israel and Moses.

He acknowledged the supremacy of the God of Israel and even brought sacrifices to be made in the presence of the Lord along with Aaron and the Israelite elders.

Then Jethro gave Moses needed advice concerning his service as Israel's judge; hearing their cases needed wise settlements.

Jethro advised Moses to teach God's laws to dependable men, then assign those trained men as judges along with Moses, over thousands, hundreds, and fifties, and smaller groups of ten.

Moses accepted Jethro's advice and planned to put it into practice in behalf of the Israelites.

Moses showed wisdom in giving careful consideration to the advice given to him by Jethro, and he accepted it to Israel's benefit and put it in use.

Israel and Moses at Sinai

In the third month after leaving Egypt, Israel camped at the desert of Sinai. There God called Moses up into the mountain where He gave Israel His Ten Commandments. These were given amidst manifestation of God's greatness and holiness. There was a trumpet blast and thunder and lightning and shaking of the mountain and a dark cloud over the mount of Sinai.

The people were instructed to prepare themselves to receive the law. They carefully obeyed and assembled, ready to receive God's holy law amidst the manifestations of His awesome presence at Sinai (Ex. 19–20).

Moses and Israel confirm
their covenant with God

Moses went with Aaron, Nadab, and Abihu and seventy elders to Mt. Sinai. Moses read some of God's laws to the people who agreed to obey them all.

Next day, Moses built an altar and set up twelve stones representing Israel's twelve tribes.

He sent young men to make sacrifices.

Moses soon sprinkled blood on the people, the blood of the covenant they were confirming with the Lord.

Then Moses, Aaron, Nadab, and Abihu and the seventy elders saw the Lord in His holiness.

After this God called Moses up into the mount with Joshua going part of the way with him.

Then God gave the Ten Commandments to Moses for all Israel. He remained on the mount forty days by himself (Ex. 24).

God then began instructing Moses concerning the tabernacle and all its furnishings, all to be built according to the heavenly pattern God would give to him. The people were asked to bring the materials for the tabernacle and all its furnishings.

God supplies skilled helpers

To take the lead in constructing the tabernacle and all its furnishings, God raised up a skilled and Spirit-filled craftsman named Bezalel and an assistant named Oholiab. These two leaders were assisted by several more skilled craftsmen in constructing the tabernacle (Ex. 31:1–11).

God, for us today, also, will provide skilled helpers to help us fulfill and complete the work God gives us to do, people with specialized skills, abilities, and experience, God will send along to help us with our assigned tasks.

While Moses was on the mount receiving the law, staying there for forty days, the Israelites, growing restless and impatient, persuaded Aaron to make an idol for them. After it was made the people held a festival with sacrifices being made to the idol Aaron had made. They than ate and drank and indulged in pagan revelry and sin.

When Moses and Joshua learned what the Israelites were doing, Moses in anger, broke the law tablets and destroying the people's calf idol, ground it to powder, and burning it, made the people drink the resultant beverage.

Israel's pagan actions at this time so angered the Lord that He was ready to destroy all the people. But Moses pled in intercession for a sinning Israel and God relented, deciding to allow the Israelites to continue living (Ex. 32).

Because the original law tablets were broken, it was necessary for Moses to go into the mount again for new tablets.

Moses requested that the Lord go with him in a special way, even that God show Himself to Moses more visibly.

God agreed to a part of Moses' request, showing His hinder part to Moses. Moses was kept from seeing God's face, for no man can see God's face and live (Ex. 33).

The ten holy law tablets were given to Moses a second time, along with some additional laws and a review of God's covenant with Israel (Ex. 34).

The glow on Moses' face after receiving the old covenant law in God's presence was so bright that Moses placed a veil over his face when in view of the people of Israel. This was a glow that was to be far surpassed by the glory of the new covenant. See 2 Corinthians 3:7–18.

The craftsmen followed the specifications for building the tabernacle with all its furnishings.

This was as the Lord and Moses had instructed them. Finally it was completed. Moses inspected their work and it was all well done, so he blessed them (Ex. 39; 43).

Now the tabernacle was set up and on the first day of the first month of the second year, all of the furnishings were put into place and all was anointed with oil, consecrating everything and making them holy to the Lord.

Then Aaron and his sons came and were dressed and prepared to do service for the Lord and the people.

Finally, after all was ready, a cloud covered the tent of meeting and the glory of the Lord filled the tabernacle.

This cloud of glory remained over the tabernacle from that time forward, a cloud by day and a fire by night as God's people made their journeys in the desert wilderness for the next forty years (Ex. 40:34–38).

God was with His people during all this time, and Moses their godly leader was with them, by their side as God's representative and servant.

In receiving the law and the tabernacle specifications and overseeing the tabernacle's construction, Moses continued to show his faithfulness to the Lord.

MOSES AND THE CENSUS

Numbers 1:1–5; 46

On the first day of the second month after coming out of Egypt, God told Moses to take a census of all the men twenty years old and older, by name, of eleven of the tribes.

Aaron and twelve leaders from the twelve tribes were to assist in this census.

These men were to serve in the army. The total number was 603,550 men (Num. 1:46).

All the people were organized by divisions, and each tribe had instructions as to their position whenever Israel moved from place to place. Each tribe had its leader and banner so there was a clear sense of order and belonging among all the tribes.

The tribe of Levi was not to be included in the census.

Their assignment was to always take care of the tabernacle and its furnishings.

In the census, also, Moses showed his obedience, patience, and care.

MIRIAM AND AARON OPPOSE MOSES

Miriam and Aaron began to criticize their brother, Moses, saying that God could speak through them as well as through Moses. This showed an attitude of jealousy and rebellion, angering the Lord. As a reprimand, Miriam was made leprous and confined outside the camp for seven days. Afterwards, Moses prayed for her healing and God restored her to health (Num. 12).

CANAAN EXPLORED AND THE PEOPLE REBEL

At God's command Moses sent twelve men to spy out Canaan. Upon their return ten of the men, a majority, discouraged the people from going into Canaan. Only Caleb and Joshua believed God would enable them to successfully conquer the Promised Land.

As a result of the bad report of the ten spies, the mass of the people rebelled and refused to believe and obey the Lord. This response angered the Lord and caused the eventual death of all the men over twenty years of age during the next forty years of Israel's life. Only Caleb and Joshua would successfully enter Canaan forty years later—this, after all their contemporaries had fallen dead in the wilderness desert because of their rebellion and unbelief. The ten unbelieving spies were stricken of a plague immediately and died before the Lord.

The negative influence of the ten spies on the Israelites illustrates the detrimental effect that unbelief expressed publicly, can have on large groups of God's people.

Somewhat later, Korah, and two-hundred-fifty Levites rebelled further against the Lord, accusing Moses and Aaron of usurping leadership power beyond what they should. This rebellion was also met with God's wrath and judgment. All two-hundred-fifty were swallowed up as the earth opened and swallowed them alive (Num. 16).

PRACTICAL LESSONS TO BE LEARNED FROM ISRAEL'S EXPERIENCES AFTER EGYPT

Had the ten spies reflected upon God's great display of His power in dividing the waters at the Red Sea, they would now believe that such a God would enable Israel to defeat the giants in Canaan, so they could possess the Promised Land themselves.

But these ten did not so reflect and so did not believe that God would fight for them. Only two men of the twelve had done right thinking about Israel's golden opportunity to possess Canaan. These men were Caleb and Joshua.

These two men remembered clearly and vividly what God had done in Egypt by the ten plagues upon Egypt and then God's massive miracle at the Red sea, saving Israel and destroying Pharaoh and his threatening forces behind them.

Also other miracles had been witnessed since their leaving Egypt: the provision of water from a rock, of manna and quail for food, and the manifestation of God's power on Mt. Sinai.

These two men were of a different spirit than the rest of their contemporaries.

But the faith of these two men showed that such faith was well within the realm of possibility of the rest of the twelve having it as well, had their hearts been open to it. But as it turned out, their unbelief was their undoing and resulted in their eternal loss.

The influence of the then unbelieving spies and the consequent rebellion among the mass of the remaining Israelites, serves as a solemn warning to the church of Christ of the last days.

The lesson is that faith in God will allow the unleashing of His power for the advancement of His kingdom, while unbelief in God will prevent and postpone the advancement of His kingdom.

God must have humble obedient and believing men for His kingdom to advance as He would like to see it advance. When God discovers some more good men with faith like that of Caleb and Joshua or Jonathan and David, to encourage His people by their attitude and example, God's people will follow their lead and His kingdom will be advanced.

Let those who are reading these lines ask God to enable them to adopt the example and spiritual faith and attitudes of men like Caleb and Joshua, two of the twelve spies sent out by Moses, men who had faith from the beginning to the end of their reconnaissance patrol into the Promised Land of Canaan.

Caleb wholeheartedly followed the Lord and so did Joshua, his good friend (Num. 14:24; 30; 38; Deut. 1:35–36; Josh. 14:6–15).

Dear Lord, from among the readers of these lines, let there be raised up a few good men, who will acquire the faith, courage, and attitudes of men like Caleb and Joshua or Jonathan and David. Through the faith, courage, and leadership of these few good men, let the power and influence of your kingdom and gospel be taken to the millions of yet unsaved souls in the world in the last days! Let them help "rescue the perishing."

"RESCUE THE PERISHING"

Fanny J. Crosby,   W.H. Doane

1. Rescue the perishing; Care for the dying; Snatch them in pity from sin and the grave. Weep o'er the erring one; Lift up the fallen; tell them of Jesus, the Mighty to Save.

2. Tho' they are slighting Him, Still He is waiting, Waiting the penitent child to receive. Plead with them earnestly, Plead with them gently; He will forgive if they only believe.

3. Down in the human heart, Crushed by the tempter, Feelings lie buried that grace can restore. Touched by a loving, Wakened by kindness, Chords that are broken will vibrate once more.

4. Rescue the perishing; Duty demands it. Strength for thy labor the Lord will provide. Back to the narrow way Patiently win them; Tell the poor wand'rer a Savior has died.

Chorus: Rescue the Perishing; Care for the dying. Jesus is merciful; Jesus will save.

Moses strikes the rock
when told to speak to it for water

Numbers 20:1–13

At the desert of Zin and Meribah, which means quarrelling, the Lord instructed Moses to speak to a rock. Instead, in his disgust with the people's fault finding, he struck the rock twice with his rod. Water came out for the Israelites but Moses' actions showed unbelief in the Lord. The Lord was seriously displeased with Moses' actions. As a consequence, Moses and his brother Aaron, too, were not allowed to cross over into the Promised Land.

The Lord however, allowed him to view the land as a whole, from atop a high mountain, east of the Jordan River.

Miriam died here at Kadesh.

This incident of Moses striking the rock for water instead of speaking to it, as the Lord had instructed him, was a serious mistake by Moses. It had some serious consequences. For Moses it set a bad example for others. His mistake serves as a solemn warning for believers today not to lapse in our obedience to the Lord, but to remain obedient and faithful to the end, even in old age.

Moses' Request of the Edomites

Numbers 20:14–21

Despite Moses' courteous request for passage through the country of Edom on the king's highway, the Edomites denied his request; a second request was also denied, the Edomites even coming toward Israel with a threatening army force, so Israel turned away to another route.

Moses' response to the Edomites' denials and refusals showed his moderation in temperament.

Aaron's death

Numbers 20:22–29

Leaving Meribah, Moses, Aaron, and Aaron's son, Eleazar, ascended Mr. Hor. Here Aaron died and his garments were put on Eleazar.

Aaron, like Moses, was kept from entering the Promised Land because of their joint unbelief at the waters of Meribah

Arad Destroyed

Numbers 21:1–3

The Aradites attacked the Israelites, so God gave all the Aradites over to destruction at the hands of Israel.

This incident was another demonstration to Israel of victory when the Lord leads and provides such victory. Under God's direction and leadership, Israel was learning increasingly that with God's leadership success would be ensured to them in a later conquest of all their enemies in Canaan.

The Bronze Snake

Due to Israel's grumbling as they traveled near Edom, God sent venomous snakes that bit and killed some of the Israelites.

Acknowledging their sin in grumbling against God and Moses, God told Moses to make and erect a high brass snake on a pole amidst the Israelites. All who looked at this brass snake, after being bitten by the venomous snakes, were cured of their venomous snake bite.

Jesus made mention of this brass serpent that was raised up in the wilderness in these words, "Just as Moses lifted up the snake in the desert, so the son of a man must be lifted up, that everyone who believes in him may have eternal life" (John 3:15).

When people look today at the cross of Christ, the power and destructive force of sin is removed and life replaces an eternal death and suffering. See the song about the cross of Christ.

"At the Cross"

Isaac Watts	R. E. Hudson

V. 1   Alas! and did my Saviour bleed, and did my Sovereign die? Would He devote that sacred head For such a worm as I?

V. 2   Was it for crimes that I have done He groaned up-on the tree? Amazing pity, grace unknown, And love beyond degree!

V. 3   Well might the son in darkness hide, And shut his glories in When Christ, the mighty Maker, died For man, the creatures' sin.

V. 4   But drops of grief can ne'er repay The debt of love I owe. Here, Lord, I give myself away; 'Tis all that I can do!

Chorus   At the Cross, at the Cross where I first saw the light, And the burden of my heart rolled away, It was there by faith I received my sight, and now I am happy all the day!

Defeat of Sihon and Og

Numbers 21:21–35

Israel met Sihon's army that came out against Israel and completely destroyed it and then, occupied their land. Next, with God's encouragement, Moses and Israel met Og's attacking army and completely destroyed it, as they had done to Sihon and his army.

But immediately prior to the destruction of these two kings and their armies, God had carefully prepared Israel and Moses their leader for this unusual campaign.

There was a careful timing to the Lord's orders given to Moses and Israel.

When the last of the rebellious generation of Israelite men had died, and not until then, did God tell Israel to turn north. See Deuteronomy 2:16. Also God said, "This very day I will begin to put the terror and fear of you on all the nations under heaven" (Deut. 2:25).

Moses, at God's command, moved north, past Edom, past Ammon and Moab into the lands of Sihon and Og.

Moses and Israel obeyed the Lord and totally destroyed Sihon, Og, and all of their people. They salvaged only their flocks and material possessions. Moses obeyed the Lord fully, having success for Joshua and all of young Israel to see as an example for them. Young Israel was obedient in everything Moses told them to do in defeating the two kings and all their people.

Moses, Israel's aged and faithful leader, along with the young and upcoming generation of Israeli fighters had a new faith, unlike the older generation that had died off in the wilderness. This new generation, along with their aged leader, found success in defeating Sihon and Og, while not infringing upon the people of Edom, Ammon, Moab, and some other nearby peoples, all at Moses' command (Deut. 2:36–37).

All Israel, along with Joshua, saw this example of tremendous success and blessing, under aged Moses' last days of leadership.

The entire enterprise they all witnessed and participated in most likely served to encourage them as they were about to enter and occupy Canaan on the west side of the Jordan River.

The Lord had brought about a believing Israel's success in this era, giving them full success against Sihon and Og and their powerful armies (Deut. 2:25, 31, 33, 36).

After these great victories, Moses called Joshua's attention to them as examples of what the Lord would do for him and all of young Israel west of the Jordan in the near future.

Moses said to Joshua, "You have seen with your own eyes all that the Lord your God has done to these two kings. The Lord will do the same to all the kingdoms over there where you are going. Do not be afraid of them; the Lord your God himself will fight for you" (Deut. 3:21–22).

Moses had pleaded with the Lord to allow him to cross over the Jordan River and see God do more exploits there for Israel. But God would not allow him to do this. Rather, he was to commission Joshua and strengthen and encourage him to prepare to lead Israel in possessing the land of Canaan (Deut. 3:23–29).

In addition to preparing Joshua, his longtime aide, for his special time of leadership, Moses now instructed all Israel to faithfully obey the Lord's commands.

He reminds them of what happened to all who had rebelled against the Lord at Baal of Peor—death, in the wanderings of a desolate desert. But those who "held fast to the Lord," were all still alive (Deut. 4:3–4).

Continuing to speak to the Israelites, Moses says that in years to come, if when they are scattered abroad among the nations of the world, they turn and seek the Lord with all their heart and soul, they would find Him (Deut. 4:28–31).

Also, Moses stressed over and over again to the Israelites that the blessing, prosperity, security, and happiness of Israel in the years to come will depend upon their remembering the Lord and carefully keeping all His commandments. All will go well with them under these conditions. A humble, obedient, and believing relationship with God will ensure that all will be well with them.

As a "devouring fire," Moses says, the Lord will go before Israel's army to route and utterly destroy the mighty nations, many made up of giants, who live behind mighty walled cities in Canaan.

Israel's army, much smaller and weaker than those forces in Canaan, shall nonetheless destroy the united forces of the Canaanite nations. This is because God fought for them and because He intended to bring judgment upon the wickedness of those in Canaan. It was not because of Israel's righteousness, but because of the Canaanites' unrighteousness and wickedness and because the Lord was fighting for the Israelites, who are still a stiff-necked people (Deut. 9:1–6).

After the defeat of Sihon and Og, and the general atmosphere among the Israelites had quieted down, Moses spoke to all the people, reviewing for them the main events of the past forty years.

Speaking to them on the plains of Moab, he repeated the main laws and teachings that God had given to the people of Israel. This new presentation of God's laws for Israel was particularly for the sake of the younger generation who had come into their full adulthood.

He called all Israel to live close to the Lord and to keep all His commandments faithfully.

By doing this, their future lives would be blessed and secure, but to forsake the Lord and His will would bring havoc and loss and be a national tragedy.

These discourses by Moses were given about a month before his death.

He did all he could do in preparing Israel for their future before he would leave them in death.

He gave a clear prediction of a coming prophet, the Messiah, through whom God would speak words of life and salvation (Deut. 18:15–19).

Finally, the time for the departure of Moses from his earthly journey had come.

Moses had served his generation in the will of God and died in peace. The Lord Himself "buried him in Moab in the valley opposite Beth Peor . . ." (Deut. 34:6).

"The Israelites grieved for Moses in the plains of Moab thirty days, until the time of weeping and mourning was over" (Deut. 34:8).

Summary of Moses' life

From the reading of Psalm 90, which Moses wrote, one cannot help but be impressed with the breadth and range of his mind as he speaks about God, the earth, the universe and mankind, of time and space and creation.

Moses had one-hundred-twenty years to experience life in the world, to reflect on human nature in its fallen state, upon God our Creator, upon those of the human family he came to know, in Egypt, his fellow Israelites and those of other nations.

He had an unusually close relationship with God, one unlike that of most other men.

In reading Psalm 90, who can plumb the depth of meaning in some of his words when the psalmist says,

> "Lord, you have been our dwelling place throughout
> all generations. Before the mountains were born or you

brought forth the earth and the world, from everlasting to everlasting you are God."

(Ps. 90:1–2)

What wonderful words and thoughts Moses expressed in the psalm he wrote, and in the Song of Moses, which he spoke in the hearing of all Israel (Deut. 31:30–32:43), and the blessings he spoke to the twelve tribes immediately before his death (Deut. 33).

Also Moses wrote the complete and blessed writing, preserved for us, which we call the Pentateuch and Torah, consisting of the first five books of the Old Testament.

Speaking again of some of the events in Moses' life when he had grown to adult maturity, at about the age of forty years, he had decided to come over on the side of God and His will and plan for his life.

He began to trust God and to learn to obey God and to be faithful to God as His servant.

He persevered in his walk with God, becoming for all of us an example of obedience, faith, humility, meekness, and faithfulness, over a long period of time, doing God's will for his life serving as Israel's leader and ruler.

Like his friend and acquaintance, Caleb, whom he often mentioned, Moses wholeheartedly followed the Lord to the day of his death. His record was not without mistakes, but nearly so.

As a leader Moses became an example to all Israel and some among them caught his example and spirit. Among these were his brother, Aaron, Caleb, Joshua, and very largely the younger generation of the Israeli men who were with Joshua when they crossed the Jordan and conquered Canaan and settled in their new land of freedom.

Moses also was strongly a man of prayer, calling upon God whenever Israel had a special need.

He prayed for his sister Miriam to be restored to health after she had been punished with leprosy for seven days, having to live outside the camp.

Also Moses was a leader who interceded strongly in prayer for his people when they deserved to be killed by God for their idolatry and for their rebellion and frequent unbelieving attitudes and grumbling.

He also interceded for Aaron that God would not kill him for his part in Israel's idolatrous actions.

Moses loved his people and he loved God.

He, like St. Paul, was willing that his name should be blotted out of heaven's Book of Life if God would not forgive Israel's sins. See Exodus 32:31–32 and Romans 9:1–5.

May God grant that both the writer of these lines and the reader of these lines shall profit much and be encouraged much by the many-sided example of this great man of God, Moses. Moses, who was so much like our Lord and master, the Lord Jesus, our supreme example.

Jesus, for whose love and approval Moses left the ease of pleasures of sin in Egypt, to suffer with Christ and God's people.

Moses' reward will be great and eternal, as will be ours, too, if we follow the Lord in our lifetime as Moses did in his.

JOSHUA

Phase I
Joshua as a Leader-Trainee
From the Exodus to Moses' death

From his youth Joshua had been Moses' loyal aide. Aaron was Moses' close brother-partner, like Barnabas and Silas had been St. Paul's partners much later. But Joshua was Moses' "Timothy," a young leader in training (Ex. 17:8–10; 32: 17–18; Num. 11:28).

Joshua's original name was "Hosea," but Moses renamed him "Joshua" (Num. 13:16).

There are several lessons to be learned as we look at Joshua's life.

Lesson number one: He learned to take orders

Joshua was chosen by Moses because of his obvious leadership abilities; he learned early to take orders.

That Joshua was learning obedience became apparent when Moses ordered him to choose some men and fight against the Amalekites at Rephidim.

Joshua moved immediately, chose some men and fought the Amalekites. While Moses, Aaron and Hur prevailed together before the Lord, with Moses' rod being held up before the Lord, the Lord gave Joshua and his men a steady and gradually increasing victory in the battle with these enemies of Israel. By sundown Joshua's forces had prevailed and defeated the Amalekites.

Joshua was quickly learning that military victories over Israel's enemies are gained only as the Lord fights with Israel.

This experience was undoubtedly a good lesson for young Joshua, an experience he never forgot. He knew that his victory that day over the Amalekites was due to a cooperative effort of himself, his men, and the Lord.

The presence and power of the Lord was fighting with him, for he knew that as Moses' hands were extended skyward in faith, victory was his and whenever Moses' hands were lowered and not extended skyward toward the Lord and heaven, his forces began to lose ground to the enemy (Ex. 17:11).

For us today, spiritual victories over our enemies will be gained when the Lord is fighting with us. We will begin losing whenever the Lord is not fighting with us.

In prayer and intercession, even with hands raised in prayer before our Lord, we shall have victories for the Lord over our enemies (Eph. 6:10–20; Phil. 1:3–11; Col. 1:3–4; 1 Thess. 1:2–3; 1 Tim. 2:1–8).

Paul and his associates exemplified the counterpart of Moses' actions and prevailing prayer with his associates, Aaron and Hur.

Continuing the discussion of lesson number one, learning to take orders, please note the following:

> Noah, earlier, had been given on order to "make an ark of cypress wood . . ." *he obeyed and all went well* (Gen. 6:14, 22).

> Prior to Noah's time Adam had been given an order to eat from only specified fruit trees in the garden where God had placed him. *He disobeyed and all did not go well* (Gen. 2:16–17).

Abraham had been given an order to leave his country and his father's household and "go to the land I will show you" *he obeyed and all went well* (Gen. 12:1).

Moses had been given an order to bring the Israelites out of Egypt's bondage. God had said, "So now, go. I am sending you to Pharaoh to bring my people the Israelites out of Egypt" (Ex. 3:10). *He obeyed, despite initial discouragements* and opposition and all finally went well.

In all branches of the military services men must learn to take orders from those in authority over them.

Joshua was now given an order by Moses, the man in authority over him. He immediately obeyed and things went well for him.

Joshua was learning an early lesson that prepared him for his later calling in life after Moses died.

After Joshua and the Israelites crossed the Jordan, the commander of the armies of heaven Himself appeared to Joshua. Joshua began to receive a series of orders from the Lord Himself. Order number one was "take off your sandals for the place where you are standing is holy" and Joshua did so (Josh. 5:15). Then this heavenly commander gave Joshua further orders and a plan as to how to conquer city number one—Jericho. Joshua obeyed, Israel obeyed, and Jericho fell.

Joshua continued receiving and obeying the orders of this commander from heaven and more of Canaan's cities fell. Finally all of Canaan's cities fell in defeat before Joshua and the armies of Israel. Joshua had learned well and Joshua had learned early to take orders from Moses and from the Lord. As a result Joshua did very, very well.

He is a great example for us today, so we can do well also.

Lesson number two

Joshua with Caleb believed that if Israel pleased the Lord, the Lord would lead them and be with them, enabling them to conquer Canaan (Num. 14:6–9).

Lesson number three

Joshua, with Caleb, the Lord said, *"followed the Lord wholeheartedly"* (Num. 32:12).

After the twelve men returned from spying out the land of Canaan, the ten unbelieving spies discouraged the people from going in and occupying it.

But in the face of this discouraging report, Joshua and Caleb sought to encourage the people to go ahead with the original plan and occupy Canaan.

Don't be afraid of the inhabitants there, they said. The Lord will lead us and be with us.

Joshua and Caleb combined a wholehearted faith in the Lord with a wholehearted following of the Lord.

What the ten spies of the "bad report" lacked and what the mass of the other Israelites was shown to lack was that they had never committed themselves to follow the Lord with all their hearts.

The Lord Himself testified that this was the case with the people of Israel at that time. Please note: The Lord's anger was aroused that day and he swore this oath: "Because they have not followed me wholeheartedly, not one of the men twenty years old or more who came up out of Egypt will see the land I promised on oath to Abraham, Isaac and Jacob—not one except Caleb son of Jephunneh the Kenizzite and Joshua son of Nun, for they followed the Lord wholeheartedly. The Lord's anger burned against Israel and he made them wander in the desert forty years, until the whole generation of those who had done evil in his sight was gone" (Num. 32:10–13).

The living faith and wholehearted commitment of Joshua and Caleb was something that was completely lacking in the hearts and lives of the great mass of the rest of the Israelite men from twenty years old and over.

Only Joshua, Caleb, Moses and most likely Aaron possessed this strong faith and commitment to the Lord who had rescued them from Egypt's bondages.

They could have had what Joshua and Caleb had but they did not have it. They chose not to have the spirit of Joshua and Caleb. As a consequence, they suffered dearly and eternally. It cost them their lives. They all died in the desert. They never saw the Promised Land.

The people of Israel at Kadesh Barnea set a terrible example of unbelief and disobedience in turning away from the Lord and refusing to believe the Lord's promise to go with them in conquering the land of Canaan (Heb. 4:11).

But Joshua, with his friend Caleb, set a commendable and good example for all Christian believers to follow today.

Let us have a full believing heart of faith and a wholehearted commitment in following the Lord to the end of our lives. See Hebrews 3:6–4:16.

If we commit ourselves to following the Lord to the end of our lives here on earth, as Joshua and Caleb did, the Lord will work through us. His gospel will be powerfully spread among all the nations. Multitudes will be saved and brought into God's kingdom, their lives cleansed and prepared for heaven.

Does Joshua's life, along with that of Caleb, have some practical lessons for us as Christian believers to learn today? Yes! Yes! Yes!

By God's grace let us learn the lessons their lives and experiences were intended to teach us—lessons to make us wise and strong and very effective for the Lord.

Let us learn from their experiences and learn the lessons well, with God's help.

Let us, with God's help, commit ourselves to becoming "the Joshua and Caleb generation" and so be the Lord's very profitable servants in these last days.

A further point we would make is this:

Was there any connection between the fact of Joshua and Caleb's "following the Lord wholeheartedly" and their having a heart full of faith and confidence in God's power and His willingness to bring that power to bear upon an undertaking so vast as defeating a large number of powerful kings and their armies with a much smaller force, such as Israel possessed?

Certainly, there must be a connection between the two spiritual traits we are discussing.

For both men had a great faith and courage, and both men were wholehearted followers of the Lord.

But their ten compatriots had no faith, but only sinful unbelieving hearts and they influenced all their fellow Israelites to have the same. And we have already been told by the Lord, when describing all of the other Israelites over twenty years of age at that time, "they have not followed me wholeheartedly" (Num. 32:1).

The psalmist in Ps. 95:7–11 and the writer of the New Testament book of Hebrews describe the Israelites at length during their time at Meribah and Massah. See Hebrews 3:7–4:16.

Israel's unbelief and hardness of heart becomes a pitfall that we must avoid.

Israel's experience is a solemn warning to all Christian believers today against a departing from the Lord and going off into unbelief, disobedience, and rebellion and ruination of our spiritual standing with the Lord.

But the journey together of a wholehearted following of the Lord and a wholehearted and courageous faith, as we have seen modeled in the lives of Joshua and Caleb, will enable the Lord to work through us with power as He worked through them.

JOSHUA

Phase II
Joshua as the leader of Israel from the death of Moses to the death of Joshua
Joshua 1–24; Hebrews 11:29

JOSHUA'S COMMISSION

Joshua 1:1–9

After Moses died, the Lord Himself spoke directly to Joshua. He promised him full success in leading Israel against the Canaanites, if he would be strong and very courageous. Also, he was to obey all the laws Moses had given him, reading the book of the law and meditating on its laws day and night, so he would be able to do everything written in it. Doing this, he would be prosperous and successful.

So God's promise of prosperity and success was conditional on Joshua's doing his part in knowing and always doing the will of God for his life and in his place of leadership.

The Lord would be with him as he was with Moses. Then, after the Lord had named the boundaries of the Promised Land, He said Joshua would be able to take it all if he would obey the Lord's will fully and be strong and courageous. Certainly, Joshua was being offered a delightful future and a golden opportunity to be of immense service to his God and to God's selected people, the people of Israel. The sacrifices and restraints of submission and obedience to God's laws would be fully worth the discipline involved, for the Lord Himself would be with Joshua to ensure victory over the most powerful enemies that would come against him and his forces.

With the large task ahead of him, Joshua was given this commissioning charge by the Lord. He had been in training for this upcoming task for forty years.

Now he was to assume his new place of responsibility and leadership. Now is his opportunity. Moses had trained eighty years for his task. Joshua had lived and trained perhaps eighty years also for his forthcoming task.

Both men were mature and experienced before God called them to their places of leadership. God promised He would be with them both.

Joshua had seen what God did in Egypt and all God had done between Egypt and his present charge and opportunity.

With such a momentous task before him, it was not a time for fear and timidity, but a time for strength, courage, and dedicated hourly and daily obedience to the Lord and all His Word—so the Lord would be completely by his side and with him constantly, until the land was conquered and allotted to the tribes of Israel.

JOSHUA, THE SPIES AND RAHAB

Joshua 2:1–24

Joshua sent out two spies to explore the land, especially Jericho (Josh. 2:1).

Rahab, a harlot lady, whose house was built on the wall of Jericho, hid these two spies and she made a mutual agreement with the two men as follows: she will not tell anyone in Jericho's city leadership about the two spies coming into her house, if in return the spies and the Israelites will save her life and the lives of all of her family when they capture the city of Jericho. The agreement was mutually made and agreed upon by her and the two spies.

After the spies had left Rahab's house, they went into the hills for three days. Afterwards they returned and gave Joshua an optimistic report about the city.

JOSHUA AND THE JORDAN

Joshua 3–4

Beginning with the preparatory instructions and then throughout the crossing of the Jordan River, Joshua issued orders to the priests and the people. Finally, the river crossing was completed and the Israelites camped at Gilgal on the first day of the month. Here Joshua set up the twelve stones that had been taken from the dry bed of the Jordan River. These stones were to serve as a memorial for the people in years to come, a help to remember how the Lord had dried up the Jordan River that was at flood tide during the harvest season in the area.

The Jordan was opened up for the Israelites as the Red Sea had been opened up miraculously, so all the nations would know that the Lord is powerful and so Israel would always fear the Lord their God (Josh. 4:19–24).

Another purpose of the Jordan River miracle was to exalt Joshua in the eyes of the Israelites as he had now been appointed their new leader. The Lord wanted the Israelites to know that He would be with Joshua in the same way He had been with Moses. The miraculous opening of the Red Sea had helped the Israelites know that the Lord was with Moses, their earlier leader. See Exodus 14:31. Now, with Joshua, their new leader, the people needed to look to him and respect and follow his orders and leadership. See Joshua 3:7–8; 4:14.

Today, too, the Lord desires that all the nations of the earth know Him, the Creator of the heavens and earth, and to know that His hand is powerful.

Events in the world's future will also demonstrate the power of the Lord's hand.

Gog and Magog, Armageddon, and other events in view of the nations, will demonstrate to them that the Lord's hand is powerful as it was in the days of Moses and Joshua.

We bless you Lord, the great and holy God, Creator of us all and our gracious Savior.

JOSHUA AND ISRAEL AT GILGAL

Joshua 5:1–12

At Gilgal the Lord instructed Joshua to circumcise all the men. Joshua obediently did this. While the men were healing, all Israel celebrated the Passover, The circumcision and Passover celebrations were steps taken as obedience to God and steps that would help prepare Israel spiritually before they began the military conquering of all of Canaan. God would certainly be with Israel if they were right with Him spiritually.

JOSHUA AND JERICHO

Joshua 5:13–6:27

While here also, near Jericho, the commander of heaven Himself appeared to Joshua personally with his sword drawn.

Joshua, upon seeing the commander of the Lord's army, "fell face down to the ground in reverence" and asked what he must do. The commander had many orders to give him but the first order was to remove his sandals. This Joshua did immediately. After this the commander gave Joshua a clear plan as to how he was to proceed to take over the city of Jericho. Joshua received this heavenly-conceived strategy and orders, and as soon as possible the plan was placed into operation.

With seven priests following an armed guard and the Ark of the Covenant, following the priests and a second armed guard following the Ark, the Israelites marched around Jericho once each day for six days. All the time, the priests were blowing their trumpets. On the seventh day the procession circled the city seven times. Then, at Joshua's signal, all the people on the seventh time around the city shouted loudly, for Joshua said, "For the Lord has given you the city." When the people shouted, the city walls all collapsed inwardly and the Israelite soldiers entered the city and destroyed and killed everyone alive in the city along with all the animals. Only the silver, gold, and bronze articles were brought out of the city. Along with these articles, Rahab and her entire family were saved alive as had been promised by the two spies.

Joshua, Ai, and Achan

Joshua 7–8

Disaster came on Israel in the first attempt to conquer Ai, because Israel had sinned in taking some devoted things from Jericho. Achan and all his family were stoned, they and all their possessions were burned, then all were covered with rocks (Josh. 7).

Afterwards, speaking to Joshua, the Lord encouraged him concerning Ai, telling him it had been delivered into his hand. The Lord instructed Joshua to use an ambush behind the city.

Joshua now gave clear strict orders to his army concerning the use of an ambush. The men obeyed; soon the city was open and set on fire and all of Ai's men were killed along with all the city's occupants. Only the plunder was taken (Josh. 8:1–29).

Joshua and his men, thus far, were receiving and carrying out the orders they all had been given. Success was coming to them. All was going well, because they were obeying the Lord and because they were trusting the Lord.

JOSHUA AND A RENEWED COVENANT

Joshua 8:30–35

Following Ai's destruction, Joshua, the Lord's servant, built an altar on Mt. Ebal, constructing it as he had been told by Moses.

In the presence of all Israel, with its officials and judges and elders, he copied on large stones the laws of Moses.

The people stood on both sides of the altar, facing the Levites; half the people were in front of Mt. Ebal, and half of the people were before Mt. Gerizim. This arrangement also, was according as Moses, the Lord's servant, had commanded when he gave instructions to bless the people of Israel.

After these preliminary arrangements were completed, Joshua read every word of the law of the Lord to the people, in the hearing of all the Israelites.

Joshua, therefore, was thus far, as Israel's new leader, doing everything as he had been ordered by the Lord and Moses. Yet there was still an important lesson for him to learn. We shall see what that lesson was in the very next situation that was faced by Joshua and the other leaders.

JOSHUA AND THE GIBEONITES

Joshua 9:1–27

In the experience of the Gibeonite deception, came an important lesson that Joshua had not fully learned as yet—the lesson? To consult the Lord earnestly prior to making any important decisions as a leader of other people.

But this time, Joshua and his associates did not inquire of the Lord about these Gibeonites.

The Gibeonites were deceiving and they lied to the Israelites. The Lord would have informed the Israelite leaders about the Gibeonites deception had they inquired of Him.

For lying to Joshua and his officials, the Gibeonites were placed under a curse and made to be woodcutters and water carriers for Israel from that point on in history.

But Joshua and Israel honored the treaty not to kill the Gibeonites nor destroy their cities (Josh. 9:1–27).

JOSHUA AND THE FIVE AMORITE KINGS
Joshua 10:1–15

There were five Amorite kings who were angry because the Gibeonites had made a peace treaty with the Israelites. These kings were kings over Jerusalem, Hebron, Jarmuth, Lachish, and Eglon. These five kings, joined together, planned to attack the Gibeonites and destroy them.

But the Gibeonites, learning of this plan, called upon the Israelites for protection.

Joshua responded to their call for help and went immediately against the five Amorite kings and their joint armies. Joshua soundly defeated them. The Israelites destroyed all their men except a very few who escaped to their fortified cities. Also, the five kings were hiding in a cave together. They were soon discovered, captured, and brought before Joshua and his men.

Joshua's men placed their feet on the necks of the five kings and Joshua gave a demonstration lesson to his men by saying to them, ". . . this is what the Lord will do to all the enemies you are going to fight" (Josh. 10:25).

Then Joshua himself killed all five kings and had their bodies hung on trees until sundown. Afterwards they were taken down from the trees and thrown into the cave where they had been previously hiding.

In the battle with the five kings, God Himself fought with Israel, raining down large hailstones and stopping the sun as signs that He was fighting with them.

JOSHUA AND THE SOUTHERN CAMPAIGN
Joshua 10. 29–43

Joshua and his men then continued fighting against all the kings and their cities in a southern campaign.

One after another they fell before Joshua and his forces, because the Lord was fighting with them.

They took Makeedah, Libnah, Lachish, Hebron, Debir, and subdued the entire southern region, putting to death all the occupants as the Lord had instructed them. They left no survivors.

It was the judgment of God on all these kings and their people. The Lord was using Israel to carry out His judgment upon these people for their sins and iniquities (Josh. 10:29–42).

After these extensive military battles and phenomenal victories, Joshua and his men returned to their headquarters and Israel's base at Gilgal (Josh. 10:43).

Joshua and the Northern Campaign

Joshua 11:1–22b

A very large army composed of the men of numerous kingdoms and their kings in the north, in the west and eastern parts of Canaan, joined forces together to fight against Israel. They had with them also many horses and chariots.

God told Joshua not to be afraid of them, but that by the evening of the next day all would be defeated.

So Joshua went forth in confidence with his army and "suddenly" attacked this large force near the waters of Merom. He routed them and soon defeated them all. No survivors were left.

Then Joshua and his men hamstrung all their horses and burned their chariots as the Lord had instructed him.

Joshua made war against all the royal cities and their forces for a long period of time, until he and his men had subdued all the enemy forces. They killed them all as he had been commanded to do.

Joshua and the Rest from War
Some Totals

Joshua 11:22c–12

Finally after several years of fighting, Israel's wars came to an end.

A complete list of the kings that were defeated by Moses and Joshua in the occupation of the Promised Land is given in Joshua chapter 12. There were thirty-one kings in all.

But notwithstanding the defeat of these thirty-one kings, there still remained much land to be taken over.

The occupation of those remaining lands would be the responsibility of the separate tribes of Israel after they had become settled in their allotted tribal districts.

JOSHUA AND HIS POST-WAR DUTIES

After the several years of war had ceased and all of Canaan had been conquered, there still remained some important tasks for Joshua to face and give his attention to.

Among these tasks were the division of the land (Num. 34:13–29; Josh. 13:8–19:51) the naming and designation of six cities of refuge, three of these on the west and three on the east of the Jordan River (Josh. 20:1–9) the assignment of forty-eight towns and their pasture lands to the Levites, for their use (Josh. 21) and the supervision of the men from the two-and-one-half tribes, whose homes were to be east of the Jordan. These men departed safely to their homes and families after the fighting in Canaan had ceased (Josh. 22).

Finally, after the above tasks were completed, Joshua gave a farewell speech to the leaders of Israel (Josh. 23).

Following this address to the leaders, he called all the tribes together and presented a summary statement of all God's actions in founding the nation of Israel.

He began with Terah, the father of Abraham, tracing his account up to Israel's present situation in the land of promise.

This address again called all Israel to a fresh renewal of their covenant with the Lord.

The people responded with a well-intentioned joint statement saying, "We too will serve the Lord, because He is our God" (Josh. 24:18).

A Summary of the Practical Lessons to be Learned from Joshua's Life

Phase I—Exodus to Moses' death

Lesson no. 1—He learned to take orders

Lesson no. 2—He, with Caleb, believed that if Israel pleased the Lord, the Lord would be with them and enable them to take Canaan.

Lesson no. 3—He followed the Lord wholeheartedly.

Phase II—Moses' death to Joshua's death

Lesson no 4—His seeing Jericho's fall and defeat must certainly have confirmed to him the total wisdom of receiving and acting on God's instructions to ensure continued success in his task.

The same lesson must have been more fully learned by all of Joshua's fighting men.

This lesson is one that we, as the body of Christ, will do well to take to heart and learn from, and make an integral part of our service for God and His kingdom.

Lesson no. 5—The incident with Achan's sin and Israel's defeat at Ai, confirmed to both Joshua and all Israel, the absolute necessity of full obedience to the Lord to ensure His blessing and their success in all future military ventures.

It is thus, certainly, a vital lesson to be learned for success in the church today.

Success at Ai, after Israel's sins were purged, proved the absolute necessity of full obedience to the Lord to ensure success.

Lesson no. 6—In the renewing of the covenant at Mts. Ebal and Gerizim, coupled with a full and complete reading of all the law of the Lord before Israel, we see the vital importance of such reading. It was important with the Lord, with Moses and with Joshua, and to the people.

This reading was from the same Book of the Law that was pointed out by the Lord to Joshua at the time of his commissioning (Josh. 1:1–9).

An intimate knowledge of and heeding of this law was fully as important to the followers as well as to the leaders of the people of Israel. Hence the care and attention Joshua gave to this careful reading of the will and laws of God to all the people at this time.

Somewhat later, after Canaan was conquered and occupied, Joshua would hold a second renewal of the covenant before all of Israel.

A periodic renewal of Israel's covenant with the Lord was wholesome and beneficial to their spiritual lives.

A periodic renewal of the Christian believer's commitment to the Lord and His will and teachings, is also beneficial for us today as it was to God's people in Joshua's day.

This practice of a periodic renewal of Israel's covenant with the Lord and the practice of a public reading of the law to all the people underlined the vital importance and benefit of a widespread knowledge of the Word of God among the common people as well as among the leaders of the people of Israel.

These practices that were being instituted during the early years of Israel's history should certainly have their counterpart in our churches today.

Periodically the church will profit from a fresh reassessment of its basic commitment and relationship to its Lord and Master, Jesus Christ our Savior.

Also the frequent public reading of the Holy Scriptures along with minimal, yet appropriate and helpful comments as the reading proceeds, will be very beneficial to the people in our churches. Did not St. Paul counsel young Timothy as follows? "Until I come, devote yourself to the public reading of scripture, to preaching and to teaching" (1 Tim. 4:13).

And the apostle John referring to the reading and hearing read of the book of the Revelation, said, "Blessed is the one who reads the words of this prophesy, and blessed are those who hear it and take to heart what is written in it, because the time is near" (Rev. 1:3).

Such knowledge and the voluntary, personal commitment to the Lord and to His law and His Word will promote general righteousness and godliness among the members of our churches.

Lesson no. 7—Joshua learned the importance of consulting the Lord prior to making all important decisions as a leader of God's people.

His failure to do this led to a serious failure in his dealings with the Gibeonites, who deceived Israel's leaders telling them they had come from many miles away. But in reality the Gibeonites lived close at hand in Canaan.

Joshua and his associates entered into a pact with them that they should not have made (Josh. 9:1–27).

Joshua's mistake with the Gibeonites is a mistake from which we all can learn. Joshua's mistake was made, along with the men with him. We read, "The men of Israel sampled their provisions but did not inquire of the Lord. Then Joshua made a treaty of peace with them to let them live, and the leaders of the assembly ratified it by oath" (Josh. 9:14–15).

Before we, as the Lord's people, make important decisions, it is wise that we consult the Lord in earnest and believing prayer so we may find the mind of the Lord. Only after doing this we should make our decisions.

CALEB

Caleb, of the tribe of Judah, was one of the twelve spies who were sent to spy out the land of Canaan (Num. 13:6).

After the report of the mission, a report listing all the large walled cities and the giants, many of whom inhabited these cities, Caleb recommended that Israel go up immediately and occupy the land. He said, "We can certainly do it" (Num. 13:7).

In another meeting the day following the initial report of the spies, Caleb, Joshua, with Moses and Aaron present, tore their clothes and spoke to the Israelites, urging them not to rebel against the Lord or be afraid to go into Canaan. God would be with them, they said (Num. 14:5–9).

The Lord in replying to Moses' plea for Israel, pointed out Caleb, then Caleb and Joshua as the only two of all the Israelites who would ever see the Promised Land (Num. 14:24,30).

Of the twelve spies, only Caleb and Joshua survived. God put the other ten to death by a plague (Num. 14:36–38; 26:65). Moses, much later, while addressing the leaders of the trans-Jordan tribes of the Reubenites, Gadites, and one half-tribe of Manasseh, reminded them that it was only Caleb and Joshua who had followed the Lord wholeheartedly. But none of the other Israelites had wholeheartedly followed the Lord, hence they all had to die in the desert (Num. 32:6–13).

Caleb and Joshua were both given assignments by Moses to help assign the land of Canaan to the twelve tribes after Canaan was conquered (Num. 34:16–19). For both men these assignments were assignments of trust and importance for Israel's future.

Immediately prior to his death, Moses made note of Caleb as one who would inherit the land for himself and his children and heirs—the very land he had explored while part of the original Canaan reconnaissance patrol (Deut. 1:34–36).

After Canaan was conquered, Caleb went to his friend Joshua and asked for the land of Hebron that the Lord had promised him. This promise had been made to Caleb forty-five years earlier after the spies returned from exploring Canaan. Joshua blessed him and gave him Hebron.

After taking over Hebron, according as he had been promised, Caleb drove out the Anakites, Sheshai, Ahiman, and Talmai. Then he marched against the people of Debir. Here he promised his daughter Acsah in marriage to the man who would capture Debir for him.

Othniel, his nephew, succeeded in doing this and so was given Acsah as his wife.

Caleb at eighty-five was still vigorous and strong enough to undertake the physical occupation of these territories, which included driving out those people who had previously lived there.

Soon Acsah asked her father for springs of water, so Caleb gave her two springs of water to add to the lands that she and Othniel had thus far been given (Josh. 15:13–19, Jud. 1:11–15).

Caleb's son-in-law, Othniel, later became a deliverer and champion for all Israel, delivering them from the control of the king of Aram.

Aram had oppressed Israel for eight years, during which time Israel had peace (Jud. 3:7–11).

Caleb was a thoroughgoing family man. He had three sons by a concubine name Ephah (1 Chron. 2:46).

In addition, he had three wives and two other concubines. From these five women, Caleb had eleven sons and one daughter. He later had many heirs (1 Chron. 2:18–20; 42–55).

What are the main practical lessons to be learned from the life of Caleb?

Lesson no. 1—*Caleb wholeheartedly followed the Lord*, and he combined this wholehearted devotion with a heart full of courage and faith.

While the Israelites were at Kadesh Barnea, and the twelve spies had returned from exploring Canaan, the ten unbelieving spies gave a "bad report" that discouraged all the people from going in to conquer the land.

But Caleb's opinion was quite different. It is said of him, "Then Caleb silenced the people before Moses and said, 'We should go up and take possession of the land, for we can certainly do it'" (Num. 13:30).

The next day in a joint statement given by Caleb and Joshua, they said,

> "The land we passed through and explored is exceedingly good. If the Lord is pleased with us, He will lead us into that land, a land flowing with milk and honey, and will give it to us. Only do not rebel against the Lord. And do not be afraid of the people of the land, because we will swallow them up. Their protection is gone, but the Lord is with us. Do not be afraid of them."
>
> (Num. 14:7–9)

So Caleb approached his task with faith and the golden opportunity that Israel had to occupy their promised land early, with a wholehearted following of the Lord.

He and his friend Joshua both believed God would help Israel take the land of Canaan immediately after coming out of Egypt. They both

137

believed the task need not be postponed for any reason. As the Lord said of Caleb, he "has a different spirit and follows me wholeheartedly" (Num. 14:24).

Because of his different spirit and attitude, he would be allowed to enter the Promised Land forty years later along with Joshua and Israel's younger, believing generation. He would not die in the desert along with all the unbelieving, older generation of the Israelites.

God will bless and favor us, too, as He did Caleb, if we will follow Him wholeheartedly during our Christian walk. He will certainly bless us as He did Caleb along with his friend Joshua.

Lesson no. 2—Caleb respectfully, yet boldly, claimed those things that he had been promised, namely the hill country of Hebron. It was the land he had personally seen when he had helped explore Canaan forty-five years earlier. The King James Version refers to the land that Caleb was asking for at this time as "this mountain."

Caleb was saying, "Now therefore give me this mountain whereof the Lord spake in that day" (Josh. 14:12, KJV).

He loved the land area he had seen years previously when he was forty years of age. Now he was eighty-five years old. He had endured faithfully, following the Lord for another forty-five years, along with his poor condemned unbelieving brothers in the desert.

But now after Canaan was conquered and he was eighty-five years of age, he remembered and he reminded his friend, Joshua, who was now Israel's victorious leader, that he had been promised a special land area in Judah's allotted district.

Joshua honored Caleb's request and claim and gave him Hebron and it's surrounding hill country.

"This mountain" and the lands around it became the country of Caleb and his heirs after him.

Hebron became Caleb's inheritance.

The practical lesson for believers today is that we as Christian believers can respectfully yet boldly claim and receive all those things that God has promised us, and having claimed them, we may receive them as Caleb received Hebron that had been promised him.

ISRAEL

The nation of Israel began with one man Abram, whose name later became Abraham, and Sarai, whose name later became Sarah.

This couple came from Mesopotamia into Canaan. They had no children, as a couple, until Sarah reached ninety and Abraham one hundred.

With God's help they then had a son, Isaac.

At maturity, Isaac married Rebekah. This couple had twin sons, Esau and Jacob.

Jacob lived with his uncle Laban at Paddan Aram, Syria where he had twelve sons and one daughter.

After twenty years, Jacob, with his family, returned to Canaan. His sons and their wives had children until there were seventy Israelis. And because of famine in Canaan, all moved to Egypt when they multiplied and lived for 430 years.

The Egyptians enslaved the Israelites. Finally God sent Moses, who with God's help, brought them out of their bondage, and after forty years they conquered all of Canaan under Joshua's leadership. They then moved into their own land of freedom and blessing.

But during the forty years from the time Israel left Egypt until they crossed over the Jordan and began to conquer Canaan, Israel had several experiences that serve as good examples for us believers today, and they had several experiences that serve as bad examples for us believers today.

The good experiences serve as encouragements for us.

The bad examples serve as warnings for us.

Israel's good examples were times when their actions were pleasing to the Lord and Moses. They were obedient.

Israel's bad examples were times when their actions were displeasing to the Lord and Moses. They were disobedient.

AT THE PASSOVER

At the first Passover, *Israel was obedient to the Lord* and Moses. They placed blood on their door posts and ate the feast in peace in readiness to leave Egypt quickly. The Passover feast prepared them to leave Egypt. *They obeyed. Things went well!* (Ex. 12:1–30).

AT THE EXODUS

The *Israelites obeyed* and asked the Egyptians for gold and silver articles, clothing and dough for bread. The Israelites obeyed Moses' instructions and miraculously crossed the Red Sea, on their way to freedom. *They obeyed. Things went well!* (Ex. 12:31–14:31).

AT MARAH AND ELIM

God now made a conditional promise to Israel: "If they would listen to God's voice and obey His commands, He would keep them from all the diseases of Egypt for 'I am the Lord who heals you,'" God said (Ex. 15:25–26).

AT THE DESERT OF SIN

After Elim, the people were hungry so the Lord provided manna and quail for them. But this provision by the Lord was given amidst Israel's grumbling, grumbling, grumbling. In reality, their grumbling was not against Moses and Aaron, but against the Lord.

The manna was given to Israel not only to provide for their physical nourishment but also as a means of testing their daily obedience to the Lord, for there were instructions given as to its collection each day and to avoid looking for it on the Sabbath (Ex. 16:20,27).

Whenever Israel grumbled it manifested unbelief and it greatly displeased the Lord.

The Lord would daily supply all their needs even though their geographical circumstances would seem to discourage such a firm and hopeful faith in adequate supply.

The Lord was with Israel every day and knew their needs and would be faithful in providing their needs. The manna was provided for the Israelites during all their wilderness life until they finally reached their promised land in Canaan. God was faithful to Israel as He, our Father, will be faithful to us as Christian believers as long as we place God's will and kingdom first in our lives. See Matthew 6:25–34.

AT REPHIDIM

At Rephidim, Israel again, because they had no water, grumbled against Moses and the Lord, even threatening to stone Moses. When Moses cried to the Lord, he was told to take some of the elders and stand with them by the rock at Horeb.

With the Lord also standing with all the men, Moses struck the rock with his rod and water came out for all the Israelites to drink. Day by day God was teaching Israel to learn to consult Him and to trust Him. Some of Israel's actions and attitudes pleased the Lord. Some of Israel's actions and actions were displeasing to the Lord. To please the Lord would bring peace and happiness. To displease the Lord would bring turmoil and unhappiness and sometimes death. Here at Rephidim, Israel tested the Lord by saying, "Is the Lord among us or not?" (Ex. 17:1–7).

Also at Rephidim the Amalekites attacked the Israelites, especially those who were among the last columns when the Israelites were on the move to a new location.

Moses told Joshua to choose some men and fight the Amalekites. He was victorious over them, defeating them soundly. This, Israel's first military engagement and victory was made possible with the Lord fighting with Joshua's forces. As long as Moses' hands and arms were held up in faith to the Lord, Joshua's forces prevailed. Whenever Moses would lower his arms, the Amalekites prevailed. So two men, Aaron and Hur, helped Moses hold his arms skyward until the raging battle was brought to an end with Israel's forces victorious.

Israel's experience with the Amalekites carries with it a lesson and example for God's people today: That lesson is that in our battles to extend God's kingdom today through evangelism and gospel preaching, and against the obstacles we often encounter in building our churches and families for the Lord, we shall prevail against Satan and carnal forces as we maintain our contact with the Lord by our hands being raised to the Lord in faith, and by careful obedience to Him. We too shall be victorious as was Israel against the Amalekites.

Israel's triumph over the Amalekites was only the first of many subsequent triumphs over more powerful enemies, all because the Lord was fighting with them (Ex. 7:8–15).

AT HOREB

At Mt. Horeb the golden-calf incident took place.

The Israelites grew tired of waiting for Moses, who remained in the mount with God for forty days. So they persuaded Aaron to make a calf-idol for them. The people brought sacrifices to this idol, worshiping in a pagan style. Afterwards they organized a matching pagan festival and rose up in a wild, frenzied pagan revelry with dancing, hilarity, with a large amount of fornication mixed in with the revelry.

The actions went boldly against what they knew about the Lord by this time. It was an evil "corporate fling" which denied their commitment to the Lord and caused God to be very angry with them. It resulted in the punishment of death for about three-thousand people.

Moses interceded for the rest of the Israelites and God forgave their sin. Moses also interceded for his brother Aaron, whose life was also saved from death at that time.

By Israel's idolatrous example at Horeb with its dire consequences, Christian believers are solemnly warned to avoid idolatry of any kind and fornication, sins which are destructive of God's glory and holiness (Ex. 32:1–25; Deut. 9:7–21; 1 Cor. 10:6–13).

AT TABERAH, AT MASSAH
AND AT KIBROTH HATTAAVAH

Here too, the Israelites made the Lord angry. See Numbers 11:1–3; Exodus 17:1–7; Numbers 11:4–35, and Deuteronomy 9:22.

At Kadesh Barnea

Numbers 13–14; Deuteronomy 1:19–46; 9:23–29

From Kadesh Barnea, Moses sent out twelve men on a reconnaissance-exploring expedition. For forty days these twelve men explored the land of Canaan. This patrol was in preparation for Israel's conquering the land and occupying it for themselves.

Upon the return of the exploratory spies, they said that land was indeed beautiful and very desirable, yet ten of the twelve spies joined together in saying that the prospects of Israel's conquering the land were deplorable and hopeless. They pointed out the vast number of walled cities and that the cities' occupants were oversized human beings—giants. The Israelites up against these odds, they said, would be defeated. They did not consider God and His power in their equation, but only the visible human factors, the giants and the walled cities and all other humanly reasoned obstacles. Only Caleb and Joshua recommended that Israel proceed with plans to conquer Canaan immediately. The other ten men's report seemed only to discourage the mass of the people of Israel.

As a consequence, all the Israelites rebelled against the Lord and refused to believe in Him and refused to move ahead with a willingness to occupy the land.

Now, because of the people's rejection of their golden opportunity to enter the Promised Land, all the men twenty years and over, must die in the wilderness-desert during the next forty years, and the younger generation of Israelis would be the ones who would conquer and occupy Canaan. God said of them that they "disobeyed me and tested me ten times . . ." (Num. 14:22).

Only Caleb and Joshua would finally enter the land along with the younger generation of the people of Israel, for they were of a different spirit than were all the others of the unbelieving people of Israel.

Israel's mass unbelief and rebellion against God's plan for their lives at this time warns believers today in our churches not to do the same, but to follow the example of the two better men, Caleb and Joshua, who believed God and were prepared to enter and occupy Canaan under God's banner and power and on His time schedule.

The Lord said, "Not one of you will enter the land I swore with uplifted hand to make your home, except Caleb son of Jephunneh and Joshua son of Nun" (Num. 14:30).

And speaking further of these two men, Moses said, "of the men who went to explore the land, only Joshua son of Nun and Caleb son of Jephunneh survived." All the others who had explored with them "died of a plague before the Lord" (Num. 14:37–38).

But of the unbelieving Israelites, God said, "Because they have not followed me wholeheartedly, not one of the men twenty years old or more who came up out of Egypt will see the land I promised in oath to Abraham, Isaac, and Jacob—not one except Caleb son of Jephunneh the Kenizzite and Joshua son of Nun, for they followed the Lord wholeheartedly. The Lord's anger burned against Israel and he made them wander in the desert forty years, until the whole generation of those who had done evil in his sight was gone" (Num. 32:11–13).

AT ARAD

Recovering somewhat from their tragic unbelief at Kadesh Barnea, the people of Israel made a vow to the Lord that they would totally destroy the cities of Arad if He would deliver them into their hands. The Aradites had attacked Israel and taken captive some of their people.

The Lord heard Israel's plea and gave the Aradite-Canaanites into their hands. The Israelites totally destroyed these Canaanites in accordance with their vow to the Lord (Num. 21:1–3).

ENROUTE AROUND EDOM

Numbers 21:4–9

After leaving Mt. Hur, the Israelites were traveling around Edom and they became impatient and began to speak against God and against Moses. They believed they were going to die in the desert. They said there was no bread or water. They called the manna "miserable food."

As a punishment of the peoples' miserable attitudes, the Lord sent venomous snakes among them. Many of the people died from the snake bites. When they came to Moses acknowledging their sin, the Lord told Moses to make and erect a large brass serpent on a pole in the midst of the Israelites. Moses did as God commanded him.

Whenever an Israelite who had been bitten by a venomous snake looked at the brass serpent, his affliction was healed.

Jesus in later years referred to this incident in these words, "Just as Moses lifted up the snake in the desert, so the Son of Man must be lifted up, that everyone who believes in him may have eternal life" (John 3:15).

AT THE DEFEAT OF SIHON AND OG

Numbers 21:21–35; Deuteronomy 2:13–3:29

After the last of the older generation of the unbelieving Israelites had died, God told Moses to turn north. He obeyed and turned north with all of the Israelites. They passed by several nations while moving northward. Finally they reached a valley near Moab. Here Israel sent messengers to Sihon, a king of the Amorites, requesting permission to pass through his land. Sihon refused this request. Sihon came out against Israel with his army. God told Moses to fight against them and soon Israel totally destroyed Sihon and all his forces and conquered all his land.

Soon Og, a second Amorite king, with his army, came against Moses and the Israelites. God also delivered this king and his army into Moses' and the Israelites' power as well. He was completely defeated and all his people were killed and his country completely taken over and occupied.

In the case of both these Amorite kings, the Lord fought with the Israelites, giving them complete victory. These two victories became examples to the younger generation of the Israelites and to Joshua, their future leader, of what the Lord would do for His people when they obeyed His commands with faith in the Lord (Deut. 3:21–22; 31:1–8).

The older generation was unbelieving and disobedient.

The younger generation was believing and obedient.

God abundantly blessed the believing and obedient generation whereas the unbelieving, disobedient, and rebellious generation of Israelites had all suffered rejection and death in the desert. This younger generation would see many more victories in the near future, serving the Lord under Joshua's leadership.

As God was beginning to bless a believing and obedient nation of Israel, and continued to bless them as they later crossed over the Jordan and finally conquered all of Canaan in triumphant campaigns, so God will bless His obedient servants today as well who, with a command to preach and plant new churches, go forth and bring thousands of lost and hopeless souls into the kingdom of Christ, delivering them from the kingdom of darkness and of Satan (Col. 1:12–13).

SUMMARY OF PRACTICAL LESSONS TO BE LEARNED

from Israel's experiences, beginning with the exodus
from Egypt to their settlement in Canaan.
The older generation and the younger generation.

THE OLDER GENERATION

Being able to see the ten mighty plagues in Egypt, the Red Sea opening, the water purifying miracle at Marah, the water from the rock and the revelation of God on Mt. Sinai, Israel's witnessing and experiencing these great manifestations, gave them an unparalleled opportunity to learn much about the true God, the Creator of the heavens and the earth.

Mighty deeds, an awesome holiness, a Gracious Protector and Provider of their needs all these manifestations of Him who was becoming their God, Israel's God, they had seen.

This message was coming through to some of this generation of the Israelites, but to only a very small number of them—to Moses, to Caleb, to Joshua, to Miriam, and perhaps to Aaron, Moses' brother.

At the Passover all Israel obeyed the Lord and Moses.

At the exodus, all Israel obeyed and plundered the Egyptians as they had been instructed. The Egyptians cooperated in this, with the Lord assisting.

At Marah Israel grumbled, yet by a miracle bitter waters were made sweet and all had water.

At Elim all was well.

At the desert of sin, amidst grumbling, Israel was miraculously given manna and quail.

At Rephidim, water was miraculously provided, again amidst much grumbling.

Also at Rephidim, Israel experienced a significant military victory over the Amalekites, due to the power of God being honored along with faith on the part of Moses, Aaron, and Hur.

Joshua, Moses' young aide and understudy, selected a few dependable men and fought valiantly against the Amalekites and defeated them.

At Horeb, with Moses in the mount getting the laws of God, Israel reverted to gross idolatry and carnality, going completely counter to what they already clearly knew about God's holiness and goodness. In other words, they knew much better than to do what they were now doing.

Soon after at Taberah, at Massah and at Kibroth Hattaavah, Israel angered the Lord once again.

Finally, at Kadesh Barnea came the tragic climax of the unbelieving and rebellious attitude of the older generation of the people of Israel.

For, upon the return of the twelve spies from exploring the Promised Land, ten of the men, a majority of the twelve, gave an unbelieving, pessimistic and fully discouraging report to all the other Israelites.

As a consequence, the entire older generation of Israel's men, twenty years and older, rejected their opportunity to go in and occupy the land.

All of Israel's previous grumbling, threats and discontent were only preliminary signs that something was not right with the hearts and lives of this early generation of Israel's people. And the situation did not seem to be improving with the passage of time.

The people, it seems, were gradually allowing wicked unbelief to expunge from their minds and memories all they had seen thus far that should have built their faith to a tremendous high point.

The growth of such powerful faith and courage had only been taking place in the hearts of a few men—Moses, Caleb, Joshua, and perhaps Aaron.

God said of all the others of this older generation, "They have disobeyed me and tested me ten times" (Num. 14:22).

Of all the unbelieving Israelites of this older generation God also said, "Because they have not followed me wholeheartedly, not one of the men twenty years old or more who came up out of Egypt will see the land I promised an oath to Abraham, Isaac, and Jacob, not one except Caleb son of Jephunneh the Kenizzite, and Joshua son of Nun, for they followed the lord wholeheartedly. The Lord's anger burned against Israel and he made them wander in the desert forty years, until the whole generation of those who had done evil in his sight was gone" (Num. 32:11–13).

Such was the punishment of this older generation of Israelites.

This punishment, destruction, loss and death was brought on Israel by themselves.

God would have been much more pleased had this generation abandoned their unbelief and rebellion and been of the spirit of Moses, Caleb and Joshua, and gone in and conquered and occupied Canaan at this time. But God could not work with this older generation as He would have liked to do.

He must abandon this unbelieving generation and await a forthcoming generation that perhaps would have a spirit of faith and obedience that will match that of Moses, Caleb and Joshua, the three men of the older generation who possessed the kind of faith and wholehearted devotion to the Lord that exemplify the type of men God needed to work through to conquer Canaan.

Finally, after forty years of desert wandering, all the older unbelieving generation of Israelites had died and were gone.

THE YOUNGER GENERATION

After the last man of the older, unbelieving generation had died, God told Moses, "you have made your way around this hill country long enough; now turn north" (Deut. 2:3).

This Moses did with all Israel. The younger, believing generation was now going to come into their own. This younger generation was composed of men whose ages ranged from twenty years up to sixty years.

They came north and were soon challenged by the first of two Amorite kings on the east side of the Jordan river.

Moses marshaled his army, and with the Lord with him and his believing obedient men, soon defeated Sihon.

Next came King Og with his army.

Moses and his believing, courageous army, made up of the younger generation of Israelites, soon had defeated this king along with all his forces. He took over sixty cities and all his territory (Deut. 3:4).

Soon after this Moses died and Joshua became Israel's new leader.

Leading the younger generation of believing Israelites, with the Lord, by his side and directing him, he soon crossed over the Jordan River and began conquering Canaan west of the river.

The first city to fall, Jericho, then later, Ai. Afterwards, over the course of several years, king after king, with their armies and people, fell in defeat before Joshua and his men.

When the wars finally ended, there were thirty-one kings in all who had fallen in defeat before Moses and Joshua: two under Moses' command, and twenty-nine under Joshua's command (Josh. 12:1–34).

The Lord finally had found a combination of men through whom He could advance His kingdom. These were leaders of the older generation of Israelites, but men who had the right spirit, the spirit of faith and who were wholehearted followers of the Lord, first Moses, then Joshua. Both of these older but believing leaders were at the head of a generation of younger, but believing and obedient men, who fought valiantly.

And the Lord fought with these men, godly leaders and obedient, believing followers. This was a winning combination then, and such an arrangement of men today, too, will also be a winning combination in gospel preaching and church planting.

The Lord who went ahead of Israel's armies and fought with Israel's armies on both the east and west sides of the Jordan River, will go before his men today, too, and will be with his men today too who go at His direction and have the same spirit of faith and obedience as did the men in Moses' and Joshua's time.

The Lord bared His mighty arm for all these mighty military exploits that were called for in that day and age on both sides of the Jordan River, east and west, until the long-promised land of milk and honey was in Israel's possession.

Israel's' experience, under Moses and Joshua, in subduing these lands, has a clear lesson for the church of Christ today—the lesson? It is this:

God will work mightily through and for a group of men who are called by Him and prepared and who move at His command and maintain a wholehearted faith and devotion to God and His Word.

That was the spiritual posture of Moses, Joshua, and the men who were fighting with them, to conquer and occupy the land of Canaan for all of Israel.

And when we, as God's servants today, in gospel work, make the posture of these early men our spiritual posture, God will indeed work with us mightily, too, bearing His mighty arm on behalf of His kingdom's advance. Thousands and thousands of lost souls will be rescued from satanic darkness and be brought into the light of Christ and His kingdom.

Dear Lord, let this grace be granted to the church of Christ in these last days!

Some of you men who are reading these sentences and paragraphs today may look upon yourselves as older men and you love the Lord and want to see God's kingdom advanced. But you may wonder how extensively God can use a man of your age and strength. You may think that your best years are behind you.

To any such men my reply is this: please go back and reread the section that begins with the heading, *The younger generation*. See how God used Moses who was very old at the time. God gave two powerful kings and their kingdoms into his hands, kings and kingdoms east of the Jordan River.

Then a second man, Joshua, who was an older man by that time, when compared with all the other men of Israel, led Israel across the Jordan and he and his army conquered twenty-nine more kings and their kingdoms.

Between these two older men they conquered a total of thirty-one kings and thirty-one kingdoms and their armies.

These two older men had the right spirit, the spirit of faith and obedience, something which all those of the older generation of men who died in the wilderness could have had but did not have, and now they, with their mighty Lord alongside them were leading a younger generation of men who were willing to believe and obey these older men, along with the Lord.

This was a winning combination, older men with obedient and believing spirits, leading younger men who were rapidly acquiring and growing in the same spirit as the older leaders already possessed.

This combination that was a winning combination for Moses and Joshua can be a winning combination for God's servants today, as well, as we endeavor to advance God's kingdom and the gospel.

Let us follow the orders of our commander-in-chief, the commander of the armies of heaven, and see mighty triumphs for our Lord in these last days, moving out with courage and faith with our mighty Lord going ahead of us.

The kind of triumphs and successes these believing men saw were largely military triumphs, but not entirely. There were other manifestations of God's power as well even a great variety of miraculous manifestations were seen by the people of Israel, both in their early years and in their later years as a nation.

But it was not merely because they were older men that had qualified them for such leadership and phenomenal success, nor was it merely because they were of the older generation of the Israelites; rather it was because these men had remembered and believed that the God they were serving was indeed the kind of God He had shown Himself to be, from the plagues in Egypt, the crossing of the Red Sea and from the other miracles He had done for Israel during the forty years in the wilderness.

All the men who had come out of Egyptian slavery along with Caleb and Joshua had seen the same mighty miracles, signs and wonders that Moses, Caleb, and Joshua had seen, but they had either forgotten what they saw or for other reasons had refused to carry over its implications to a new set of circumstances, namely, that that same God would show the same kind of power in their conquering and occupying Canaan.

But Moses, Joshua, and Caleb had not failed to make the carryover in their memories, thinking, and faith.

That is what made these men of a different spirit than the others who had died in the wilderness. And it was this belief and memory of the kind of God they had seen in action, that qualified them for the leadership and success they were given in occupying the Promised Land.

Those men who lay dead in the wilderness-desert could have had the same faith as Moses, Caleb, and Joshua had, but they did not allow it to formulate in their hearts and minds.

Likewise today it is not the age factor that will qualify men to see great things for God, but rather whether we allow there to formulate in our hearts and minds a full knowledge of the kind of God that He showed Himself to be in Egypt and the wilderness and, yes, in the conquering and occupation of the Promised Land and during later manifestations of God's power during Israel's history.

In other words, our God today is the same God that showed His mighty power in behalf of the people of Israel from the time they left Egypt until they settled in the Promised Land—a God of wonders and power. Even as Gideon said, "Where are all his wonders that our fathers told us about when they said, 'Did not the Lord bring us up out of Egypt?'" (Jud. 6:13).

Young men as well as older men can qualify to see great manifestations of God's power, as soon as they allow to formulate in their hearts and minds a knowledge of the kind of God that He showed Himself to be in Egypt and the wilderness. Note the experiences of two young men who illustrate this point. They are Jonathan and his friend David (1 Sam. 14, 17).

A good safeguard for the man who is going to see great manifestations of God's power in any work of the kingdom is that he first become deeply anchored in his Christian character and walk with God. Lacking in such spiritual depth will make such a man vulnerable to pride and other attacks of Satan. The notoriety and attention can be destructive to him unless he is trained beforehand as Jesus trained his twelve men before the great power came to them at Pentecost. After they had been trained sufficiently, they were ready for the power and they had sufficient character so as to know how to be good stewards of it and not to be ruined by it.

ACHAN

Joshua 7
Achan's sin

Achan, of the tribe of Judah, took some of the devoted things out of Jericho, when it was being subdued by Joshua's men. All had been told not to do this. All gold, silver, bronze, and iron articles were to be put into the Lord's treasury and not taken into anyone's personal possession (Josh. 6:17–19; 24).

Achan hid these stolen items in his tent and it was viewed as a sin not only by one man, Achan, but as a sin committed by the entire body of the Israelites.

As Israel proceeded to capture city number two on the west side of the Jordan River, they suffered a defeat because the Lord was not with them. This was because of Israel and Achan's sin.

It was soon discovered that Achan had committed this disobedience, and as his judgment, he, his sons and daughters, and all his animals were stoned to death. Then his tent, the things he had stolen, along with the dead bodies were burned up. Then over everything, a large pile of rocks was thrown.

The place afterwards was called the "Valley of Achor," which means "disaster."

So Achan's covetous act brought not only a defeat to Israel and the loss of thirty-six Hebrew fighters at Ai, but Achan and all his family and possessions were destroyed (Josh. 7).

Such was the great loss and defeat that was brought upon all Israel by one man's sin. It was Israel's loss and Achan and all his family's judgment and loss that also resulted.

Some lessons to be learned from Achan's life and death: Only strict obedience to God's instructions ensures victories and success in God's enterprises. Disobedience to the Lord brings defeat and tragic loss.

This experience of Israel at the outset of their campaign of occupying the Promised Land serves as a pointed and solemn warning to the church of Christ in these last days as we seek to advance his kingdom.

Let us be wise and learn from the experiences of Israel and from the experience of Achan.

IV

Patterns from the Judges to the
Kings of United Israel

IV
Judah and the Simeonites

Judges 1:1–21

After Canaan was occupied, these two tribes experienced victory in fighting side-by-side, in driving out the Canaanites in their areas. This victory was because they were obeying the Lord. Hence the Lord was with them (Jud. 1:1–21; Josh. 13:1–ff).

Lesson: These men had victory and success because they were obedient. Therefore the Lord fought with them and gave them good successes.

JOSEPH

Judges 1:22–26

These men also had victory, conquering Bethel with the Lord's help.

Lesson: With the Lord's help they had victory.

The tribes of Manasseh, Zebulun, Asher, Naphtali, and the Danites all failed to drive out the original inhabitants in their areas. Hence this accounted as disobedience. These people began to worship the idols of these people to their detriment.

The next generation of Israelites after Joshua and the elders died, began to disobey the Lord, departing from obedience to the Lord's covenant and commands. They stopped listening to the Lord and began neglecting the covenant they had made with God. As a consequence of this disobedience, they were unable to drive out the remaining inhabitants of Canaan. The Lord stopped fighting with them.

Othniel

With Israel made subject to the king of Aram Naharaim for eight years, they cried to the Lord. The Lord raised up Othniel, Caleb's son-in-law. The Spirit came upon him and he, with some obedient men, overpowered Aram Naharaim and delivered Israel from his power.

Othniel served as Israel's judge for forty years, while Israel had peace (Jud. 3:7–11).

Lesson: While in bondage, Israel cried out to the Lord, their true God. He brought them again out into freedom and peace, by a godly, spirit-empowered Othniel.

Ehud

Being subject to Moab for eighteen years due to departing from the Lord, Israel cried to the Lord again. He raised up Ehud. Ehud killed Eglon, the king of Moab, escaped, then blowing a trumpet in Ephraim, said, "Follow me." "For the Lord has given Moab, your enemy, into your hands" (Jud. 3:28).

The men followed Ehud and they defeated Moab, killing ten thousand strong and vigorous men. None escaped. Moab became subject to Israel with peace for eighty years (Jud. 3:12–30).

Lesson: No idol, but only the true God of Israel, is able to provide freedom, happiness, and peace. This time through an obedient Ehud and a people who were willing to call out to the true God, at the same time turning away from their false gods, eighty years of peace followed Ehud's and the Lord's deliverance.

SHAMGAR

Judges 3:31

This man, with an oxgoad, struck down six-hundred Philistines and saved Israel.

Lesson: Shamgar's deeds against six-hundred troublesome Philistines, marks him as a true hero and champion, worthy of enough note to be named for all-time in Israel's early history and Holy Scripture. With a single weapon, he killed six-hundred men, truly a phenomenal feat! His contribution? "He, too, saved Israel" (Jud. 3:31).

DEBORAH AND BARAK

Judges 4–5

Deborah, a godly prophetess in Israel, would hold court to settle people's disputes.

Israel, because of their sins had suffered under the control of king Jabin, a king of Canaan for twenty years. But because the Israelites cried to the Lord, he spoke to Deborah with a message for Barak. It was this,

> "The Lord, the God of Israel, commands you: Go, take with you ten thousand men of Naphtali, and Zebulun and lead the way to mount Tabor. I will lure Sisera, the commander of Jabin's army, with his chariots and his troops to the Kishon River and give him into your hands."
>
> (Jud. 4:6–7)

Barak told Deborah he would go if she went with him.

Deborah agreed to go with him, but the glory of victory would not be his, because of his attitude.

The two went to Kadesh together, where Barak procured ten-thousand men as fighters.

Sisera, Jabin's general commander, brought his men with his iron chariots to the Kishon River.

Deborah then told Barak, "Go! This is the day the Lord has given Sisera into your hands. Has not the Lord gone ahead of you?" (Jud. 4:14).

At Barak's advance near Mt. Tabor with his men, the Lord routed Sisera and his men and chariots and all his men were killed.

Sisera fled on foot from his chariot into the tent of Heber's wife, Jael.

She fed him clabber, and covering him, he fell asleep, exhausted.

Then Jael came quietly and drove a tent-peg through his temple with a hammer, killing him.

Barak soon came by and found Sisera in Jael's tent, dead.

That day, the Lord subdued king Jabin and as Israel's strength grew, Jabin's decreased until he was finally destroyed (Jud. 4:1–24).

We bless you, great and wonderful Lord! Through a godly prophetess and an obedient military leader, with ten thousand Naphtalite and Zebulunite volunteers, God rid a repentant Israel of her oppression of twenty years.

The Lord worked through the yielded prophetic gift and faith of Deborah, to receive and pass on a message of instructions to Barak, one who was willing to receive and believed her message.

Barak, with Deborah at his side, raised an army of volunteers and went to a designated location, Mt. Tabor, near the Kishon River.

Here the Lord drew Sisera and his forces and the Lord routed him at Barak's advance "Not a man was left" (Jud. 4:15–16).

Barak is named as a man of faith in Hebrews 11:32–40.

He, with godly Deborah, "became powerful in battle and routed foreign armies" (Heb. 11:34).

Faith in God, courage, and obedience, were boldly manifest in the lives of the prophetess Deborah and the military leader, Barak, and also in the bold actions of Jael, Heber's wife, into whose hands the Lord delivered the life of king Jabin's military general, Sisera. God gave Jael the honor of killing the leader of the very forces that had for twenty years been oppressing the Israelites.

Summary of lessons to be learned from the lives of the two women and the man Barak

1. Deborah was living a godly and holy life and with a prophetic gift, was open to messages from the Lord when they were given.

   As Israel cried to the Lord, she heard from the Lord and delivered the message on to the designated man of God, Barak.

2. Deborah was the wife of Lappidoth and a mother in Israel (Jud. 5:7).

   Prior to king Jabin's defeat, conditions in Israel were deplorable, due to King Jabin's oppression of the Israelites.

Note:

"In the days of Jael, the roads were abandoned;
travelers took to winding paths.
Village life in Israel ceased,
ceased until I, Deborah, arose
arose a mother in Israel.
when they chose new gods.
and not a shield or spear was seen
among forty thousand in Israel.
my heart is with Israel's princes,
with the willing volunteers among
the people. Praise the Lord!"

(Jud. 5:6–9)

3. Both Deborah and Barak were ready and willing to be of service to the Lord and to their people Israel. When the Lord spoke to them after the people of Israel had cried out to Him, these two responded and obeyed the Lord's instructions. As a result a great and marvelous deliverance was accomplished for God's people.

   They blessed the Lord along with their friend Jael and many other happy and free again Israelites.

   After Deborah, Barak and Jael's service, Israel had peace for forty years (Jud. 5:31c).

GIDEON

Judges 6–8; Hebrews 11:32

Due to departing from the Lord again, Israel was given into the hands of the Midianites for seven years.

When they cried to the Lord, the Lord sent a prophet who spoke to them as to why they were being oppressed.

Then the angel of the Lord appeared to Gideon with a call to leadership.

He was being called to undertake a large leadership task. But he first wanted proof that it was the God of Israel who was talking to him (Jud. 6:11–16).

He obeyed when told to place the meal on the rock (Jud. 6:20).

The consuming of the meal that Gideon had prepared, by fire from the rock, was good proof that it was the angel of the Lord speaking to him. Immediately after this the angel disappeared (Jud. 6:17–22).

The Lord continued giving instructions as to destroying the Baal idol and the Asherah pole, and replacing those with a proper altar and an appropriate sacrifice on it, the seven-year-old bull that was his father's.

Gideon obeyed the Lord concerning the altar and sacrifice. It endangered his life with the Baal worshiping townspeople, but Gideon's father spoke in defense of him and so his life was preserved from death for destroying the Baal idol.

This incident resulted in a name change for Gideon. Some now called him "Jerub-baal," meaning, "let Baal contend" (Jud. 6:33).

As the enemy unified and formed a campsite in the valley of Jezreel, the Spirit of the Lord came upon Gideon.

He blew a trumpet calling his family clan to follow him.

He then sent messengers to call volunteers from four other tribes: Manasseh, Asher, Zebulun, and Issachar. Many of them came to him, thirty-two thousand in number (Jud. 6:33–35).

With the Spirit on him he moved into action, organizing his volunteers into an army and locating them in a campsite at the spring of Harod. The camp of the Midianites was north of them in the valley.

He now requested of the Lord further confirmation that He would indeed deliver Israel by His hand. He asked for a double-fleece proof. God gave this double proof to him (Jud. 6:36–40).

The Lord, speaking to him, told him he had too many men and to reduce their number. Gideon obeyed, speaking to all who were fearful to go home. Of the thirty-two thousand men, all went home except ten thousand who stayed with Gideon.

Then the Lord reduced the ten thousand all the way down to three-hundred men only.

This was so Israel would not say they had brought about the victory, but that the Lord had done it.

Gideon accepted the Lord's changes with no objections (Jud. 7:1–8b).

He was further encouraged to lead against the enemy by overhearing a conversation of two Midianites during the night, about a dream one of them had.

Hearing the conversation abolished any fears he may have had about attacking the enemy. After hearing the dream and its interpretation, he worshiped God (Jud. 7:8c–16).

He returned to his men and shouted, "Get up, the Lord has given the Midianite camp into your hands" (Jud. 7:15).

He now divided his three-hundred men into three groups of one hundred each; he places a trumpet and pitcher with a torch inside of it, in the hand of each man.

They surrounded the camp during the second watch of the night, with orders to "Watch me," "follow my lead. When I get to the edge of the camp, do exactly as I do. When I and all who are with me blow our trumpets, then all around the camp blow yours and shout, 'For the Lord and for Gideon'" (Jud. 7:17–18).

At Gideon's signal all broke their pitchers and blew their trumpets. When all three hundred blew their trumpets, and called out, "For the Lord and for Gideon," the Lord caused the men in the Midianite camp to turn on each other and kill one another (Jud. 7:22).

The entire Midianite army fled and was blocked from crossing the Jordan River by the other Israelites who had been called to help pursue the enemy.

A mighty victory was gained over Israel's enemies, for the Lord had fought with them.

Gideon again sent messengers to the other tribes for their assistance. Men from Manasseh, Asher, Naphtali all helped in the pursuit and defeat of the army. The men of Manasseh captured and killed two Midianite leaders, Oreb and Zeeb (Jud. 7:24–25).

Gideon refused an offer to become Israel's king, but Midian was no longer a problem for Israel.

Israel had peace for forty years during Gideon's lifetime. He died at a good old age and had seventy sons and a seventy-first son by a concubine. His name was Abimelech (Jud. 8:22–35).

In defeating the Midianites, Amalekites and people from the east, one-hundred-twenty-thousand men had been killed. Gideon and his three hundred continued to pursue the fifteen-thousand men who still remained of the armies of the enemy.

He crossed the Jordan and finally he encountered Zeba and Zalmunna, two kings of the Midianites and their fifteen thousand remaining men. Gideon caught them unawares and routed them, capturing the two Kings.

Gideon's pursuing as he did showed his determination to finish the defeat of a cruel enemy.

He also punished the Succoth men and killed those at Peniel, for refusing to help Gideon's three-hundred men with needed food (Jud. 8:4–17).

He killed the two Midianite kings (Jud. 8:18–21).

After this massive victory Israel enjoyed peace for forty years (Jud. 8:28).

PRACTICAL LESSONS TO BE LEARNED
FROM GIDEON'S LIFE

Lesson no. 1

The story of Gideon and Israel's defeat of the Midianites and their allies with only 300 men illustrates what mighty deeds are possible when a man follows God's instructions and the Lord is working along with that man.

As in the case of Moses and Joshua and the earlier Israelites, and their defeat of thirty-one kings and their armies, so Gideon's defeat of one hundred and thirty-five-thousand men with three hundred men shows that when God and his power are in the equation with only a small human force, we may expect unimaginable and astounding results.

Lesson no. 2

God delights to take the "weak things of the world to shame the strong" (1 Cor. 1:27).

So when men boast, they can "boast in the Lord" and not in human prowess (1 Cor. 1:31).

There may be a man reading these lines, a young man, a middle-aged man or an older man, and you may believe God is calling you to a great task, a task way beyond your perceived abilities to accomplish in the natural. Like Gideon you are saying to the Lord, so to speak "My clan is the weakest in Manasseh, and I am the least in my family." But the Lord answers you as He answered Gideon, "I will be with you," and He will say the equivalent to you as He said to Gideon when the Lord said, "You will strike down the Midianites as if they were but one man" (Jud. 6:15–16).

In other words, the Lord is saying to you, "You will be able to accomplish completely and successfully the large task I am calling you to undertake."

Gideon finally became fully convinced that the God of Israel was the one calling him to his large assignment. After he had become convinced of that fact, he then moved with confidence and dispatch, being assured that success was up ahead for him and his men.

When you or I become fully convinced that the same God of Israel is the one calling us to our large assignment, we too will be able to move forward with confidence and dispatch, being assured that success is up ahead for us too, as it was for Gideon.

ABIMELECH

Judges 9

From the account of Abimelech's beginnings, it appears that he was only a wicked, despotic man, ambitious for sovereign power. He was certainly a demagogue, appealing to his mother's brothers and her clan for support.

They in turn, presented his proposal for power to the citizens of Shechem, all of whom were followers of Baal worship. These people then gave him seventy pieces of silver from the Baal temple to help him finance his campaign for political power. The suggestive thrust of this gift was apparently to help Abimelech do the very wicked deed that he now proceeded to do—kill in cold blood his seventy blood brother competitors for the position of king that he wanted for himself.

No angel appeared to Abimelech's parents nor to him with a call to lead a campaign against any common enemy of Israel. Nor had the Spirit of God come upon him asking him to launch a movement of any kind against a threatening enemy of Israel.

The proposal to fill the vacuum of leadership in Israel after his father's death, had come, it would seem, from himself alone.

Gideon, his father, had declined the offer of being crowned Israel's king (Jud. 8:22–23); but now Abimelech was seeking to be crowned a king of Israel.

With the financial assistance he had received from the Baal worshipers of Shechem, Abimelech hired some riff-raff followers, and going to his brothers' hometown, he killed all his brothers, sixty-eight or sixty-nine of them, in cold blood.

Then he was publicly crowned king by the citizens of Shechem and Beth Mello (Jud. 9:1–6).

But Jotham, Abimelech's youngest brother, had escaped and hid himself while his brothers were being killed.

This brother one day climbed atop Mt. Gerizim and shouted a long speech to the citizens of Shechem.

In his speech he denounced Abimelech and the citizens of Shechem for their joint wickedness in killing all of Abimelech's brothers and their failure to show gratitude to Gideon for all he had done for Israel. Also he denounced them for their rebellion against the house of Gideon in making Abimelech their king only because he was their flesh and blood.

If in all their actions they had not done honorably, he said, let fire come out of Abimelech and burn the citizens of Shechem and Beth Mello, and let fire come out from the citizens of Shechem and Beth Mello and burn Abimelech. Thus a double curse was pronounced on Israel's "new king" and upon those who had made him king.

It was said that Abimelech "governed" Israel for three years but one commentator reports that the original Hebrew word used here for "governed" is a particular word meaning to rule as a despot over a despotism i.e. as a tyrant and not as a ruler with divine approval and a divine call.

As a sign of God's disapproval of Abimelech's rule, He sent an evil spirit between him and the citizens of Shechem.

This evil spirit caused trouble and contention between the ruler and those being ruled.

A new would-be ruler came into Shechem, named Gaal. This man stirred up dissention and serious armed conflict between Abimelech and all those in Shechem.

Finally, Abimelech turned against all those in Shechem and killed nearly all of its people. Then he burned the city and scattered salt over it.

He then burned about a thousand men and women who had sought refuge in the stronghold of the temple of El Berith.

Next, he and his men, continuing on in their hellish rampage of hate, went to a nearby city named Thebez. They besieged and captured this city and were about to set fire to a strong tower filled with people seeking refuge and safety there.

As Abimelech and his men were about to set the stronghold on fire, a woman up above threw a large millstone down upon Abimelech's head and fractured his skull.

A young man close by, at Abimelech's request, thrust him through with a sword, to finish him off, killing him (Jud. 9:50–55).

"Thus God repaid the wickedness that Abimelech had done to his father by murdering his seventy brothers. God also made the men of Shechem pay for all their wickedness. The curse of Jotham son of Jerub-Baal came on them" (Jud. 9:56–57).

PRACTICAL LESSONS TO BE LEARNED FROM ABIMELECH'S LIFE

1. A carnal, selfish ambition for public position and prominence, being sought without God's approval or call, is no good way to serve one's fellow-citizens.
2. Public service is a noble calling for a Christian believer when he is prepared for it and called by the Lord to enter into it.

But to seek public office as Abimelech did with a mass-murdering of his competitors, and without God's call, was a bloody, wicked, satanically, and worldly way to proceed.

His evil, self-centered approach to a career of pubic service on Israel's behalf was shown to be a failure as he proceeded. God's curse fell upon him and his people and the relationship that developed between him and those he would serve resulted only in grief, war, and death.

The entire population of those who had made him king was put to death by their own ruler and king.

Finally, a heavy millstone was cast down from above and fractured this king's skull, and a young man's sword finished the job of killing him.

TOLA
Judges 10:1–2

JAIR
Judges 10:3–5

IBZAN
ELON
ABDON
Judges 12:8–15

Tola, of the tribe of Issachar, rose to save Israel. He was Israel's leader for twenty-three years.

Then came Jair, from Gilead, who led Israel for twenty-two years. He had thirty sons, who rode thirty donkeys and controlled thirty towns in Gilead, east of the Jordan River.

A few years later, following Jephtha's six-year rule, Ibzan became Israel's ruler for seven years. He had thirty sons and thirty daughters.

Then came Elon, a Zebulunite, who led Israel for ten years.

Then came Abdon from Pirathon, who led Israel for eight years. He had forty sons and thirty grandsons. They rode on seventy donkeys.

The writer of Judges, in reporting about these men, is careful to identify the tribe they came from, and at times their fathers or other ancestors. Also, care is given to tell the number of years they served as Israel's leader, and each time we are told where these men were buried.

Only five paragraphs were required to describe the public careers of these five men, but they all contributed significant service as Israel's leaders for several years.

Three of the five were outstanding family men, having, most likely, several wives and many children.

The total number of years of Israel's leadership that was contributed by these five men was seventy years.

PRACTICAL LESSONS TO BE LEARNED FROM THE LIVES OF THESE FIVE LEADERS

1. These five men, although seeming to be of perhaps less spectacular importance than some of the other judges of Israel, yet together, they led Israel for seventy years, an average of fourteen years for each man.

To be a public servant of the entire nation of Israel for any length of time would be an honor for any man at any time.

And these five men all had that honor, an opportunity of a lifetime, to be a leader of God's chosen people, the people from whom came many godly kings and prophets and finally, the Messiah-Savior Himself.

To serve the Lord and people in any public capacity whether in a local church or in a governmental position is an honor. It presents one with a great opportunity to further God's kingdom by one's influence and presence (Prov. 29:2; Rom. 13:4).

JEPHTHAH

Judges 10:6–12:7

The Israelites, again forsaking the Lord, began foolishly worshiping the gods of five neighboring peoples of Aram, Sidon, Moab, the Ammonites, and the Philistines.

As a result, the Lord allowed the Philistines and Ammonites to oppress Israel for eighteen years.

Finally, Israel cried out to the Lord and began to forsake their idols.

The Gileadites sent for Jephthah, a mighty warrior, asking him to lead them against the Ammonites. Finally, agreeing to their request, he sent messengers to the Ammonites in an effort to persuade them to cease attacking Israel.

The Ammonites would not listen to his requests.

Then the Holy Spirit came upon Jephthah and he led his people against the Ammonites in battle.

Soon he had subdued them, freeing Israel from their oppression. But in the course of his enterprise against the Ammonites he made a foolish vow to the Lord. It resulted in his killing his only daughter as a sacrifice when he returned home.

Afterwards Jephthah and the Gileadites in a bloody dispute with the Ephraimites, killed forty-two thousand of them at the Jordan River. Jephthah led Israel for six years (Jud. 12:1–6).

PRACTICAL LESSONS TO BE LEARNED FROM THE LIFE OF JEPHTHAH

Jephthah gained a great success in his battle with the Ammonites after the Spirit of the Lord came upon him. Israel was thus delivered from their eighteen years of oppression.

Like Jephthah, so in our Christian ministries for the Lord, we shall have great success only as we are empowered by the Holy Spirit. That which was true for Jephthah will also be true for us.

Rash vows to the Lord should be avoided by God's servants today as we see and learn from Jephthah's experience (Jud. 11:29–40).

SAMSON

Judges 13–16

Due to Israel's sin again, the Lord delivered them into the hands of the Philistines for forty years.

SAMSON'S BIRTH

Judges 13:1–25

Now the angel of the Lord appeared to a man named Manoah of the tribe of Dan. The angel said that his wife who was barren would have a son. Neither she nor the son was to use any grape product. The son would be a Nazirite, never cutting his hair, nor using wine or any grape product or other strong drink or eating anything unclean. He would begin delivering Israel from the Philistines.

The mother was to obey the Lord in all that was commanded her by the angel concerning diet, drink, and hair.

The angel came a second time to Manoah and his wife. He talked with him. After placing a burnt offering and a grain offering on an altar, the angel ascended in the flame coming from the altar, then disappeared.

Manoah and his wife fell on their faces, learning it was an angel of the Lord. He feared, but his wife allayed her husband's fears.

Samson was born; he grew up with the Lord's blessing and the Spirit began stirring him at his maturity.

SAMSON'S MARRIAGE

Samson saw a young Philistine woman he wanted as his wife.

Finally a wedding ceremony was scheduled. It was to be seven days in duration.

Somewhat before the ceremony, Samson had encountered and killed a lion that was about to attack him. Following this, a swarm of honey bees lodged inside the dead lion's carcass.

Coming into this area later, Samson took some honey that the bees had produced within the lion's carcass. He ate some of the honey and shared some of it with his parents.

Then in the wedding ceremony he told a riddle to his thirty Philistine attendants.

These attendants were finally told the meaning of the riddle with the help of Samson's new wife.

For interpreting the meaning of the riddle within the seven days Samson must supply thirty linen garments and thirty additional suits of clothing for his wedding attendants.

To procure these clothes, Samson went to a Philistine town, killed thirty Philistines and took their clothes and gave them to his thirty wedding attendants.

Meanwhile his bride's father gave Samson's new bride to another man, a Philistine.

This so angered Samson that he tied three hundred foxes, tail-to-tail, attached torches to their tails, and turned them loose in the Philistines dry and ready-for-harvest grain fields.

After learning why Samson had done this, the Philistines burned up both Samson's wife and her father.

In retaliation, Samson now slaughtered many of the Philistines, then left and hid in a cave.

Men from Judah soon came and delivered Samson over to the Philistines. But Samson grasped a jawbone of a donkey and killed one thousand Philistines with the jawbone.

All of his attacks against the Philistines were made after the Spirit of God had come on him, for Samson was God's new and unique champion of the Israelites to fight against Israel's long-time enemies, the Philistines, who had oppressed them for well over forty years.

Finally, Samson's new girlfriend, Delilah, persuaded him to tell her the secret of his mighty strength.

She passed this secret on to his Philistine enemies. They cut off all his hair and with it the Lord departed from him.

They then gouged out his eyes and placed him in a hard-labor prison, grinding grain, this along with brass shackles on his wrists.

But after a while his hair grew long again and at a great Philistine celebration where they had Samson performing for their entertainment, he prayed to the Lord, asking the Lord to strengthen him once more.

The Lord heard and answered his prayer.

He then placed his two arms on strategic supporting pillars where the festival was being held, and the entire building fell down, killing multitudes of the Philistines. He killed more at his death than he had killed during his entire lifetime. Samson ruled Israel for twenty years and delivered Israelites from the cruel oppression and rule of their longtime enemies the Philistines.

PRACTICAL LESSONS TO BE LEARNED
FROM SAMSON'S LIFE

1. God's supernaturally empowering a single man to accomplish the rescue of His people from cruel oppression shows the vast versatility and unique variety of means in the accomplishing of His purposes.

One time the Lord commands an army to march around a walled city for seven days and the city is captured.

One time it is one man killing six hundred Philistines with an oxgoad and this man "saved Israel" (Jud. 3:31).

Another time a thirty-two-thousand-man-volunteer army is reduced to three hundred men and with the three hundred an army of one hundred and thirty-two thousand is destroyed and routed, with some called in assistance from nearby tribes to help in the pursuit (Jud. 6–8).

Now Samson is empowered to throw off the oppression of the Philistines and he "led Israel for twenty years in the days of the Philistines" (Jud. 15:20).

The Lord only needs a fully yielded and obedient man or woman to do great things in the progress of His kingdom.

Empowered by God's Holy Spirit there is no limit to what He can do through yielded servants of His choosing.

He will use a Deborah, a Barak, a Gideon, a Samson, a Jonathan, or a David.

He will use a Reinhard Bonnke, or some unknown man named perhaps Bob, Mike, or a Joe, a George or a Richard and multitudes of others whose names we could list.

Any and all who have placed their bodies and lives on God's altar as a living sacrifice, God will use in accordance with their gifts and callings (Rom. 12:1–2; Eph. 2:10).

God loves to take the man who is weak and unpromising in his own eyes and empower him to do a useful and blessed work in the lives of needy people.

Jesus called twelve ordinary men and trained and empowered them, making them into twelve useful and effective church-planting Apostles. God chooses "the foolish" things of the world to shame the wise, the "weak things," the "lowly things" so that "no one may boast before him" (1 Cor. 1:26–29).

ISRAEL

DURING THE TIME OF THE JUDGES

Israel served the Lord while Joshua lived, also while the elders lived who had known Joshua.

But after that generation had died, the new generation came who had not seen the Lord's great deeds for Israel.

This generation turned from the Lord and worshiped Baal and other gods of the nations nearby. This grieved the Lord and angered Him.

Habitually, the later generations of Israelites turned away from obeying the covenant that they had been given by their forefathers (Jud. 2).

After occupying the Promised Land, about one half of the twelve tribes failed to drive out the original inhabitants of Canaan, hence they were disobeying the Lord in this way. God had told the Israelites to completely eliminate all of the original inhabitants as a judgment upon them for their wickedness.

As a consequence of Israel's incomplete obedience in leaving many of the original inhabitants in the land, they began intermarrying with these people and adopting their idolatrous worship (Jud. 2:1–3:1–5).

Israel's evil apostasy occurred prior to the rise of Israel's first judge, Othniel (Jud. 3:7).

They finally cried to the Lord; Othniel delivered them from the oppression of king Aram Naharaim of eight years. Israel had peace now for forty years.

Israel's evil apostasy occurred prior to the rise of Ehud. King Eglon of Moab oppressed Israel for eighteen years. Israel cried to the Lord and Ehud delivered them (Jud. 3:12–30).

Israel had peace for eighty years.

Israel came under attack by the Philistines.

Shamgar came to their rescue, killing 600 Philistines with an oxgoad. "He, too, saved Israel" (Jud. 3:31).

Israel's evil apostasy occurred prior to the rise of Deborah and Barak. Israel had been oppressed by king Jabin for twenty years. Israel again cried to the Lord and God spoke to a woman prophetess, Deborah, and a military leader, Barak, a second woman, Jael, also had a part in the victory.

King Jabin and his forces under the leadership of his commander, Sisera, were defeated. Israel now had peace for forty years (Jud. 4–5).

Israel's evil apostasy again occurred prior to the call of Gideon.

The Midianites, Amalekites and the other peoples from the east dominated and harassed Israel for seven years.

God raised up Gideon and after Gideon had called out an army of thirty-two-thousand volunteers, God caused it to be reduced to three hundred men. With these three-hundred men, Gideon defeated an enemy of one-hundred-thirty-five-thousand men.

Israel now had peace for forty years (Jud. 6–8).

Israel being again in trouble, Tola "rose to save Israel." He led Israel for twenty-three years (Jud. 10: 1–2).

Jair "led Israel" for twenty-two years (Jud. 10:3–5).

Israel's evil apostasy again occurred prior to the call of Jephthah. Israel suffered for eighteen years under the oppression of the Philistines and Ammonites.

He led Israel for six years (Jud. 10:6–12:7).

Ibzan, Elon, and Abzon together led Israel for twenty-three years (Jud. 12; 8–15).

Israel left the Lord and did evil in the eyes of the Lord. Thus the Lord allowed the Philistines to dominate Israel for forty years. God then raised up Samson who fought the Philistines and led Israel for twenty years (Jud. 13–16).

"In those days Israel had no king; everyone did as he saw fit" (Jud. 21:25).

In Judges chapters seventeen through twenty-one, the story is told of Micah's idols and a treacherous crime of rape and murder committed by some wicked men of Gibeah, of the tribe of Benjamin.

All Israel learned about this crime in Benjamin and demanded that the Benjamites bring the suspects out to be tried and killed.

When the war ended more than ninety-one thousand men on both sides had been killed.

These were very, very tragic and trying times for the young nation of Israel, a nation that was only slowly learning to walk in harmony with their Lord and Savior.

SUMMARY OF PRACTICAL LESSONS
TO BE LEARNED FROM THE ISRAELITES

1. During the early years after occupying Canaan, Judah and the Simeonites and the tribe of Joseph had success in clearing their areas of the original inhabitants because they were remaining obedient to the Lord and thus the Lord fought with them.

2. Israel would serve the Lord while their deliverer judge was living. When he died they would depart from the Lord and turn to idolatry.

3. When the Lord would send another nation in to oppress Israel, they would forsake their idols and call upon their true God, their Deliverer and Savior. Their idolatrous gods would not rescue them from their troubles and oppression. Only Israel's true God could do this.

4. If Israel could have become more regular and constant in their worship and service of their Lord, they would have experienced a constant peace and blessing. And this without interruptions of foreign nations being sent to oppress them. Christian believers need to be constant and persevering, as well, in their walk with the Lord, enjoying His peace, His joy and creative presence over the span of a lifetime. In addition to this, wise and careful measures need to be taken to introduce each succeeding generation of young people to the Lord, inspiring them to come to know the Lord as the older generation had come to know Him.
    Young people's programs and activities of various kinds need to be devised constantly in an effort to bring our young people under the influence of the kingdom of God and our Savior, Jesus Christ. Our failure to make these special efforts will result in a loss of our succeeding generations to a secular and God-denying world.

5. The people of Israel failed to show gratitude to Gideon and his family for all he had done for them (Jud. 8:35). This failure was to Israel's discredit as it will be also to Christians' discredit in our time if we fail to show constant appreciation to the Lord and to His faithful servants for work well done on our behalf.

NAOMI
RUTH
BOAZ

Ruth 1–4

Elimelech and his wife Naomi lived in Bethlehem, Judah, during the days of the Judges.

They had two sons Mahlon and Kilion. A famine came into the land so the entire family moved to Moab, hoping to live there until the famine came to an end in Judah.

While living in Moab Elimelech died and Naomi's two sons married Moabite women. After about ten years the two sons died also, leaving Naomi living with her two daughters-in-law.

Finally the famine in Judah ended and God provided food there again. Naomi therefore decided to return to Bethlehem.

She started out on her journey alone with her two daughters-in-law Ruth and Orpha.

After they had traveled a short distance Naomi urged both to go back and return to their Moabite people. Finally Orpha, one of the two, agreed to this and returned to her own people. But Ruth did not like the idea of returning for she had an unusually deep love for Naomi and also, it seems, for Naomi's God, the God of Israel. So she refused to turn back to her own land and people. She was determined to go with Naomi and finally Naomi stopped urging her to do otherwise.

So Naomi and Ruth came together to Bethlehem.

The townspeople were greatly stirred when Naomi returned home again after being away for so many years. They said "Can this be Naomi?" but Naomi told them to no longer call her Naomi, which means "pleasant," but rather call her Mara, which means "bitter," for Naomi had suffered such great losses by the death of the love of her life, Elimelech, and her two sons Mahlon and Kilion. She believed the Lord had brought misfortune upon her.

Now Naomi had a relative on her husband's side named Boaz. He owned property and raised farm products, among them barley and wheat.

Ruth asked Naomi if she could go and glean for grain on one of the nearby farms. Naomi thought this was a good idea and encouraged her to do this.

It was at the time of the barley harvest so she went out to pick up the leftover grain that she would find behind the harvesters.

Now it so happened that she fell in behind the men who were harvesting the grain fields of Naomi's relative, Boaz. After Boaz came to observe the progress of his men, he noticed Ruth gleaning in the field and he inquired who she was. He was told that she was a Moabitess and had returned from Moab with Naomi and that she had shown Naomi, her mother-in-law, great kindness.

Upon hearing this, Boaz was pleased to have her glean behind his men and cautioned the men against stopping her or harming her in any way.

He, after meeting and talking with Ruth, told her to return in the days following and continue gleaning grain. He asked the men to drop some extra grain for her, intentionally, so she would have plenty to pick up. Also, that she should follow with Boaz's servant girls and feel free to drink from the men's water jars when she was thirsty.

Finally, it developed, through Naomi's arrangements, that Ruth became wife to Boaz, who was by no means a young man at that time.

Boaz was a godly and respectful man, a man of good standing in the town of Bethlehem.

He was Naomi's kinsman-redeemer and he bought the property and took over the social prerogatives that had belonged to Naomi's husband Elimelech.

Boaz and Ruth were married and had a son, Obed. Naomi enjoyed holding little Obed in her lap and her women friends would say to her when they saw this, "Naomi has a son."

Obed grew to manhood and became the father of Jesse, and Jesse grew up and became the father of seven sons, one of whom was David who became a famous king of united Israel.

Practical Lessons to be Learned from the Lives and Examples of the Following:
Naomi, Ruth, Boaz

Lesson no. 1

The entire story of Ruth brings before us a heart-touching description of the sovereign and providential grace of God in ordering events to accomplish His great purposes.

First, we are given an account of how the Lord provided a link to the line to King David, and then ultimately to Jesus the Messiah-Savior Himself.

Reading the story of Ruth, Naomi, Boaz and little Obed causes us to say of our Lord,

> "Praise the Lord, O my soul.
> I will praise the Lord all my life;
> I will sing praise to my God as long as I live."
>
> (Ps. 146:1–2)

Lesson no. 2

That Ruth, a Moabitess and non-Jew, was so honored and blessed as she was to become an integral part of the line leading to both David and the Messiah, may well have happened because she honored the Jewish people through her love for Naomi, a bereaved woman, a member of the Jewish race.

Ruth also came to love the God of Naomi, the God and Savior of Israel.

She left Moab where idols were worshiped to go to Israel with Naomi, who knew the true God.

In Israel Ruth worshiped and served this true God along with her godly husband Boaz, and her former mother-in-law Naomi and others.

Did not God say to Abraham, "I will bless those who bless you and whoever curses you I will curse"? (Gen. 12:3).

Whoever blesses and loves the Jewish people, whether he is a man or a woman, God says, "I will bless."

Ruth, a non-Jew, loved Naomi her Jewish mother-in-law and in so doing she blessed her.

The two women, Ruth and Naomi, had both suffered the loss of their husbands and so had a shared grief, but Ruth was devoted to Naomi and showed her great kindness and support. God honored her for this and she became the happy mother of little Obed, who became the grandfather of king David and part of the line that finally led to Jesus the son of Mary and Joseph.

Lesson no. 3

The experience of Naomi was similar in many ways to that of Job.

When she departed from Bethlehem, notwithstanding the famine, her life in many ways was full. She had a husband and two sons with her to provide her with support.

Her name "Naomi," meaning "pleasant," was quite descriptive of her circumstances at that time. But when she returned to Bethlehem after many years, her life felt empty.

She asked her friends who greeted her upon arrival to call her "Mara," meaning "bitter." She said, "Why call me Naomi? The Lord has afflicted me; the almighty has brought affliction upon me" (Ruth 1:21).

She felt that the name "Mara" was much more descriptive of her circumstances now than "Naomi" would be.

But later on, after Ruth had married Boaz, a little Obed was born as a result of God's blessing their union, Naomi would take the child at times and lay him in her lap and care for him.

A smile, now, was most likely seen on Naomi's face and laughter must have returned to her life as her friends seeing this said, "Naomi has a son."

The grief and sorrow of the past years was beginning to be replaced with joy, hope and happiness. Her friends said of little Obed, "He will renew your life and sustain you in your old age" (Ruth 4:15).

Naomi was beginning to learn like Job learned and as multitudes of other afflicted saints have learned down through the years the truth of the words of St. Paul who said, "And we know that all things work together for good to them that love God, to them who are the called according to his purpose" (Rom. 8:28, KJV).

Eli

1 Samuel 1:9–18; 21–21; 2:11–4:21

Eli was presiding high priest in Shiloh when Elkanah came there with his two wives, Peninnah and Hannah. They came to Shiloh year after year to worship and sacrifice to the Lord. Eli was of the family of Ithamar.

Eli observed Hannah praying to the Lord for a son, whom she promised to give to the Lord's service for his entire lifetime.

Eli said to her, "Go in peace and may the God of Israel grant you what you have asked of him" (1 Sam. 1:17).

Eli was a guide to young Samuel who later came to Shiloh to learn to serve the Lord there.

Eli was in many respects a good man but he had failed to guide his two sons properly in their priestly ministries. His two sons despised the sacrifices and dishonored the Lord by the way they conducted themselves in their priestly offices. They stole the best parts of the sacrifices from the people for their own personal use. They also had sinful sexual relations with the women who were serving at the entrance of the tent of meeting. They were very wicked men and Eli was too lax in his attempts to rebuke them.

Also he partook of their stolen offerings, fattening himself and his sons on this meat.

Eli was rebuked by the Lord for scorning the Lord's sacrifice and offerings that had been prescribed for God's dwelling, also for honoring his two sons more than the Lord by fattening himself with the choice parts of the offerings made by the people of Israel. 1 Sam. 2:29.

Eli knew fully about the sins his two sons were doing, but failed to restrain them sufficiently, hence he and his household would be punished forever.

This was a most serious sin against the Lord and could not be atoned for by sacrifice or offering (1 Sam. 3:11–14).

Eli's culpability in this spiritual situation that had developed in Shiloh was very, very serious and deep. A great judgment from the Lord at the hands of the Philistines was God's way of punishing not only Israel, but Eli, and his sons.

Two invasions and battles with the Philistines resulted in two tragic defeats for Israel.

In battle number one, four thousand Israelis were killed.

In battle number two, thirty-two thousand Israelis were killed.

The Ark of the Covenant was taken; Eli's two sons were killed and Eli himself died of shock and a fall when he heard of the news of the deaths of his two sons, of Israel's extensive losses and that the Ark of the Covenant had been taken.

Also Eli's daughter-in-law died in childbirth when she heard the report of her family members being killed and also that the ark had been taken (1 Sam. 4:1–22).

ELI HAD LED ISRAEL FOR FORTY YEARS PRACTICAL LESSONS TO BE LEARNED FROM ELI'S LIFE

He was entrusted with a high and responsible office, priest of God's people of Israel, but he failed in discharging the responsibilities of his trust. In two main respects he failed:

1. He failed in training his two sons to properly fulfill their duties as his assistants in the work of priests.
   Both he and they failed to respect the high significance of the sacrifices that the people were bringing into the tabernacle at Shiloh.
2. He failed to restrain his two sons in their evil ways they were handling both the people of Israel and the sacrifices they were bringing with them as they came to worship the Lord.

   In both these ways he dishonored the Lord and caused much grief among the worshipers of the people of Israel.

   He had led Israel forty years but died a failure and without God's approval upon his ministry.

But not only did Eli die without God's approval on his ministry, he also incurred God's wrath and anger for the great amount of evil and wickedness that happened under his auspices, an evil and wickedness which he had full power to put a stop to if he had wanted to do so.

But Eli fell far short of his duties as God's high priest for the people of Israel, duties which were his from the first day of his appointment to his office.

The practical lesson of Eli's life is quite clear and exceedingly important, which is: for a man of God to be called to the work of apostle, prophet, evangelist, pastor or teacher, or any other high calling of God, he must accept a correspondingly high degree of responsibility to which he must be faithful, and a trust for which he must answer to God at its conclusion.

HOPHNI AND PHINEHAS
1 Samuel 2:12–36; 4:17; 19–22

The writer of 1 Samuel states in an outright manner, in an opening summary statement, "Eli's sons were wicked men; they had no regard for the Lord" (1 Sam. 2:12).

This disregard for the Lord was shown by the disrespectful manner by which they dealt with the sacrifices the people would bring with them as they came to worship the Lord.

The priests and their servants would take from the boiling meat of the sacrifice portions of the meat in an inappropriate manner. Also before the fat was burned, the priest's servant was told to take from the sacrifices the best raw portions of the meat before it was sacrificed. These choice portions were used by the priests themselves in a selfish manner.

All in all, the priests, the two sons of Eli, were making a fiasco of the office of the Israelite priesthood.

Men who were supposed to be holy representatives of a holy God were acting like satanic charlatans and satanic priests. They were harming the cause of the Lord.

These two men were also sleeping with "the women who served at the entrance to the tent of meeting" (1 Sam. 2:22).

Reports of the misdeeds of these two sons of Eli were coming back to Eli from the people themselves.

Eli reprimanded them but his rebuke was very weak and certainly not strong or effective.

As a consequence, the sons paid no regard to their father's rebuke and the evil only continued.

It was God's will that these two sons would soon be put to death and the time soon came that the Lord allowed Israel's enemies, the Philistines, to attack Israel. These two wicked priests were among those who were killed at that time.

The Philistine attacks brought about a crushing defeat for all Israel with thirty-four thousand killed.

And the Ark of the Covenant was taken away from Israel, as well.

Among the large number of Israeli dead, not only were Eli's sons killed but Eli himself, upon hearing of their deaths and that the Ark was taken, went into shock and falling backwards from his seat, broke his neck and died.

His daughter-in-law also died in childbirth upon hearing of the deaths of her husband, her father-in-law and of the Ark's being taken away (1 Sam. 4).

LESSONS TO BE LEARNED FROM THE LIVES OF ELI'S TWO SONS

These two men had no regard for the Lord, yet were serving in an office that called for only holy and righteous men.

God's judgment on them in the end was swift and just.

Their otherwise godly father should have acted much sooner and with greater sternness and dispatch than he did to put an end to their wicked deeds in the priesthood. But he was morally lax and soft and tolerated a situation that caused him to share greatly in their guilt and led to the ultimate downfall of his entire family and priesthood.

He and his two sons were to be replaced by a faithful priest who would serve according to God's heart and mind. That man was Samuel.

Samuel was a young man who was growing up in the presence of the Lord and was learning to handle the Word of God and the offices of prophet, priest, and judge with faithfulness and integrity and honesty.

Samuel served to please God all his life.

Samuel's character and service and example, and not that of Eli, are certainly our patterns to follow in service for our Lord.

The lives of Eli, Hophni, and Phinehas serve as solemn warnings to us to steer clear of their ways and their mistakes.

ELKANAH AND HANNAH

1 Samuel 1–2:11

Elkanah was an Ephraimite from Ramathaim, in the hill country of Ephraim.

He had two wives, Hannah and Peninnah.

Peninnah had children, several boys and girls, but Hannah was barren.

Each year, Elkanah took his two wives to Shiloh to sacrifice to the Lord to worship.

Peninnah constantly provoked Hannah because she had no children and it made Hannah sad and upset.

Elkanah had a special love for Hannah and he tried to console her in not having any children, but she remained grief stricken and sad because of it.

At Shiloh, not eating because of her sorrow, Hannah prayed to the Lord, asking for a son, promising to give him to the Lord for life if the Lord would grant her request.

After returning home she soon became pregnant and gave birth to a son. She named him Samuel, meaning "heard of God."

Hannah remained home until her son was weaned.

Elkanah provided a free hand for Hannah and a safe life for her saying, "Do what seems best to you" (1 Sam. 1:23).

Elkanah was a God-fearing and reverent husband and father, leading his family in regular worship before the Lord.

In this he was setting a good example for all his family and had taken Hannah to a place before the Lord where she could pray and a place where she could leave her son, dedicated and given to the Lord.

Elkanah and his godly wife Hannah became the parents of one of Israel's greatest men, the prophet Samuel.

Elkanah established the environment for godly living and a Samuel for the people of Israel.

Elkanah and Hannah were like the godly Christian farmer parents of Billy Graham, from the Charlotte, North Carolina area. They brought God into their home, worshiped Him regularly, and provided an atmosphere for good things to happen to God's people.

After young Samuel was given to the Lord in Shiloh, Elkanah "went home to Ramah, but the boy ministered before the Lord under Eli the priest" (1 Sam. 2:11).

Each year Hannah made Samuel a little robe and brought it to him (1 Sam. 2:19).

Hannah being barren and full of sorrow and grief because of it had sought the Lord earnestly in Shiloh for a child promising to dedicate her child to the Lord's service all of his lifetime.

When her prayer was answered she kept her promise and gave Samuel to the Lord.

Her dedication is an example for parents of all time to also dedicate their children to God's will and service for all their lifetime.

Elkanah's life and conduct, along with the holy and dedicated life of his wife Hannah, are two examples of a couple, yielded to the Lord and used by the Lord to advance God's cause and kingdom.

HANNAH'S PRAYER

1 Samuel 2:1–10

Hannah was given by the Spirit of God a beautiful and significant prayer in connection with the dedication of her son to God for his life of service to the Lord and to Israel.

Her Spirit-inspired prayer deserves our careful study, thought, and meditation, for it exalts our great God, our Savior and King.

Hannah's willingness to give her son to God's service from the time of his early childhood and for the whole of his life was a most pleasing sacrifice to the Lord.

Her husband, Elkanah, deserves equal credit for such dedication, for he was in full compliance and support of that which Hannah wanted to do for the Lord and for his people Israel.

God blessed not only this godly couple, but all Israel for years to come as Israel was struggling to find stability and usefulness in God's plan of salvation for the entire world.

After Samuel, Hannah was given three more sons and two daughters (1 Sam. 2:21).

She thus became a true mother in Israel with her firstborn becoming a great and godly priest, prophet, and judge in Israel, a guide to Israel for many years.

Hannah, was a godly and prayerful mother and a loving wife, the kind who delight the heart of God and delight the hearts of their godly husbands and become an eternal blessing to their children and grandchildren. May God grant that there may be raised up a multitude of such godly holy wives and mothers to serve their Lord in these last days.

And also may there be raised up a multitude of godly husbands and fathers like Elkanah to serve the Lord in these last days, yes godly couples to serve the Lord and His kingdom together in these last days.

Practical lessons to be learned from the lives and examples of Samuel, Jonathan, and the following Kings of United Israel

Saul—40 years
Ishbosheth—2 years
David—40 years
Solomon—40 years

SAMUEL AND SAUL

1 Samuel 1–16:13; Psalm 99:6; Jeremiah 15:1; Hebrews 11:32

SAMUEL'S BIRTH AND DEDICATION TO THE LORD

Samuel's conception and birth were the result of a prayer of faith and desire by his mother Hannah.

He was given to the Lord and to his priestly and prophetic services from the time he was weaned.

Hannah, his mother, was prayerful and godly. Her prophecy-prayer is recorded in 1 Samuel 2:1–10 and is reminiscent of the prophecies given by Mary, Zechariah and Simeon at the births of Jesus and John the Baptist (Luke 1:46–55; 68–79; Luke 2:29–32).

Samuel grew up in the presence of the Lord (1 Sam. 2:21); and he grew in favor with God and man (1 Sam. 2:26).

It was said by a prophet sent by God concerning Samuel even during his boyhood and formative years, "I will raise up for myself a faithful priest, who will do according to what is in my heart and mind. I will firmly establish his house, and he will minister before my anointed one always" (1 Sam. 2:35).

SAMUEL'S CALL

1 Samuel 3

Prior to a certain night in young Samuel's life, he did not know the Lord. Then during this particular night the Lord spoke to him and he finally received God's prophetic message. The prophetic message concerned God's coming judgment upon Eli. Next morning Samuel, at Eli's urging, told him of Eli's coming judgment.

The Lord from this point on began to appear at Shiloh and He revealed Himself to Samuel more and more through His word.

Samuel began to grow in spiritual stature and power. All Israel began to learn about him that he was to be a true and great prophet of the Lord.

Samuel was careful to not let any of the Lord's revelation to him go unnoticed or unheeded. He kept close record and contact with all God said to him (1 Sam. 3:19–21).

He began to pass on to Israel the messages that God gave to him (1 Sam. 3:21c).

ISRAEL'S DEFEAT BY THE PHILISTINES

In Israel's tragic defeat at this time by the Philistines there were two main battles. In battle number one 4,000 Israelites were killed. In battle number two 30,000 Israelites were killed.

The Ark of the Covenant was taken and Hophni and Phinehas were killed (Eli's two sons) and Eli died as a result of shock and a fall. Phinehas' wife died at childbirth when she heard of the deaths of her husband and father-in-law, and the capture of the Ark by the Philistines (1 Sam. 4).

The Ark was taken first to Ashdod then Ekron (1 Sam. 5). Then the Ark was later returned to Israel (1 Sam. 6).

THE PHILISTINES SUBDUED

1 Samuel 7:2–17

After twenty years of Philistine oppression, the Israelites began to cry for relief. The Ark during these twenty years was in Kiriath Jearim and the Israelites began to put away their idols and confess their sins at Mizpah.

Meanwhile the Philistines came up to attack at Mizpah.

Samuel sacrificed a burnt offering and as he prayed for Israel, God intervened against the attacking Philistines with a mighty thunderstorm, throwing them into a panic. The Israelites pursued and defeated the Philistines at that time.

Israel had freedom as long as Samuel was their leader.

Samuel traveled a three-town circuit as Israel's judge until he was very old, going to the three towns of Mizpah, Bethel and Gilgal, always returning to his home in Ramah (1 Sam. 7:15–17).

ISRAEL ASKS FOR A KING

1 Samuel 8:1–22

Samuel's two sons Joel and Abijah were appointed to serve as judges for Israel at Beersheba. But they were unlike their godly and honest father. For dishonest gain they would take bribes and pervert justice.

Due to the dishonesty of Samuel's two sons, and it becoming known to Israel's leaders, these leaders began asking for a king. Samuel was now old and these leaders were looking to Israel's future after Samuel would die.

This request displeased Samuel but the Lord said, finally, go ahead and give them a king.

Israel has rejected me, the Lord said, not you, Samuel.

Samuel had been an honest, just judge and leader of Israel all his life, but somehow, his two sons had not seen fit to follow the Lord as their father had, just as Eli's two sons did not follow the Lord as Eli had.

SAMUEL ANOINTS SAUL

1 Samuel 9–10

Under God's direction, Samuel now became a kingmaker.

Samuel providentially meets Saul, eats with him and gives him several signs that tell Saul that God has good plans for his future.

Samuel later anoints Saul as Israel's first king.

The spirit comes upon Saul; he prophesies with the prophets.

Samuel brought all the tribes together at Mizpah and explained to the people concerning their king and introduced Saul to them.

He gave to the people a copy of the regulations for a kingship, bearing a written copy before the Lord, and then sent the people to their homes (1 Sam. 10:17–27).

Saul also went to his home in Gibeah accompanied by some valiant men whose hearts God had touched (1 Sam. 10:26).

But some troublemakers despised him and brought no gifts to him, doubting his suitability as their future king (1 Sam. 10:27).

After Saul and Israel's successful rescue of Jabesh Gilead, Samuel joined Israel at Gilgal to reconfirm Saul as Israel's king. God had given a great victory against the Ammonites in defending Jabesh Gilead (1 Sam. 11).

More victories over Israel's all-too-frequent enemies could have taken place had Israel's new king determined to faithfully obey and follow the Lord, but king Saul's heart was never disposed to humbly follow the Lord and as a result, his later career as king became a tragic failure. The kingdom soon had to be taken away from him and given to a better man.

SAMUEL'S FAREWELL SPEECH

1 Samuel 12

In Samuel's farewell address to the nation of Israel, he begins by focusing the people's attention on the honesty and integrity that he maintained during all his years of leadership in Israel. The people immediately agreed to his character claim and testified to its truth along with the testimony of Saul to the same thing.

He then reviews Israel's history from Egypt to Canaan and notes God's many deliverances of Israel during the time when they were oppressed and cried to the Lord. He notes Barak, Gideon, Jephthah and Samuel as some of those who delivered a repentant Israel.

Now, although having God as their King, they asked for and now have their first human king. Asking for a king was a sin for Israel, yet notwithstanding this sin, if they and their king would serve the Lord with all their hearts, God will keep and bless them. If they do not serve the Lord with all their hearts, judgment will result.

Hence, Israel's full blessing is contingent upon their wholehearted obedience and serving the Lord alone.

Idolatry and backsliding from the Lord must be put away from their national life.

SAMUEL REBUKES SAUL

1 Samuel 13

Saul and his army were ready to fight the Philistines at Gilgal. Samuel within the seven days time limit did not come to Saul to sacrifice prior to the battle, so Saul stepped in and he himself sacrificed the offerings before the battle began. But this was against God's regulations for a king to do. Saul performed a function that only a priest was supposed to do. Hence, what Saul did was a serious disobedience to the Lord and it disqualified Saul for a long prosperous reign as Israel's king (1 Sam. 13:1–15). Later on, Saul also was disobedient in reference to his command to fully destroy the Amalekites (1 Sam. 15; 28:18).

Israel had no fighting weapons to use against the Philistines, except the two swords of Saul and Jonathan (1 Sam. 13:16–22).

Saul's commitment to obey the Lord's commandment was weak and under a stressful and testing time he failed the test and disobeyed the Lord.

Obedience to the Lord was a criterion for success in his new office. He failed the test. Unlike Abraham who passed his test with Isaac, Saul failed his obedience test with the Lord.

So once again, the test of strict obedience to God disqualified an otherwise promising and talented man for high office in God's kingdom in Israel.

Love and strict obedience to God is the greatest requirement for success in service to God and His church and kingdom.

This strict obedience to God has been a basic qualification for success for men in both old and New Testament times and it is one of the basic requirements for God's blessing in our service for God today, as well.

SAUL REJECTED AS KING

1 Samuel 15:1–35

Saul was given clear instructions from the Lord through Samuel to destroy the Amalekites completely. But Saul refused to obey the Lord's command. He saved their king alive and many of the best sheep and cattle from the plunder, Saul thought, to use as sacrifices to the Lord.

Saul had allowed the soldiers to talk him into doing this, because "he was afraid of the people and so I gave in to them," he said (1 Sam. 15:24).

Thus he disobeyed the Lord and was rejected from being Israel's king, although he remained in the office as king for nearly forty years.

Saul was unlike Joshua as a leader. Saul placed too little importance on God's commands to him, thinking he could put them aside if it suited him.

Not so with Joshua who took all God's orders seriously to be carefully obeyed.

Samuel anoints David

1 Samuel 16:1–13

Samuel was told by the Lord to go to Bethlehem to the house of Jesse. God had chosen one of Jesse's sons as Israel's new king.

Samuel immediately obeyed the Lord, going to Bethlehem where arrangements were made for a sacrifice to be held there. Jesse and all his sons were invited to the sacrifice.

After Samuel had seen seven of Jesse's sons it was determined that God's choice for Israel's next king was not among the seven.

Did Jesse have any more sons? Yes, there was another son, the youngest, who was outside caring for the family's sheep. David, son number eight, was called in from the sheep and he was the one.

God said to Samuel after he had seen David, "He is the one." So Samuel anointed him as Israel's next king in the presence of his brothers

Choosing a man for Israel's king, God looked upon the heart of the man for His choice, and not on his outward appearance. Although, David had a handsome and pleasing outward appearance, God was looking on the heart condition as his first criterion.

"From that day on the Spirit of the Lord came upon David in power" (1 Sam. 16:13).

DAVID

1 Samuel 16–31; 2 Samuel 1–24; 1 Kings 12:12; Psalm 1–72 and others 1 Chronicles 3:1–9 (his sons)

DAVID IN SAUL'S SERVICE

1 Samuel 16:14ff

The Spirit of the Lord had left Saul; then an evil spirit from the Lord came upon Saul and tormented him.

His attendants advised that he find a man who could play the harp and have this man play before Saul when he was troubled by the evil spirit.

One of Saul's' servants had learned of David who could play a harp and was a brave warrior and could speak well and was a fine looking man. Moreover, the Lord was with him, the servant reported.

Saul sent for David who entered Saul's service. He would play before Saul and it would calm him.

David soon became one of Saul's armor bearers. Saul was very pleased with him (1 Sam. 16:22).

DAVID AND GOLIATH

1 Samuel 17:1–58

David in the name of the Lord struck down and killed Goliath, the giant warrior champion of the Philistines.

The Philistines and the world saw this giant idol worshiper and his fellow Philistines routed and defeated by the Lord working through a mere youth who was fighting with the Lord with him. This youth had no weapons except a sling, some stones and a staff.

This victory over the Philistines, sparked by young David's actions was similar to that which had been triggered by young Jonathan's actions somewhat earlier. Both men acted in the name of the Lord and God worked with both of them to bring about a successful victory over Israel's long-time enemies.

DAVID AND JONATHAN

1 Samuel 18:1–4

Saul kept David in his service full-time after David had killed Goliath.

David was given a high ranking in Saul's army. He was made a commander.

David began to go out against Israel's enemies and was very successful in all he undertook for Saul. This was because the Lord was with him.

Due to David's rising fame in Israel, and particularly because of the words of a song the women of Israel were singing, "Saul has killed his thousands, and David his tens of thousands," Saul became jealous and afraid of David.

Saul soon tried twice to kill David by throwing his spear at him when he was in his presence.

Finally, David married Michal, Saul's younger daughter.

SAUL TRIES AGAIN TO KILL DAVID

1 Samuel 19

Saul, a third time, tried to kill David with his spear (1 Sam. 18:10–11; 19:9–10).

He failed in every attempt. So David escaped from Saul's presence and went to Ramah and talked with Samuel (1 Sam. 19:10), with Saul and his men still seeking for David.

Jonathan, one of Saul's sons, who loved David, made a covenant between himself and David. They agreed that they both would love, care and always protect one another (1 Sam. 18:1–4; 20:16–17; 41–42).

Jonathan looked out for David's life when his father Saul wanted to kill David (1 Sam. 20:1–42).

In speaking up for David, his friend Jonathan's own life was placed in jeopardy, for Saul in his anger and jealousy, at one time hurled his spear at Jonathan, attempting to kill him. 1 Sam. 20:30–33.

David and Jonathan had an abiding love and sworn friendship for one another's families.

They wept together at David's departure from Jonathan for the sake of safety from Saul (1 Sam. 20:41–42).

DAVID AT NOB

1 Samuel 21:1–9

From Abimelech the priest, David obtained some consecrated bread and Goliath's sword.

This was one stop in David's flight from Saul.

Saul's servant Doeg saw David here at Nob. His seeing David would later have tragic consequences.

DAVID AT GATH

1 Samuel 21:10–15

Another stop in David's flight from Saul was the Philistine city of Gath, where he met Achish the king of Gath. Out of fear of this king, however, since David was recognized by some of the king's men for who David was in Israel—a champion fighter and leader—David feigned insanity. So he was asked to leave Gath.

DAVID AT ADULLAM AND MIZPAH

1 Samuel 22

At Adullam was a cave where David now went. His friends and family joined him there, also the discontented and debtors, about 400 men. David became their leader.

He asked the king of Moab to provide for his father and mother.

Then at the advice of the prophet Gad, David went back into Judah and lived in the forest of Hereth (1 Sam. 22:5).

Because Abimelech the priest at Nob had helped David, news of that happening was reported back to king Saul and it resulted in the killing of all the priests of Nob; eighty-five men were killed in cold blood. In addition to these killings, Doeg, Saul's aide, killed all the inhabitants of Nob, including the women, the children and all the animals (1 Sam. 22:18–19).

DAVID SAVES KEILAH
1 Samuel 23:1–6

The Philistines were attacking and looting Keilah. David inquired of the Lord whether he should fight against the Philistines and try to save Keilah.

The Lord said twice, "Yes," to go and the Lord would rescue Keilah by David. David and his men then went and defeated the Philistines and took much loot.

Saul, hearing that David was in Keilah, came after him. David left Keilah and went into the desert of Ziph and Saul continued his search.

Finally, due to news of a Philistine invasion elsewhere, Saul left off his pursuit of David and went away.

God was protecting David during these critical days.

DAVID SPARES SAUL'S LIFE
1 Samuel 24

After returning from his pursuit of the Philistines, Saul continued his pursuit of David in the desert of En-Gedi.

He and his men entered a cave and fell asleep.

David and his men meanwhile were deep in the same cave, and while Saul slept, David came and cut off a piece of his robe but refused to kill him.

David was conscience stricken after he had cut the piece from Saul's' robe.

Then David spoke to Saul and Saul spoke to David, Saul realizing that later David would be Israel's king. Saul now returned home and David and his men returned to their stronghold.

DAVID, NABAL AND ABIGAIL

1 Samuel 25

Samuel now died and was mourned and buried at Ramah (1 Sam. 25:1).

David and his men moved to the desert of Moan.

Nabal, a wealthy man with large flocks of sheep, refused David's request for assistance for his men, which would have been appropriate inasmuch as David and his men had helped Nabal's shepherds.

David planned to kill him and his men in revenge, but Nabal's wife Abigail intervened and persuaded David to spare the bloodshed. Nabal soon died and Abigail became David's wife.

God had providentially intervened in preventing David from his vengeful intent and plan to kill all of Nabal's men and perhaps Nabal himself.

DAVID AGAIN SPARES SAUL'S LIFE

1 Samuel 26

Saul went down to the desert of Ziph with 3,000 men, intending to capture David.

Being asleep with his men in a camp there, David and Abishai crept into Saul's camp, where all the men were in a deep sleep. David took Saul's spear and water jug but turned aside from his second opportunity to kill Saul, since Saul was the Lord's anointed.

David then addressed Abner and Saul from a nearby hill.

Saul acknowledged his sin. Then he and his men withdrew and went home. David also left from there.

DAVID AMONG THE PHILISTINES

1 Samuel 27; 1 Samuel 21:10–15

David returned again to Achish, King of Gath. He and his men lived in Ziklag, a town king Achish had suggested he use as a place of temporary residence.

From Ziklag David and his men made regular raids against the Amalekites and other nearby Negev peoples, each time returning to Achish and Ziklag.

He remained at Ziklag for one year and four months. He had hoped Saul would not pursue him in Philistine territory and he did not.

SAUL AND THE WITCH OF ENDOR

1 Samuel 28

Samuel was now dead. The people had mourned for him and buried him (1 Sam. 28:3).

The Philistines were preparing again to fight Israel.

Fearing the Philistines, Saul inquired of the Lord by dreams, by Urim, and by prophets, but the Lord did not answer. Therefore, he sought a spiritualist witch at Endor.

She, having called up Samuel, Samuel told Saul that he, his sons and Israel's army would be delivered into the hand of the Philistines by the following day.

ACHISH SENDS DAVID BACK TO ZIKLAG

1 Samuel 29

King Achish was well pleased with David and David and his men agreed to go with king Achish and the Philistines in fighting against the Israelites, yet king Achish's commanders demanded that David and his men not fight with them against the Israelites—not trusting him. So David and his men returned to Ziklag.

DAVID DESTROYS THE AMALEKITES

1 Samuel 30

David and his men recovered all that had been taken by the Amalekites who had attacked and burned Ziklag.

God had providentially caused David to turn back from fighting with the Philistines, and when he returned to Ziklag he found a situation that badly needed his attention. The Lord promised him success in pursuing the Amalekites.

Starting out, he and his men met an Amalekite slave who led David to the Amalekites.

David defeated and routed many and recovered all of his people.

God blessed David at every turn.

Thank You, Lord, for being with David during these trying days and preserving his life for future service to Your kingdom and people.

At the outset of the trial of Ziklag, when David's men were so grieved and angry at David, David "found strength in the Lord his God" (1 Sam. 30:6).

SAUL TAKES HIS LIFE

1 Samuel 31

Saul and three of his sons and his armor bearer and many other Israelite soldiers died on the battlefield in one day in a vicious battle with the Philistines.

Israel was badly defeated.

The three sons of Saul who were killed at that time, along with their father, Israel's king, were: Jonathan, Abinadab and Malki-Shua.

Saul's death had resulted from an initial serious wounding by the Philistines, then he himself fell on his own sword and then an Amalekite finished the killing by running him through with his sword or spear (1 Sam. 31:1–6; 2 Sam. 1:1–16).

PRACTICAL LESSONS TO BE LEARNED
FROM THE LIFE OF SAMUEL

1. From his boyhood days Samuel had a reverent and receptive attitude toward the Word of God. This was God's Word from direct prophetic revelation or, most certainly, from God's Word and law from the written covenant laws of Moses.

We are told of Samuel that, "He let none of his words fall to the ground," and the Lord "revealed himself to Samuel through his word" (1 Sam. 3:19–21).

The Lord continued to appear at Shiloh and spoke to Samuel about many things as young Samuel grew up to maturity.

"But Samuel was ministering before the Lord, a boy wearing a linen ephod" (1 Sam. 2:18).

"He grew up in the presence of the Lord" (1 Sam. 2:21).

"And the boy Samuel continued to grow in stature and in favor with the Lord and with men" (1 Sam. 2:26).

"The Lord was with Samuel as he grew up" (1 Sam. 3:18).

"The Lord continued to appear at Shiloh, and there he revealed himself to Samuel through his word" (1 Sam. 3:21).

2. Samuel not only continued to receive the word of God for himself, but he began sharing what he received with the people of Israel. The people began to recognize that Samuel was a prophet of God.

3. As Israel's leader from youth to old age, Samuel never stole from the people or cheated them in any way. He never took a bribe as their judge. He was honest and upright during all his years as their leader.

    All the people testified that this was true of Samuel (1 Sam. 12:1–5).

4. Samuel faithfully obeyed the Lord in whatever he was told to do. Like Joshua, he obeyed the Lord faithfully and willingly. Hence he was a success as Israel's leader and the Lord was with him to the end of his life on earth. Only his two sons did not follow their father's teachings or example. They became dishonest judges, taking bribes and perverting justice.

5. Samuel prayed and sacrificed for a repentant Israel after they began to turn from their idols. The Lord heard his prayer for protection from attacking Philistines and the Philistines were routed and stayed away as long as Samuel was Israel's leader (1 Sam. 7:2–17).

6. Samuel adhered to a loving and close faith in God and he adhered to a willing, loving, and strict obedience to all God's

commands from his youth to old age. As a result Samuel became a great and lifelong blessing to his fellow Israelites and a pleasure to God, his Savior and Lord.

JONATHAN

1 Samuel 14

Jonathan was one of the several sons of king Saul, king of Israel. Israel had numerous battles with the Philistines during their early years as a nation.

In one of these battles with the Philistines, Saul, Jonathan and three thousand Israelites were preparing to fight the Philistines. Israel lacked the necessary weapons with which to fight well and the Philistines had not only myriads of men but also three thousand chariots and six thousand charioteers and plenty of weapons.

Saul's men were fearful and hiding. Jonathan and his armor bearer had located themselves near a pass near Micmash.

Jonathan, having courage and faith in God, decided on a courageous bold move against the enemy.

His armor bearer, devoted and also courageous, followed Jonathan's risky but faith-courageous lead.

They both showed themselves in the pass to the observant Philistines, with a verbal fleece sign. The sign developed in favor of believing the Lord, who they believed would fight with them.

God did fight with these two young believing men. They killed twenty Philistines. Then God Himself brought an earthquake and created a panic among the entire assembled enemy Philistines, who then began to flee and even striking each other with their swords.

The Israelites pursued the enemy, killed many and gained a great victory against the Philistines as they were routed (1 Sam. 14:1–23).

During Israel's pursuit of the fleeing Philistines' king, Saul had caused his men to swear they would eat no food. This weakened his men. Saul's son, Jonathan, had been separated from the main body of Saul's men and had not been aware of the agreed upon fast among Saul's men, and he ate some honey to strengthen himself.

When his father later found out that Jonathan had eaten this food, he was prepared to kill his son in punishment. But Saul's men stood up in Jonathan's defense and his life was saved (1 Sam. 14:24–45).

PRACTICAL LESSONS TO BE LEARNED
FROM THE LIFE OF JONATHAN

1. Jonathan had a daring faith in God.
   In a battle situation with Israel's enemies, the Philistines, Jonathan was a young man with enough knowledge of God and enough faith in God to strike out with a bold, risky, yet faith-filled aggressive move against Israel's uncircumcised enemies, the Philistines.

   Using a verbal fleece of a sort, Jonathan and his loyal armor bearer heard the correct response from the Philistines, who had seen the two men in the open pass where they had made themselves visible to their enemies.

   The Philistines shouted to the two young courageous Hebrews, "Come up to us and we'll teach you a lesson."

   That was the signal the two were waiting to hear. It meant that the Lord was going to fight with them.

   So the two climbed up to a point of higher elevation and engaged the Philistines in hand-to-hand combat. The two had soon killed twenty Philistines in an area of about one half of an acre.

   Then a panic sent by the Lord struck the entire force of the Philistines. The Lord had brought a timely earthquake into the area and the Philistines were thrown into fear and confusion.

   The other Israelis begun to pursue their enemies and killed many.

   A tremendous defeat of the Philistines was gained that day by the greatly outnumbered and outmanned Israeli army.

This entire victory was originally set into motion by the faith and courage of two young men, Jonathan and his loyal armor bearer. They had believed God together and acted in accordance with their faith.

Their daring, their faith in God and their willingness to take a risk for God has left us with a great example to stimulate us in our attempts to do some exploits for God in these last days as well.

2. Jonathan had an abiding love for David.

After David had killed Goliath and his actions had sparked a great military over the Philistines, Jonathan was so impressed that he affirmed his love for David.

He sealed his love for David with a covenant, even giving him his robe, his tunic, his sword, his bow, and his belt (1 Sam. 18:1–4).

Jonathan's love and loyalty to David grew even more secure with the passage of time. He spoke in David's defense against his father, king Saul, and took steps to defend him from Saul's attempts to kill David.

These times we are told that Jonathan loved David as himself (1 Sam. 18:1, 3; 20:17).

This amazing love that Jonathan had for David was certainly a result of God's grace and Spirit being at work in the life of Jonathan.

That this is a safe conclusion as regards the true nature of the firm and long term personal relationship between Jonathan and David will seem to be confirmed when one remembers that, humanly speaking, Jonathan and not David was next in line to be Saul's successor as Israel's king.

Jonathan obviously had knowledge of and was in sympathy with David's future reign as Israel's king, and this, as Saul's successor.

It is clear that Jonathan had Israel's true interests at heart and desired only God's choice and God's best for His people. He did not project his own personal ambitions over and above God's own plans for Israel's future leadership.

Jonathan's father had selfish and personal ambitions for his son Jonathan, but Jonathan did not have any such ambitions. He wanted God's will for his life and God's will for the nation of Israel, and God's will for his friend David.

It would seem that the earlier fondness by which Jonathan spoke of the Lord when he and his armor bearer fought against the Philistines was the ruling passion of his entire brief life.

He was like the short-lived young men, such as Henry Martyn, David Brainard, and the five short-lived young men who lost their lives when they were very young, attempting to bring the Christian gospel to the Auca Indians in Ecuador in 1956.

Jonathan had made the following statements about the Lord at that time:

"Come, let's go over to the outpost of those uncircumcised fellows. Perhaps the Lord will act in our behalf. Nothing can hinder the Lord from saving whether by many or by few" (1 Sam. 14:6).

And

"But if they say, 'Come up to see us,' we will climb up, because that will be our sign that the Lord has given them into our hands" (1 Sam. 14:10).

And

"The men of the outpost shouted to Jonathan and his armor bearer, 'Come up to us and we'll teach you a lesson.'"

So Jonathan said to his armor bearer, "Climb up after me; the Lord has given them into the hands of Israel" (1 Sam. 14:12).

It is obvious from these several statements made at this time, that Jonathan had a living faith in the God of Israel, and that this faith in God continued to the end of his brief life. It ended on the battlefield where he was again fighting the Philistines in the name of the Lord as he had done before.

But his friend David lived on to serve the Lord as Israel's next king and servant of God.

Jonathan had certainly seen in David's actions with Goliath and the Philistines the same courageous faith that had impelled him earlier when his faith and courage had sparked a victory over the same Philistine enemies. This unanimity of faith and courage in God had brought these two young men together in an abiding and strong bond of love and kinship, a bond that was never broken.

PRACTICAL LESSONS TO BE LEARNED
FROM THE LIFE OF SAUL

After Samuel was old and nearing the end of his leadership of Israel, the people of Israel desired a king as the other nations had. So finally, due to the peoples' persistence, the Lord told Samuel to give them a king.

Saul the son of Kish, was chosen. He was anointed with oil by Samuel, and then anointed by the Holy Spirit by the Lord.

Saul's initial enterprise as king was the rescue of Jabesh Gilead from the threats of violence by the Ammonites.

The Spirit came upon Saul. He organized an army and quickly defeated the Ammonites, rescuing the people of Jabesh Gilead with great success.

Saul could easily have continued on the path of success as Israel's first king.

He had Samuel as his proven guide and advisor. He had some natural God-given abilities of leadership, and good potential as a strong leader-king for Israel at that time.

But as time went on, Saul proved unwilling to carry out strict orders that were given to him from the Lord.

He would obey in part the orders that were given to him. But the parts of the orders given to him that did not seem to suit his fancy, he would disobey and do what *he* thought should be done. As a consequence, on two major military campaigns, Saul blatantly disobeyed the specific orders that he had been given by the Lord through Samuel the prophet.

Because of this disobedience, the kingdom was taken away from him and his descendants.

The Spirit of the Lord departed from him and evil spirits began coming upon him.

His reign degenerated into a tragic failure.

Among the crimes and failures, at one point he became responsible for the killing of eighty-five priests of the Lord and all the citizen-inhabitants of an entire town of Nob. All the men, women, children, and animals were ordered killed by Saul due to his wrath against David.

Many of Israel's earlier leaders had been successful because they had godly character and when given an order from the Lord, they quickly obeyed the orders.

Some of these men were Abraham, Moses, Joshua, Othniel, Gideon, Barak, and Samuel—all men who trusted and obeyed the Lord.

But Saul was unlike these men.

If an order from the Lord did not suit him, he would disobey it. Hence his career as Israel's first king was a failure and his life ended in tragedy, a casualty and attempted suicide on the battlefield with Israel's enemy, the Philistines.

Strict obedience to the Lord is of first importance in serving in God's kingdom in any capacity whatsoever.

This is the main lesson we see clearly illustrated in the life of Saul, Israel's first king.

Would those who are reading these lines be a success in serving the Lord and would the man who is writing these lines be a success in serving the Lord? Then let us be doubly careful to give strict obedience to the Lord's commands to us, if indeed we can determine what His commands to us are. As we wait upon the Lord in prayer and faith, His commands and leading will become clear to us.

Disobedience to the Lord's instructions was the path Saul chose to follow and his career and life ended in tragedy.

Obedience to the Lord's instructions is the path, which, if we choose to follow, will end in success and God's eternal blessing.

Let us choose the path of obedience to the Lord for success, for peace and for God's eternal blessing.

Let us end our careers as did a Joshua or a Samuel or a St. Paul and not as did king Saul.

V

Patterns from the Kings of Israel

V
Ishbosheth, King of United Israel
2 Samuel 2:8–4:12

After king Saul died on the battlefield fighting against the Philistines, Abner, son of Ner, his military commander took Ishbosheth, one of Saul's sons and made him king over Israel, except Judah of the house of David over which David began to reign.

Ishbosheth was forty years old when he began to reign and he reigned two years.

But conflict began to develop between the house of Saul and the house of David. This conflict lasted a long time and "David grew stronger and stronger while the house of Saul grew weaker and weaker" (2 Sam. 3:1).

During this period Abner wanted to come over on David's side. He made a move to do this but was killed by Joab and Abishai, because Abner had killed Asahel, a third brother of Joab and Abishai.

Ishbosheth soon sent Michal, one of David's wives back to David at David's request.

After Abner was killed Ishbosheth lost courage and all Israel became alarmed.

213

Now, two of the king's leaders of raiding bands came into Ish-bosheth's house and stabbed him in the stomach while he was taking his midday rest, then they cut off his head. The names of these two men were Baanah and Recob. These men carried the head of their king all the way to Hebron and announced to David what they had done and showed him the king's head. They thought David would rejoice because of this. But David knew a heinous crime had been committed by these two men and he ordered their immediate execution, and it was done.

But notwithstanding all the killing and long-term conflict, the way was now clear for David to be made king over all of Israel.

And this soon happened. David soon was anointed king, shepherd of all Israel and he moved his place of residence from Hebron to Jerusalem where he began to rule over all Israel.

DAVID HEARS OF SAUL'S DEATH

2 Samuel 1:1–27

A young Amalekite came to David and reported Israel's defeat at the hands of the Philistines, and Saul's death along with it.

Upon hearing the news, David and his men were grief-stricken, but nonetheless, David ordered the young Amalekites execution because he had finalized Saul's death by his hand, and king Saul was the Lord's anointed.

David took a "lament of the bow" memorial poem for Saul and Jonathan and ordered that it be learned and sung by the men of Judah (2 Sam. 1:19–27).

DAVID ANOINTED KING OVER JUDAH

2 Samuel 2:1–7

A short time after Saul's death, David asked the Lord if he should go up to one of the towns of Judah. God said yes! Which one, David asked the Lord? To Hebron, God said.

This was David with an anointing to be Israel's next king, asking God for directions as to moves that would ultimately bring him into Israel's kingship (2 Sam. 2:1–4).

David, the youngest of eight sons of Jesse of the tribe of Judah, was about to begin his ascent to the kingship of the chosen people of Israel.

David immediately commended those of Jabesh Gilead for burying Saul. He called it a kindness shown to him. These same men also buried Saul's sons along with their father, the king (2 Sam. 2:5–7; 1 Chron. 10:11–12).

Why did Saul die at this time?

"Saul died because he was unfaithful to the Lord; he did not keep the word of the Lord and even consulted a medium for guidance, and did not inquire of the Lord. So the Lord put him to death and turned the kingdom over to David son of Jesse" (1 Chron. 10:13–14).

WAR BETWEEN THE HOUSES OF DAVID AND SAUL

2 Samuel 2:8–4:12

Although Saul was dead, Ishbosheth, one of Saul's sons, ruled over all Israel, except Judah, for two years. David ruled Judah for seven-and-one half-years, during which time David's house gained gradual ascendancy over Saul's former power in Israel.

David was patient and persistent, as finally all Israel would come under David's power and reign.

In the battle of Gibeon, Abner killed Asahel.

Later, in revenge, Joab and Abishai, Asahel's brother, killed Abner who was in the process of delivering all of Israel over to David.

Then, two men, Baanah and Recob, murdered Ishbosheth, and for this deed David had them both killed (2 Sam. 4:1–12).

Prior to moving on to Jerusalem, therefore, and taking over the rulership of all of Israel, David had seven years and six months of experience in being a king, learning methods of organization and leadership. This experience in Hebron and Judah undoubtedly helped him later on as his responsibilities increased.

He ruled in Hebron seven years and six months. He then ruled in Jerusalem for thirty-three years.

DAVID BECOMES KING OVER ALL ISRAEL

2 Samuel 5:1–5; 1 Chronicles 11:1–3

David began ruling in Hebron at age thirty and reigned for a total of forty years and six months, first in Hebron, seven-and-one-half years, and during the period of his reign in Jerusalem, for thirty-three years.

This was a long tenure in public life, but the Lord was with him through successes, problems, pressures, mistakes, and recovery from mistakes.

DAVID CONQUERS JERUSALEM

2 Samuel 5:6–16; 1 Chronicles 11:4–9; 14:1–7

The Jebusites had stubbornly resisted all attempts to oust them from the difficult of access fortress at Jerusalem.

But finally Joab, one of David's most courageous and innovative men, succeeded in capturing the Jebus fortress for David. David now occupied this area, naming it the city of David.

Because Joab had been successful in capturing this fortress for David he was named David's chief army commander.

David built up this fortress making it his capital and center of his administration.

David became more and more powerful because the "Lord God Almighty was with him" (2 Sam. 5:10).

In Jerusalem David took more wives and concubines and had more children.

In Hebron he had six sons and now in Jerusalem he had eleven more, making a total of seventeen sons in all.

King Hiram of Tyre built David a beautiful cedar palace in a marvelous gesture of friendship (2 Sam. 5:11–12).

DAVID DEFEATS THE PHILISTINES

2 Samuel 5:17–25

After David was established in Jerusalem, as if to test his strength, the Philistines "went up in full force to search for him."

Before answering the Philistines' challenge, David consulted the Lord. The Lord said to him, "Go, for I will surely hand the Philistines over to you" (2 Sam. 5:19).

David went and the Lord handed them over to David.

Again, the Philistines came up and camped at the same location as the first time—Rephaim.

The Lord this time gave David more specific and detailed instructions as to how to fight the Philistines.

David obeyed the Lord exactly and again defeated the enemy. "So David did as the Lord commanded him, and he struck down the Philistines all the way from Gibeon to Gezer" (2 Sam. 5:25).

With the Philistines now soundly defeated David planned to bring the Ark of the Covenant to Jerusalem.

THE ARK BROUGHT TO JERUSALEM

2 Samuel 6:1–23; 1 Chronicles 13; 15:1–16:43

The Ark was brought to Jerusalem with great praise and worship and celebration. David danced before the Lord as God's selected king and man of God.

Both David and his officials along with the priests openly showed their exuberance as the Ark was being brought into Jerusalem. David himself in his praise disrobed partly if not fully, but it was a holy gesture and in the glorious presence of the Lord.

Michal, one of David's wives, observing David's worship, despised him in her heart and made a critical remark to David when he came in to his house and saw her. Due to her judgmental criticism of her husband her womb was closed throughout the rest of her life, she never had any children by David.

GOD'S PROMISES TO DAVID

2 Samuel 7:1–17; 1 Chronicles 17:1–5

After David been made king over all of Israel, he moved his entire family and headquarters to Jerusalem.

After Hiram, his friend, completed building the palace residence for him, David began living in the beautiful cedar palace with his family. But he strongly desired to build a great temple of worship for the Lord. David had always loved the Lord and he wanted to build Him a place that would bring Him glory and honor.

In response to David's desire to build a great house of worship for the Lord, the Lord said that He Himself would build David and his descendants into a house. David and his descendants would be established as a line of kings forever.

David himself would not be the one to build a temple for the Lord, because he had been primarily a military fighting man and had shed much human blood.

Solomon, David's son, would, however, build a house for the Lord.

In David's case, some twenty kings followed David and reigned over Israel and Judah, kings all from David's line. Ultimately the Messiah, Jesus Himself, would rule in Jerusalem—He also from the line of David. See the genealogies in Matthew 1 and Luke 3.

Many of the messianic predictions came through David in the Psalms.

Also according to the gospel that was preached by St. Paul, one of the integral parts of his message was a reference to David and the promise God made to him concerning his descendent, the Christ. See Acts 13:34 and note Paul's words written to Timothy, "Remember Jesus Christ raised from the dead, descended from David. This is my gospel, for which I am suffering even to the point of being chained like a criminal" (2 Tim. 2:8–9).

DAVID'S PRAYER

2 Samuel 7:18–29; 1 Chronicles 17:16–27

David went before the Lord in prayer after he heard the full message of the Lord through the prophet Nathan.

David acknowledged God's promise of an eternal kingdom through his family line. He was inexpressibly honored and grateful to the Lord and told the Lord to go forward and accomplish his purposes through him and his descendants.

DAVID'S VICTORIES

2 Samuel 8:1–14; 1 Chronicles 18:1–17

David subdued many and powerful nations, forcing many to pay tribute to Israel. Some of these nations were the Philistines, the Moabites, Hadadezer, the king of Zoba, in the Euphrates district, the Arameans of Damascus, the Ammonites, the Edomites, and the Amalekites.

He collected many valuable metals and materials for the Lord's treasury as a result of these many victories.

"The Lord gave victory everywhere he went" (2 Sam. 8:6, 14).

Moreover, as a public ruler, David "did what was just and right for all his people" (2 Sam. 8:15).

David's actions may be a goal for every legislator and public official in our government today.

David was truly God's appointed shepherd of Israel, a man after God's own heart, setting a pattern for all of Israel's and Judah's kings who followed him on the throne.

DAVID'S OFFICIALS

2 Samuel 8:15–18; 1 Chronicles 18:14–17

David had a staff of capable men to help him administer the affairs of Israel. He was a righteous man serving in a public ruler capacity, doing an honorable work for the Lord.

DAVID AND MEPHIBOSHETH

2 Samuel 9

Mephibosheth, Jonathan's son, was crippled in both feet. David restored to him all of Saul's lands and arranged for him to eat at the king's table with David's sons.

All his lands were to be tilled by Ziba, his sons, and twenty servants. This deed was a kindness David showed to Jonathan's family and part of the pledge-agreement he had made with his close friend Jonathan.

DAVID AND BATHSHEBA

2 Samuel 11

David had sexual relations with Bathsheba and she became pregnant. To cover it up, he had Uriah, her husband, killed. Then David took Bathsheba as his wife.

"But the thing David had done displeased the Lord" (2 Sam. 11:27).

The Lord, speaking through the prophet Nathan said to David, "Now, therefore, the sword will never depart from your house because you despised me and took the wife of Uriah the Hittite to be your own" (2 Sam. 12:10).

The sins David committed at this time were forgiven by the Lord and he did not die because of it, but as the Lord said to him, "the sword will never depart from your house." The sword thrusts now began to come into David's life, into his home and into his kingly administration.

The thrusts of God's sword that came into David's life from this point on were many. I have listed some of the very apparent troubles that David experienced and there may well have been many more that are not shown in the biblical text.

Some of the apparent and obvious sword thrusts that came into king David's life are the following (2 Sam. 12–20:26);

Thrust No. 1 — The death of his first child with Bathsheba after seven days of illness from the Lord

Thrust No. 2 — Amnon's rape of Tamar

Thrust No. 3 — Amnon's murder by Absalom

Thrust No. 4 — Five years estrangement between Absalom and David

Thrust No. 5 — Absalom lay with David's wives in broad daylight

Thrust No. 6 — Conspiring by Absalom to take David's throne

Thrust No. 7 — Violent death of Absalom

Thrust No. 8 — Conspiring by Sheba to take David's throne

Thrust No. 9 — Conspiring by Adonijah to take David's throne (1 Kings 1:1–27)

Thrust No. 10 — Death of Adonijah, one of David's sons

Thrust No. 11 — Gave the Lord's enemies the occasion to show their contempt

THE GIBEONITES AVENGED

2 Samuel 21:1–14

In his nationalistic zeal, Saul had killed many of the Gibeonites. This was in violation of the oath that Joshua and the Israelites had made earlier that the Gibeonites would not be killed as Israel occupied Canaan.

David now took steps to make this mistake right with the Gibeonites. He did what the Gibeonites requested to make matters right again. Several of Saul's descendants were killed and publicly displayed by the Gibeonites. This satisfied the Gibeonites.

WAR AGAINST THE PHILISTINES

2 Samuel 21:15–22

Several Philistine giants fell at the hands of David's men. David himself was never again allowed to go out with his men, he having a narrow escape with death during this time.

DAVID'S SONG OF PRAISE

2 Samuel 22

In spite of David's sin, and after he had committed his serious sins of adultery and murder, he still loved the Lord and fully and completely confessed all the evil he had done.

After he had sinned and been forgiven, he again faithfully served the Lord to the end of his life.

Also by numbering Israel did David sin again and his people had to suffer many deaths because of it (2 Sam. 24).

But almost always David loved and obeyed the Lord and kept obedient before the Lord.

In spite of a few lapses of his faith and obedience, the vast majority of David's days were devoted to faithful service of his Lord. He truly was a man after God's own heart.

THE LAST WORDS OF DAVID

2 Samuel 23:1:1–7

David in his last words made a reference to God's call to himself as king, "The man anointed by the God of Jacob, Israel's singer of songs! The Spirit of the Lord spoke through me; his word was on my tongue."

He then described what a godly man's rule over men is like; it is like:

a. The rising sun on a cloudless morning and
b. The sun shining on the grass after a rain.

ADONIJAH TRIES TO BECOME ISRAEL'S KING

1 Kings 1:1–27

Adonijah's usurping attempt was unsuccessful, for David declared and made Solomon king as his successor.

He was later executed because of the impropriety of his request that Abishag, the Shunemmite be given to him as his wife.

DAVID MAKES SOLOMON KING

1 Kings 1:28–53

The declarations that Solomon would be David's successor on Israel's throne were in fulfillment of God's directions to David. He was one of the sons of David and Bathsheba.

David confirmed Solomon's assignment from his bed of illness as he was near death.

DAVID'S CHARGE TO SOLOMON

1 Kings 2:1–9; 1 Chronicles 22:1–9

David's main charge given to his son Solomon except for some of the personal and special instructions that were given with the general charge is as follows:

> "I am about to go the way of all the earth," he said. "So be strong, show yourself a man, and observe what the Lord your God requires: Walk in his ways, and keep his decrees and commands, his laws and requirements, as written in the Law of Moses, so that you may prosper in all you do and wherever you go, and that the Lord may keep his promise to me: 'If your descendants watch how they live, and if they walk faithfully before me with all their heart and soul, you will never fail to have a man on the throne of Israel.'"
>
> (1 Kings 2:2–4)

In conjunction with David's charge to his son Solomon, he made many preparations for the building of a temple for the Lord in Jerusalem. He appointed stonecutters to prepare dressed stone. He provided iron for nails, and bronze, cedar logs and many other materials that would be needed in building the temple.

David also instructed his officials and all of Israel to help Solomon to accomplish the building of a beautiful temple for the Lord.

He also subdivided the Levites into separate groups and gave separate and distinct duty assignments to each group.

He assigned some as supervisors in the building process; some to be judges, some singers and some players of instruments to serve later after the temple was completed.

David also had a large army organized with twenty-four thousand men from each of the twelve tribes.

The Spirit of God had also given David detailed plans for the temple that Solomon was to build. He gave these plans to Solomon.

Along with the materials that David had collected and put aside for the temple, he contributed much of his personal wealth along with that contributed by the officials of Israel (1 Chron. 23, 28, 29; 2 Chron. 6:7–8).

David had wanted to build a place for the Lord to be worshiped and properly recognized but the Lord desired to have his son Solomon build the temple for Him since David had been a military man and had shed much blood in that role. Now Israel would be at peace with its neighboring nations so Solomon could give himself to constructing the temple and building up the nation of Israel in a peaceful environment.

DAVID'S DEATH

1 Kings 2:10–12; 1 Chronicles 29:26–30

"David son of Jesse was king over all Israel. He ruled over Israel forty years—seven in Hebron and thirty-three in Jerusalem. He died at a good old age, having enjoyed long life, wealth and honor. His son Solomon succeeded him as king" (1 Chron. 29:26–28).

PRACTICAL LESSONS TO BE LEARNED FROM DAVID'S LIFE

There were many similarities between the lives of David and Joseph who had lived much earlier then David. I will note some of the similarities between the two men, then I will list some of the lessons we may learn from David's life.

First then, some of the similarities between David and Joseph:

1. Both young men learned when they were teenagers that they were destined to be rulers in their later years.

   Joseph's dreams were clear enough for him to conclude with safety that he was to become a ruler sometime, somewhere, with even his eleven brothers and his parents also being under his care and jurisdiction.

   In David's case, the prophet Samuel anointed him with oil in the presence of his seven brothers and father, to be someday king of Israel, and David certainly was aware of the meaning of Samuel's anointing that day.

2. Both young men were attractive in their physical appearance. We are told that Joseph was "well-built and handsome" (Gen. 39:6).

   Of David we are told, "He was ruddy, with a fine appearance and handsome features" (1 Sam. 16:12).

   But notwithstanding the attractive outward appearance of these two young men, God had looked upon their hearts and saw that their hearts were tender and unassuming, and humble.

   They were both men after God's own heart. So God chose them both for places of great responsibility and leadership. He knew He could trust them with power.

   After Joseph was sold by his brothers, he was taken down to Egypt and there began working as a servant-slave.

   But in Egypt,

> "The Lord was with Joseph and he prospered, and he lived in the house of his Egyptian master. When his master saw that the Lord was with him and that the Lord gave him success in everything he did, Joseph found favor in his eyes and became his attendant. Potiphar put him charge of his household, and he entrusted to his care everything he owned."
>
> (Gen. 39:2–4)

Also when he was put in prison on a false charge, we are told,

> "But while Joseph was there in the prison, the Lord was with him; he showed him kindness and granted him favor in the eyes of the prison warden. So the warden put Joseph in charge of all those held in the prison, and he was made responsible for all that was done there.
>
> The warden paid no attention to anything under Joseph's care, because the Lord was with Joseph and gave him success in whatever he did."
>
> (Gen. 39:20c–23)

Of David we are told that after Samuel had seen seven of Jesse's sons he said, "The Lord has not chosen these." But yet the Lord had told Samuel previously, after Saul had died, "Fill your horn with oil and be on your way; I am sending you to Jesse of Bethlehem. I have chosen one of his sons to be king" (1 Sam. 16:1).

So Samuel asked Jesse, "Are these all the sons you have?" "There is still the youngest." Jesse answered, "but he is tending the sheep."

Samuel said, "Send for him; we will not sit down until he arrives."

So he sent and had him brought in. He was ruddy, with a fine appearance and handsome features.

Then the Lord said, "Rise and anoint him; he is the one."

"So Samuel took the horn of oil and anointed him in the presence of his brothers, and from that day on the Spirit of the Lord came upon David in power. Samuel then went to Ramah" (1 Sam. 16:11–13).

From the day of David's being anointed with oil by Samuel, the Spirit began coming upon him with power. This Spirit anointing from the Lord meant that the Lord was with David in a powerful way as he grew into manhood.

The Lord was with David as he had been with Joseph during his early and difficult days in Egypt, first as a servant in Potiphar's household, then while he was in prison with a false charge against him.

The Lord was with David as he protected his father's sheep from prowling lions and bears.

And after he had been sent down to the battlefield when the Israelis were arrayed against the Philistines. Goliath, their giant-champion, was threatening Israel. David was astounded at seeing Goliath curse and threaten the armies of the Lord, with no Israelite to answer his evil challenge.

David said to Saul,

> "Your servant has killed both the lion and the bear; this uncircumcised Philistine will be like one of them, because he has defied the armies of the living God. The lord who delivered me from the paw of the loin and the paw of the bear will deliver me from the hand of this Philistine."
>
> (1 Sam. 17:36–37)

David attributed his triumph over the lion and the bear to "the Lord."

He soon went "in the name of he Lord almighty" against the mighty Goliath and killed him and thus sparked a mighty victory of the armies of God against the Philistines that day (1 Sam. 17:45–53).

Moreover, after David had entered full time into Saul's service, he was successful in every assignment he was given because the Lord was with him. "In everything he did he had great success, because the Lord was with him" (1 Sam. 18:14).

And "When Saul realized that the Lord was with David and that his daughter Michal loved David, Saul became still more afraid of him . . ." (1 Sam. 18:28–29).

These two young men, Joseph and David, were successful in all they undertook to do—extremely successful, having a success that was very obvious to others—Joseph in Potiphar's household and in prison, David as a shepherd, then against Goliath, later in Saul's military service against the Philistines, and even in winning the love of Saul's daughter Michal.

What is the reason given for the success of these two men?

It was because the Lord was with them both.

Yes, it is true that both of these young men had extremely high callings and destinies upon their lives. Both of their futures involved high authority and great responsibilities as rulers, one in Egypt and the other over all Israel.

But both of these men proceeded into their lives and callings with obedience and submission to God's will and to God's laws and statutes.

Joseph remained faithful to the end of his life. David remained faithful most of his life, and when he sinned he immediately confessed his sin, was cleansed and restored to fellowship, and went on to the end of his life doing God's will and depending on God's grace.

May we as God's servants and Christian believers today expect to have the kind of success that David and Joseph had in their lives? In our early lives as they did or in our later years as they did? Will we be able to live a successful and prosperous life as did David and Joseph?

The answer is yes!

As long as we seek the Lord and obey His will in all our lives, the Lord will be with us as he was with David and Joseph.

God will be with us to fulfill His calling upon our lives and we will come to the end of our lives a success in the eyes of the Lord and a blessing to those we have served.

Another man in the Bible whose life confirms this promise is Uzziah, one of the later kings of Judah.

We read of Uzziah,

"Uzziah was sixteen years old when he became king, and he reigned in Jerusalem fifty-two years. His mother's name was Jecobiah; she was from Jerusalem. He did what was right in the eyes of the Lord, just as his father Amaziah had done. He sought God during the days of Zechariah, who instructed him in the fear of God. As long as he sought the Lord, God gave him success."

(2 Chron. 26:3–5)

As long as Uzziah, you, and I seek the Lord and follow his instructions in the Word of God, God will give us success.

Beginning as a sixteen-year-old king and continuing for fifty-two years, Uzziah was king of Judah. He was successful and prospered as long as he sought and obeyed the Lord.

He became proud in his later years and performed an act that a king was not supposed to do, and his success vanished at that time in his career. But up until that time he prospered and was successful (2 Chron. 26).

PRACTICAL LESSONS WE CAN LEARN FROM DAVID'S LIFE:

Lesson No. 1

We as Christian believers, today, can have the Lord with us, who will give us success as David had in his life.

And it is wonderful to have the Lord with us, because there is much, much laughter and rejoicing and happiness and great peace.

A man is happy every day when the Lord is with him.

A woman is happy every day when the Lord is with her.

Husbands and wives get along well, with forgiveness and patience and plenty of tolerance and humor and optimism brought into their lives, when the Lord is with them.

Children in families whose parents have the Lord with them, as David had the Lord with him, these children will begin looking up to their fathers and mothers.

The sons will begin to say, "I want to be like my dad. He's always happy, kind and full of fun and he loves me so much, and he loves God so much. I want to be like my dad when I grow up, and I love my mother, too."

And the daughters will most likely begin to say, "I want to be like my mother. She's so nice and she loves me so much. We have so much fun together. She loves God, too. I love God, too. I want to be like my mother when I grow up. I love my daddy, too. He loves me so much, and he loves my mama so much."

This is the kind of talk and conversation you are going to hear around your house when the Lord is with us, moms and dads, in our homes—good talk, loving talk, encouraging talk. There will be a lot of fun in our homes, laughter in our homes, love and blessing in our homes, because the Lord is with us and gives us peace and joy and love among our family members.

If there is a young man reading these lines who had discerned God's call to enter the house construction business or law and public service, or public school teaching or some particular line of business or medicine or science or Christian ministry, will you be a success after laying the proper foundations for your career endeavor?

Yes! Yes! You will find success if you have found God's calling for your life and the Lord is with you as He was with David as you enter your career.

Of David, it was said, "In everything he did he had great success, because the Lord was with him" (1 Sam. 18:14).

And if the Lord is with you, in everything you do, you will have great success too.

The Lord was with David when he was young and the Lord remained with David as he grew older. As long as he sought the Lord and obeyed the Lord's instructions and commands, the Lord remained by David's side and blessed him and gave him great success.

Lesson No. 2

David inquired of the Lord each time he had a major decision to make.

He did not make major decisions without first consulting with the Lord. As a result of this policy he received wise counsel from the Lord and his moves brought success.

Some examples of David's following this practice are the following:

a. Whether to go against the Philistines to save Keilah (1 Sam. 23:1–6).

   This was while he was in Philistine territory. The Lord said, "Go, attack the Philistines and save Keilah." His men had reservations concerning this so David checked with the Lord a second time. God said "Go" a second time; he went and was successful.

b. Whether to pursue the Amalekite raiding party that had sacked and burned Ziklag The Lord said through the priest, "pursue them, you will certainly overtake them and succeed in the rescue" (1 Sam. 30:7–8).

   They found an Egyptian slave abandoned by his master because he was ill. He led David to the Amalekite party and the Amalekites were defeated, and all their families were rescued (1 Sam. 30:1–20).

c. Whether he should go up to one of the towns of Judah after Saul's death (2 Sam. 2:1–7).

   The Lord said, "Go up." Where? David inquired. "To Hebron," the Lord answered.

   David went up to Hebron and the men of Judah anointed him king of Judah, the first step toward becoming at a later time, the king of all Israel.

d. Whether to go and meet the Philistines challenges.

   This was after being anointed king of all Israel. He was challenged twice by the Philistines armies. He inquired both times of the Lord whether to go and meet their challenges: the Lord said at the first challenge, "Go, for I will surely hand the Philistines over to you" (2 Sam. 5:19).

   David went and defeated them.

At the second Philistine challenge David inquired and the Lord replied with a more detailed set of instructions including an ambush.

David did as the Lord commanded him and he struck down the Philistines all the way from Gibeon to Gezer" (2 Sam. 5:25).

Each time David inquired, he obeyed and met success and victory over the enemy.

If we, like David, will inquire of the Lord before making important decisions and major moves, the Lord will instruct us, too.

We can do this by claiming God's promises of guidance, using Psalm 25:9, 12; Psalm 37:5; Proverbs 3:5–6; James 1:5–6 and other similar passages that invite our asking for God's will at times of decision making. He will guide us as we wait patiently upon him for his leading.

Lesson No. 3

We are told that, "David reigned over all Israel, doing what was just and right for all his people" (2 Sam. 8:15).

He set an example in right living and administration during the vast majority of his life.

He consistently followed in the way of the God of Israel, the true God who had brought Israel out from Egyptian bondage into the Promised Land.

David had nothing to do with the Baals or any other foreign god or image made by men.

He set standards of kingly administration that became a measure by which those who later followed him on the throne in Jerusalem could compare their reigns. Had their reigns been good or evil? By a comparison of their reigns to that of David men could tell of the kind of reign they had contributed.

The names of some of the kings whose reigns were spoken of in comparison to that of David are the following: Solomon, Jehoshaphat, Hezekiah, and Josiah.

To Solomon the Lord said, "As for you, if you walk before me in integrity of heart and uprightness, as David your father did, and do all I command and observe my decrees and laws, I will establish your royal throne over Israel forever . . ." (1 Kings 9:4–5; 2 Chron. 7:17–18).

Of king Jehoshaphat of Judah it was said "The Lord was with Jehoshaphat because in his early years he walked in the ways his father David had followed. He did not consult the Baals, but sought the God of his father and followed his commands rather than the practices of Israel" (2 Chron. 17:3–4).

Of king Hezekiah of Judah it was said, "He did what was right in the eyes of the Lord, just as his father David had done" (2 Chron. 29:2). Also see 1 Kings 15:5 for a summary statement of David's overall life and record as a public servant.

Of king Josiah of Judah it was said, "Josiah was eight years old when he became king, and he reigned in Jerusalem thirty-one years. He did what was right in the eyes of the Lord and walked in the ways of his father David, not turning aside to the right or to the left" (2 Chron. 34:1–2).

Some examples of the right actions of David are the following:

1. Prior to becoming king he steadfastly refused to kill king Saul, although he had more than one opportunity to do so. He refused to kill king Saul because of his respect for the Lord and the Lord's anointing on Saul.

2. After he had become king over all of Israel, he took steps to make relations right with the Gibeonites. Saul in his nationalistic zeal had killed some of the Gibeonites. This was in violation of the oath that Joshua and the Israelites had made that the Gibeonites would not be killed as Israel occupied Canaan.

   David took steps to make this crime right with the Gibeonites, satisfying the demands they insisted upon.

3. He showed a substantial kindness to Mephibosheth, one of Jonathan's sons (2 Sam. 9).

4. He attempted to show a kindness to Hanun, the ruling king of Moab whose father had recently died. David's attempted kindness to this man was misunderstood because king Hanun

listened to the faulty advice of his advisors who suspected David's motives in showing his kindness (2 Sam. 10).

Lesson No. 4

David, although prevented from building a temple for the Lord, made many preparations for Solomon's building it.

He did this first, by receiving from the Spirit of God, plans for the temple. Second, he gathered together vast amounts of the materials that would be needed for its construction. Third, he generated much support from all of Israel to help his son accomplish the building of the temple.

David's example in making preparations for a project which he envisioned but could not personally accomplish was an action which we as God's servants may be able to repeat in our lifetimes to help our successors and others coming after us to accomplish or help finance worthwhile tasks for the advancement of God's kingdom.

F.B. Meyer, in speaking of David's desire to build the temple for the Lord, but a desire to which the Lord said no, said,

"God will credit us with what we would have been if we could. He who has the missionary's heart, though he be tied to an office chair, is considered as one of that noble band; the woman at Zarephath, who did nothing more than share her last meal with the prophet, will have a prophet's reward; the soul that thrills with the loftiest impulses, but that cares for the widowed mother or dependent relative, will be surprised one day to find itself credited with the harvest that would have been reaped had those seed germs been cast on more propitious soil. In the glory David will find himself credited with the building of the temple of Mount Zion."

"The energy that David would have expended in building the temple wrought itself out in gathering the materials for its construction. 'I have prepared with all my might for the house of my God . . .' (1 Chron. 29:2, etc.) If you cannot have what you hoped for, do not sit down in despair and allow the energies of your life to run to waste; but arise, and gird yourself to help others to achieve. If you may not build, you may gather materials for him who will. If you may not go down into the mine, you can hold the ropes."[3]

Lesson No. 5

David continued to praise the Lord and serve the Lord after his sin with Bathsheba and her husband was forgiven, cleansed, and behind him. He did not give up but got up and continued on with the Lord to the end of his life.

After the Lord had spoken to him about his sin through the prophet Nathan, David said, "I have sinned against the Lord" (2 Sam. 12:13).

In one of the well-known psalms of David, Psalm 51, a psalm he wrote after Nathan came to him about his sin of adultery with Bathsheba, David poured out his heart in a forthright confession, begging God for His mercy. David said in part,

> "Have mercy on me, O God,
> according to your unfailing love;
> according to your great compassion
> blot out my transgressions.
> Wash away all my iniquity
> And cleanse me from my sin."

(Ps. 51)

He continued in this psalm, which consists of nineteen verses, asking God for cleansing and to create in him a pure heart, and imploring God to do many other necessary things for him in his time of need.

---

[3] F.B. Meyer, *Great Men of the Bible Vol. II,* p. 56.

In verse number seventeen David says, "The sacrifices of God are a broken spirit; a broken and contrite heart, O God You will not despise."

David brought to the Lord at this time of his life, a broken spirit, a broken and contrite heart, a full repentance of his sin, a full confession of his sin and a full and complete forsaking of his sin, a sin which, to be sure, he never repeated to the end of his life. His only hope was to cast himself upon the compassions, the love and mercies of the God that he had come to know so well during his many years of walking with Him.

SOLOMON

1 Kings 1:1–11; 2 Chronicles 1–9
Proverbs; Song of Solomon; Ecclesiastes

SOLOMON'S BIRTH

2 Samuel 12:24–25

After the first child of David and Bathsheba died, David comforted Bathsheba and lay with her and Solomon was born. "The Lord loved him" and named him Jedediah, which means "the Lord loved him." This was the second son of Bathsheba and David.

This child was destined to be David's successor on the throne of a united Israel.

DAVID MAKES SOLOMON KING

1 Kings 1:28–53

King David was advanced in years and his physical energies were at a low ebb.

Adonijah, one of his sons, knowing of his father's weakened state, on his own volition, began to conspire to take over his father's throne. His conspiratorial process was well underway but it became known to the prophet Nathan who was not part of it.

Nathan told Bathsheba of the conspiracy and asked her to tell David. So she informed David and her report to David was soon confirmed by Nathan himself.

David took immediate steps to make his son Solomon king in his place.

Soon Solomon was riding on David's own white mule, was then anointed king by Zadok the priest and was seated on David's throne as Israel's new king.

Adonijah and his supporters soon learned of Solomon's enthronement by David, and so fell in fear and confusion.

Solomon was now Israel's new king, according to the plan of God and David.

David then gave a solemn public charge to Solomon along with some special instructions that he would need. Soon after this, David died and was buried in the city of David. David had reigned over Israel forty years—seven years in Hebron and thirty-three years in Jerusalem.

SOLOMON'S THRONE ESTABLISHED

1 Kings 2

Adonijah had to be executed because of his brash boldness after Solomon was made king and because of his attempt to take David's throne on his own (1 Kings 2:1–25).

Abiathar was removed from the priesthood because he had been part of Adonijah's conspiracy (1 Kings 2:26–27).

Joab was put to death and buried (1 Kings 2:28–35).

Beniah was made commander of the army in Joab's place. Zadok was appointed priest in place of Abiathar.

Shimei who had severely cursed and opposed David was put to death after he broke his vow to remain in Jerusalem or face death (1 Kings 2:36–46).

SOLOMON ASKS FOR WISDOM

1 Kings 3; 2 Chronicles 1:1–13

At Gibeon, after making many sacrifices on an altar there, Solomon during the night while sleeping, dreamed.

In his dream God said to him, "Ask for whatever you want me to give you." Solomon wisely asked for discernment, so he could rule his people well. Solomon's request pleased the Lord and the Lord agreed he would give him wisdom to administer justice well. God also would give Solomon riches and honor and long life, although he had not asked for those (1 Kings 3:1–15).

Solomon's manifestation of a God-given wisdom immediately began to show itself as he decided a dispute between two prostitutes over the right possession of an infant (1 Kings 3:16–28).

SOLOMON'S OFFICIALS AND GOVERNORS

1 Kings 4

Solomon began with a staff of key administrative officials; also he appointed twelve governors over the twelve tribes of Israel.

The twelve governors supplied provisions for the king and his royal household, each governor supplying for one month each.

Solomon's reign extended from the Euphrates River down to Egypt, ruling over all Judah and Israel and all the people from Dan to Beersheba.

Everyone lived in peace and safety having their own vine and fig tree.

SOLOMON'S WISDOM

1 Kings 4:29–34

God fulfilled His promise and gave Solomon great wisdom. He wrote three thousand proverbs, one thousand and five songs; he described plant life, taught about animals, birds, reptiles, and fish.

Men came from all the nations to hear him teach. His wisdom was greater than that of any other men and his fame spread worldwide.

PREPARATIONS FOR BUILDING THE TEMPLE

1 Kings 5; 2 Chronicles 2

Hiram, king of Sidon, provided cedar and pine logs for Solomon. Solomon, in turn provided food for Hiram's people.

God gave Solomon success in making arrangements with Hiram for temple building materials. He and Hiram made a good working agreement together and peaceful relations between the two.

Solomon had thousands of skilled and unskilled workers doing the work with Adoniram in charge of all these working men.

SOLOMON BUILDS THE TEMPLE

1 Kings 6; 2 Chronicles 3

In the 480th year after Israel came out of Egypt, in the fourth year of Solomon's reign, in the second month Solomon laid the foundation of the temple. Seven years later it was finished.

While the temple was in process of being built the Lord said to Solomon

> "As for this temple you are building, if you follow my decrees, carry out my regulations and keep all my commands and obey them, I will fulfill through you the promise I gave to David your father. And I will live among the Israelites and I will not abandon my people Israel."
>
> (1 Kings 6:12–13)

St. Paul in preaching and building the church in Corinth was thinking in terms of building the temple of the Lord—also St. Peter in 1 Peter 2:4–6, a temple made up of Christian believers. See 1 Corinthians 3:10–17.

Much beautiful cedar wood was used in the temple, along with pine, also olive wood.

Precut finished stone was used in many areas of the temple, and much gold, silver and brass was used throughout the building.

The temple was fully furnished with all the implements necessary for worship and for great beauty.

After the temple building was completed, Solomon called together the elders of Israel, the heads of the twelve tribes and the priests and other leaders in Israel. All these men in the presence of the people brought the Ark of the Lord into the temple. Solomon said at this time, "Praise be to the Lord, who with his own hand has fulfilled what he promised with his own mouth to my father David" (1 Kings 8:15).

Then Solomon offered a prayer of dedication as the temple was offered to the service of the Lord for all the people of Israel. Many thousands of sacrifices were offered to the Lord during this time of public dedication and worship.

After the temple was finished and now dedicated to the Lord and also Solomon's palace was completed, God appeared to Solomon at Gibeon. The Lord said to him, "I have consecrated this temple, which you have built, by putting my name there forever. My eyes and my heart will always be there . . . them" (1 Kings 9:3–9).

Solomon's glory and splendor were without precedent among the kings of his era.

The queen of Sheba visited him and was overwhelmed with the glory and riches and beauty of all that Solomon and his people had done in Jerusalem and in all Israel. She said of Solomon's glory and achievements after her visit in Jerusalem, "Indeed, not even half was told me; in wisdom and wealth you have far exceeded the report I heard" (1 Kings 10:7).

Solomon had gold and other riches, a great throne made of ivory overlaid with gold; he had wisdom, chariots and horses by the hundreds and thousands.

Solomon's Wives

1 Kings 11:1–13

Solomon loved many women. He had 700 wives and 300 concubines. When he grew old his wives turned his heart away from the Lord.

He built temples for his foreign wives, and even followed the worship of several foreign gods.

His heart was not fully devoted to the Lord as was David's heart. He thus displeased the Lord, making Him so angry that the Lord would tear the kingdom away from him after his forty years of rule were at an end.

He had turned away from following the Lord and turned to idolatry.

Because Solomon had turned from the Lord in his later years the Lord raised up two adversaries against Solomon and Israel. These two were Hadad the Edomite and Rezon of Zobah; both of these men, with their followers, were hostile toward Solomon and Israel—even to the end of Solomon's reign (1 Kings 11:14–25).

SOLOMON'S' DEATH

1 Kings 11:41–43; 2 Chronicles 9:29–30

Solomon died after being king for forty years and was buried in the City of David. Rehoboam succeeded him.

PRACTICAL LESSONS TO BE LEARNED FROM THE LIFE AND EXAMPLE OF SOLOMON, KING OF ISRAEL

Lesson No. 1

Solomon asked God for "a discerning heart" so he would be able to govern well and be able "to distinguish between right and wrong" (1 Kings 3:9).

This request of Solomon was made near the outset of his career as king of Israel, and was made while he was in a sleeping state, in a dream when the Lord appeared to him.

Yet the entire transaction between the Lord and Solomon, i.e. the Lord's invitation to make his request and Solomon's stating of his request—were sober and fully valid in their results, as a transaction between the Lord and Solomon.

Solomon's request came from the depths of his heart and was honest and sincere.

He was thirty years of age, inexperienced in rulership and now he was confronted with ruling a great and numerous people and a massive building project. He felt like a child in comparison with the tasks confronting him.

The Lord was pleased with Solomon's request and immediately agreed to grant it.

Likewise we, as Christian people today, when we are young and inexperienced or perhaps older in age, will do well to ask God for a discerning heart as did young Solomon, when we are facing any large and difficult tasks in our lives.

We are told that, "The Lord was pleased that Solomon had asked for this." And the Lord answered Solomon, "I will do what you have asked. I will give you a wise and discerning heart . . ." (1 Kings 3:10,12). And the Lord kept His promise to Solomon and gave him abundant discernment and practical wisdom throughout his life as a king of Israel.

For the successful accomplishment of many of the tasks that God gives us in life we, like Solomon, need a God-given wisdom.

This wisdom is available to us as it was to Solomon and the Lord will be pleased to give it to us when we, realizing our inadequacy, ask Him for the wisdom we need.

This same king, Solomon, had much to say about wisdom for God gave him an abundance of it.

Two examples are these: "The fear of the Lord is the beginning of knowledge, but fools despise wisdom and discipline" (Prov. 1:7) and, "For the Lord gives wisdom, and from his mouth come knowledge and understanding" (Prov. 2:6).

Lesson No. 2

As Christian believers we do well and are wise to avail ourselves of some of the wisdom that the Lord gave Solomon. We are told, "God gave Solomon wisdom and very great insight and a breadth of understanding as measureless as the sand on the seashore. Solomon's wisdom was greater than the wisdom of all the men of the East and greater than all the wisdom of Egypt" (1 Kings 4:29–30).

We are told that, "He spoke three thousand proverbs and his songs numbered a thousand and five. He described plant life. . . . He also taught about animals and birds, reptiles and fish."

We do not have his songs, except for two, before which his name appears—Psalms seventy two and 127. We do not have his teachings on plant life and animals, birds, reptiles and fish.

But we do have some of his public dedicatory prayers and the Lord's public responses to those prayers. And we have thirty-one chapters of his Proverbs, the Song of Solomon, and the Ecclesiastes. From these public prayers and writings of Solomon, we are able to gain much wisdom, a wisdom that God gave him to share with us.

From all the wisdom and knowledge we can learn from Solomon's writings and that which we can learn from the other Scriptures of the Old and New Testaments, we as God's people can gain an abundance of wisdom and knowledge in order that we "may be thoroughly equipped for every good work."

May God bless us as we, His people, gradually acquire more wisdom and knowledge so we may live a more holy, wise and useful life, serving the Lord and others.

Lesson No. 3

With the help of our Lord along with our holy resolve, let us maintain the level of our devotion to the Lord to be wholehearted at all times. And let us follow the Lord completely, not partially, at all times.

Solomon let down the level of his heart's devotion to the Lord and failed to follow the Lord completely to the end of his life as king (1 Kings 11:1–6).

Solomon failed to follow his own teaching all the way to the end of his life—his teaching which said, "Keep thy heart with all diligence; for out of it are the issues of our life" (Prov. 4:23 KJV).

David, his father, set a better example than did Solomon in this regard.

Solomon did well during most of his life; it was only toward its end that he fell back away from the Lord into serious disobedience.

It hurt him and certainly hurt the Lord who had loved him from his infancy, when the Lord named him "Jedediah," which means, "the Lord loved him" (2 Sam. 12:24–25).

A less than wholehearted service to the Lord was also a trait of another king of Judah who came later than Solomon. That king was Amaziah, who ruled for twenty-nine years. It was said of him, "He did what was right in the eyes of the Lord, but not wholeheartedly" (2 Chron. 25:1–21). The misdeeds of his reign, as a consequence, were many.

It would seem to be into the fourth decade of Solomon's forty-year reign that he began to depart from the path of wisdom and obedience.

He loved many women and married many women from lands outside of Israel.

He married wives from Moab, Ammon, Edom, Sidon and from the land of the Hittites.

As he grew older, these wives who worshiped idols turned Solomon's heart away from the Lord. He built facilities for worship of their idolatrous gods. He also himself followed Ashtereth, the goddess of the Sidonians and Molech, the detestable god of the Ammonites.

His heart thus turned away from the God of Israel whom he had loved and followed so faithfully throughout most of his life.

During these last five-to-seven years of his life and career, his heart was not fully devoted to the Lord. He ceased obeying the Lord's command and covenant. As a consequence, the Lord would tear ten tribes away from him after his son took over the throne. Only two tribes would be left in the hands of the descendants of David.

Also, God raised up two strong adversaries to cause him and Israel trouble until he would die. These two foreign leaders were Hadad and Razon.

Unlike Uzziah, who later ruled over Judah, and allowed pride to become his downfall, Solomon allowed love for foreign women and their idols to draw him away from the Lord.

Solomon fell into the same snare that some of the men of Judah fell into during the days of Nehemiah. These men had married women from Ashdod, Ammon, and Moab, a practice that was able to lead them into sin (Neh. 13:23–27).

Solomon's experience, then, becomes a solemn warning to all of us that we should maintain our full hearts' devotion and following of the Lord, fully to the very end of our lives, and this even into the time of old age.

To pull back and let down in our perseverance at the very end, can well put us in jeopardy of forsaking and disappointing our Lord as Solomon did.

By God's grace, therefore let us continue to the very end of our race. "Let us run in such a way as to get the prize."

Let us not run the risk of being "disqualified for the prize" (1 Cor. 9:24–27).

PRACTICAL LESSONS TO BE LEARNED FROM THE LIVES AND EXAMPLES OF THE FOLLOWING KINGS OF ISRAEL:

Jeroboam—22 years

Nadab—2 years	Jehoahaz—17 years
Baasha—24 years	Jehoash—16 years
Elah—2 years	Jeroboam II—41 years
Zimri—7 days	Zechariah—6 months
Omri—12 years	Shallum—1 month
Ahab—22 years	Menahem—10 years
Ahaziah—2 years	Pekahiah—2 years
Jehoram—12 years	Pekah—20 years
Jehu—28 years	Hoshea—9 years

Lesson No. 1

These men's lives illustrate what not to do, if you want to live with God's peace and blessing in your own life and be an influence for good in the lives of others.

Lesson No. 2

Stated previously, if you want to bring a curse upon your own life and a curse and judgment upon the lives of those under your care, then proceed through life in the way these nineteen kings did.

Beginning with Jeroboam the son of Nebat of the tribe of Joseph and Ephraim and ending with Hosea, the ten-tribed northern nation of Israel was traveling a course that each year and each decade was leading it closer to national disaster.

This nation began in approximately the year 930–940 B.C. and by the year 722 B.C. it had lost its independence and ceased to exist. Its land was taken over by a foreign power and its people were removed far away and settled in foreign lands.

Within a little more than 220 years this fine people had lost its liberties, its hope, and national life.

Refusal to obey the commands and laws of God was the reason for the downfall of both its kings and people.

Of all its nineteen kings who ruled in its capital of Samaria, not a single one of the nineteen kings submitted to the Lord and endeavored to influence His people to turn back and follow the God of their fathers, Abraham, Isaac, and Jacob. Rather, each king continued a policy of violating the Ten Commandments, especially promoting idolatry, image making and its corresponding disregard of the true God who had done so much for them in earlier days.

Many if not all of these kings had contact with God through prophets. Especially was this true of Jeroboam and Ahab, and there were others. Jeroboam had heard from the Lord through the prophet Ahijah twice.

It would seem that none of these kings except perhaps four of them, showed signs of any significant spiritual sensitivity at all. Those four were Jehoahaz, Jehu, Jehoash, and to a certain extent, Ahab, toward the end of his life.

Jehoahaz sought the Lord for a time because of the oppression of Hazael, king of Aram, and the Lord listened to his plea and raised up a deliverer for him, delivering him from the power of Aram (2 Kings 13:1–9).

Jehu was commissioned and anointed king with the special task of destroying the house of Ahab and all the Baal prophets and Baal worship. He did well in carrying out his commission, and in this respect he pleased the Lord. But he still refused to forsake the sins of Jeroboam and the evil idolatry that he had established in Israel.

Jehoash: This king, who ruled sixteen years, while visiting the godly prophet Elisha, was told to open a window and shoot an arrow toward the east. He did this, signifying he would defeat Aram, a threatening enemy of Israel.

Afterward, this king was told by Elisha to strike the ground with an arrow. He did this, but only three times, it would mean he would completely defeat and destroy Aram's forces. But now he would defeat him only three times and his power would soon recover again.

The Lord spoke to these kings and their people many times.

The names of the prophets through whom the Lord spoke to Israel were these: Ahijah, Jehu, Iddo, Micaiah, Elijah, Elisha, Hosea, and Amos.

The Lord warned Israel repeatedly through these men, urging them to turn from their false gods and sins, but neither the kings nor the people would listen to the Lord. Only a few of the people from these ten tribes would go to Jerusalem from time to time to seek the Lord when they learned that He was with the kings of Judah and bringing revival among the people there.

But the kings of Israel never turned to the Lord themselves and never tried to move their people closer to the Lord as so many of the godly kings of Judah were doing.

All the kings of Israel continued doing evil in the eyes of the Lord and continued leading their people into the same goat and calf idol worship which was instituted by their first king, Jeroboam.

As a consequence the entire nation of Israel was taken into captivity and lost their national life and identity.

"So the Lord was very angry with Israel and removed them from his presence" (2 Kings 17:18).

> "The Israelites persisted in all the sins of Jeroboam and
> did not turn away from them until the Lord removed

them from his presence, as he had warned through all his servants the prophets. So the people of Israel were taken from their homeland into exile in Assyria . . ."

(2 Kings 17:22)

JEROBOAM—A KING OF ISRAEL

Jeroboam was the first king of the newly formed northern kingdom of Israel. It consisted of ten tribes that had rebelled against Rehoboam after Rehoboam had taken the throne in Jerusalem from his father Solomon.

During the latter years of Solomon's reign Jeroboam had rebelled against Solomon but no details of this rebellion against Solomon are given us in the scriptural accounts. But the rebellion was serious enough that Solomon tried to kill Jeroboam and so Jeroboam fled to Egypt and remained there until Solomon's death.

Jeroboam had been one of Solomon's officials and was recognized by Solomon as a man of good potential leadership talent. Solomon even had promoted him and placed him in charge of the full labor force of the house of Joseph.

At about this same time, it would seem, the Lord told him through Ahijah the prophet that his household could become a great household and dynasty and that if he would obey the Lord as David did, his kingdom would become a great kingdom as enduring as that of David (1 Kings 11:38–39; 1 Kings 11:29–40).

So Jeroboam had a golden opportunity to be of service to God and to Israel, if he were willing to trust and obey the Lord and keep his commandments.

But after Solomon died, Jeroboam returned from Egypt and became the first in line of nineteen kings that ultimately ruled over the ten-tribe nation that became known as the kingdom of Israel.

But Jeroboam, coming to the throne in Samaria, turned his back on an opportunity to become a great king, and first in the line of godly kings, using his position and influence to turn the ten tribes of the northern kingdom back to the true God of Abraham, Isaac and Jacob.

Instead he now "thinking to himself" and after seeking advice, decided to make two golden calves as idols, placing one at Dan and one at Bethel. He thus was instituting an idolatrous worship for his people.

This was clearly a move that was leading his people into sin and away from a worship that was pleasing to the God of Israel. He was afraid of losing his peoples' loyalty and if his people worshiped in Jerusalem they would turn back to the house of David in Judah. So he would rather lead his people away from the true God and into the idolatrous worship of calf-idol worship.

Jeroboam's actions in this regard set a precedent that subsequent kings of Israel would never break away from. All eighteen kings who followed Jeroboam as kings of Israel continued leading their people, the people of the ten northern tribes of Israel, into a worship that dishonored and insulted the Lord who had done so much for them. It became an outlandish and disastrous sin for the northern nation of Israel.

Jeroboam continued promoting this evil worship and appointing an evil priesthood to administer it at the idolatrous altars in Israel. This sinful idolatrous worship later led to Israel's complete downfall.

PRACTICAL LESSONS TO BE LEARNED FROM THE LIFE AND EXAMPLE OF JEROBOAM, KING OF ISRAEL

Lesson No. 1

If Jesus comes to you and says, as He said to some of His disciples, "Come, follow me," then for your own sake and for the sake of those who will be served and blessed by your life, respond immediately to His call and go with Him. God is presenting to you a golden opportunity to be of service in His Kingdom. You may not know yet the line of service He is calling you into, but it will be in keeping with your natural gifts and abilities.

God will go with you all the way and give you peace and make you a blessing to many.

Do not turn away from God's call, for that will only lead to disaster for your life, as it did for Jeroboam.

Jeroboam was from the tribe of Ephraim, and an official on king Solomon's staff. He had easily recognizable talents as a potential leader. He did his work so well that Solomon promoted him to be in charge of the entire workforce of the house of Joseph.

The Lord also recognized his leadership potential and told him through the prophet Ahijah that he would be given ten of Israel's tribes after Solomon died and if he would walk in God's paths and laws, he and his family would become a dynasty to match that of David, even to humble and challenge David's line and that of the kings of Judah and Benjamin.

In other words Jeroboam was given a golden opportunity to become a great and blessed king and be an influence for great good in the kingdom of God. It was truly a unique opportunity, for Jeroboam was not of the line of David but from the tribe of Joseph and Ephraim.

But after Solomon died Jeroboam returned from exile in Egypt where he had fled from Solomon, and he did not grasp his opportunity for great blessing and service to God and Israel.

He chose instead the low road of his own personal plan of a king's career ruling over the ten-tribed nation of Israel.

He was afraid his people would transfer their loyalty back to Jerusalem to the house of David if he followed the Lord and His laws. So he set up goat and calf idols in Israel—at Dan in the north and at Bethel in the south and he ordained priests from any family who could put up a sufficient priest deposit for the office.

Jeroboam thus led all Israel into idolatry and national sin, and his practice was followed by all eighteen of the kings who succeeded him on Israel's throne in Samaria. Not a single king in the succession broke away from this evil system, and it led finally to Israel's downfall as a nation.

So for Jeroboam, it was a golden opportunity refused and the course he chose was an evil one that led to a nation's abandonment of God, the truth, God's blessing and to a final destruction and loss of their national life. In 722 B.C. the nation of Israel was taken captive by the king of Assyria and the people were taken away into foreign lands and there they lived miles away from their beloved Israel, the land of promise that God had given them.

The lesson to be learned from Jeroboam's life? For a man to refuse God's call upon his life and choose the evil path like that which Jeroboam chose, will result only in personal and career disaster as it did for Jeroboam—loss of opportunity of good service and a life lived only for oneself and in the end judgment and loss upon your life.

For Jeroboam, since he was in a high position of a ruling king, his choice led to loss for an entire nation of people because his influence was so great.

Instead of being blessed, he and his family were cursed. He was told that because of his sin and leading Israel into idolatry,

> "Because of this, I am going to bring disaster on the house of Jeroboam—slave or free. I will burn up the home of Jeroboam as one burns dung, until it is all gone. Dogs will eat those belonging to Jeroboam who die in the city, and the birds of the air will feed on those who die in the country. The Lord has spoken."
>
> (1 Kings 14:10–11)

Instead of rejecting God's call upon your life, grasp it and follow it immediately and find God with you in blessing and prosperity and success and happiness. And in the end you, like Moses and other obedient and godly saints, will go and live with God forever.

AHIJAH'S PROPHECY AGAINST JEROBOAM

1 Kings 14:1–20

Abijah, Jeroboam's son, became ill so Jeroboam sent his wife to Shiloh to ask the prophet Ahijah if his son would recover or not.

She went in disguise, but Ahijah although now blind, was told by the Lord that she was coming.

Ahijah said the son would soon die and Jeroboam and his house would soon be completely destroyed. This was because he had rejected the Lord and sinned and caused Israel to sin.

Jeroboam had been given a marvelous opportunity to be a good king with God's blessing but had failed to appreciate and grasp his opportunity. Instead, he led Israel for twenty-two years into deep idolatrous sin and rejection of the Lord.

He was a failure as a public servant of the Lord. He would be succeeded by his son Nadab.

NADAB—KING OF ISRAEL

1 Kings 15:25–32

Nadab was the son of Jeroboam. He did evil in the eyes of the Lord, walking in the ways of his father and causing Israel to sin. He reigned two years and was killed by Baasha along with all of his family after Baasha had begun to reign.

BAASHA—KING OF ISRAEL

1 Kings 15:33–16:7

Baasha reigned for twenty-four years in Israel. He did evil as had Jeroboam. He had killed Nadab, his predecessor, along with all of his family and took over the throne in Samaria.

ELAH—KING OF ISRAEL

1 Kings 16:8

Elah reigned two years in Samaria and was killed by Zimri, along with all of Baasha's family. He did evil as the other kings of Israel were doing, promoting idolatry and causing Israel to sin.

ZIMRI—KING OF ISRAEL

1 Kings 16:15

After killing Elah, Zimri reigned only seven days and then died in a fire he himself had set. He committed many sins and had caused Israel to sin in only a brief seven days.

Omri—King of Israel

1 Kings 16:29; 2 Chronicles 18

Omri reigned for twelve years in Samaria and he did evil in the eyes of the Lord as Jeroboam had done, only more so than Jeroboam had done.

Ahab—King of Israel

Ahab was the son of Omri. He reigned twenty-two years in Samaria and he outdid Jeroboam in doing evil.

He brought in Jezebel as his wife. She was the daughter of Ethbaal, the King of the Sidonians.

Ahab and Jezebel, together, instituted Baal worship throughout Israel.

Despite his seeing many miracles and a divine intervention in behalf of his military victory over Ben Hadad, king of the Arameans, Ahab never fully acknowledged the lordship of the God of Israel.

He did, however, humble himself when he heard of his personal judgment pronounced by a prophet (1 Kings 21:17–29).

Elijah fed by ravens

1 Kings 17:1–6

Elijah was the Tishbite from Tishbe in Gilead.

He told Ahab there would be neither dew nor rain for the next few years "except at my word."

Elijah was told to hide in the ravine of Kareth east of the Jordan and the Lord would send ravens with food; He went, drank from the brook and was fed morning and evening with bread and meat by the ravens.

He did what the Lord told him to do.

In obedience to the Lord he stayed there for some time, until the brook dried up.

THE WIDOW AT ZAREPATH

1 Kings 17:7–24

After leaving the ravine at Kereth, east of the Jordan River, he went by the direction of the Lord to a place near Sidon where he stayed with a widow of Zarepath.

He stayed in an upper room in the house of this widow.

The widow's flour and oil supply was at a low ebb when Elijah arrived there, but as she used what she had, the Lord multiplied it continually and there was a sufficient amount of a food supply for herself, for her son, and for the prophet Elijah for nearly three years as the prophet lived there during the period of the famine in the land.

There came a time when the widow's son died of an illness and Elijah cried to the Lord who returned the boy's life to him (1 Kings 17:17–24).

The woman said after seeing her son alive, "Now I know that you are a man of God and that the word of the Lord from your mouth is the truth" (1 Kings 17:24).

ELIJAH AND OBADIAH

1 Kings 18:1–15; James 5:13–20

Elijah stayed in Sidon for a long time, into the third year of the famine. Then the Lord told him to go present himself to king Ahab. God was going to send rain.

Elijah was intent on obeying what the Lord told him to do, so he went, and on the way he met Obadiah, a godly prophet and manager of Ahab's palace.

Elijah asked Obadiah to take a message to king Ahab; that Elijah desired to see him.

The prophet Obadiah was reluctant to do this, because he feared that Ahab would kill him if Elijah could not be found at that time. But, nonetheless, after Obadiah had spoken to the king he was able to put him in contact with the prophet Elijah.

ELIJAH ON MT. CARMEL AND THE
COMING OF RAIN
1 Kings 18:16–46

When Ahab saw Elijah he called him a "troubler of Israel," but Elijah said he had not troubled Israel but king Ahab had troubled Israel by forsaking the Lord's commands and following the Baals.

Elijah now told king Ahab to call all the people together, along with the prophets of Baal and Asherah, 850 in number.

A contest was arranged to demonstrate who the real and true God was—Baal or the God of Israel.

Two altars were built and sacrifices were placed on each altar, but no fires were ignited.

The Baal worshipers called upon Baal and nothing happened. Elijah called upon the God of Israel and God sent fire down and consumed the sacrifice the altar and the water, demonstrating that the God of Abraham, Isaac and Jacob is the real God that Israel should worship.

"When all the people saw this, they fell prostrate and cried, 'The Lord, he is God! The Lord, he is God!'" (1 Kings 18:39).

Then all prophets of Baal were taken down to the Kishon Valley and put to death.

Elijah and the Lord had won a great victory that day for the cause of His kingdom and the truth.

The overall purpose of the famine and the contest atop Mt. Carmel between the Baal worshipers and Elijah and those who worshiped the Lord was to turn back to the Lord all those in Israel who had wandered away from the truth into the spiritual darkness of idol worship and error.

A manifestation of God's supernatural power in causing fire to fall from above was effective in demonstrating the existence of the true God and that He alone should be acknowledged, served, and worshiped.

Elijah's faith and zeal for the Lord in bringing about this entire event in the midst of the spiritual darkness of an apostate people of Israel was most commendable.

It brought great honor to the Lord and most likely many were brought back to a renewed faith in the God of Israel.

The writer of the New Testament book of James refers to Elijah in the same connection.

James said,

"The prayer of a righteous man is powerful and effective. Elijah was a man just like us. He prayed earnestly that it would not rain, and it did not rain on the land for three-and-a-half years. Again he prayed, and the heavens gave rain and the earth produced its crops.

My brothers, if one of you should wander from the truth, and someone should bring him back, remember this: whoever turns a sinner from his error will save him from death and cover a multitude of sins."

(James 5:16–20)

In this passage from James 5:13–20, the Lord, through James, is encouraging Christian believers to pray for one another's needs, especially for physical healing.

We can expect the Lord to hear and answer our prayers when we pray with faith in the same way as the Lord answered Elijah's prayer for rain stoppage at one time, then for the rain to begin again at a later time.

ELIJAH FLEES TO HOREB

1 Kings 19:1–8

Traveling on foot, running, and walking from Mt. Carmel, Elijah went first to Jezreel, a twenty-five-to-thirty-mile journey. Then upon learning that Jezebel was planning to kill him, he fled south, first to Beersheba, about a ninety-mile journey, where he left his servant-associate. From Beersheba he continued traveling south, finally reaching Mt. Horeb, a forty-day-and-forty-night journey. The total distance from Mt. Carmel to Mt. Horeb is approximately 300 miles.

In a cave at Mt. Horeb, God appeared to him, asking him what he was doing there. Elijah replied twice with the same answer to the Lord's question that was asked him twice. "I have been very zealous for the Lord God Almighty. The Israelites have rejected your covenant, broken down your altars, and put your prophets to death with the sword. I am the only one left, and now they are trying to kill me, too" (1 Kings 19:10).

Then the Lord gave Elijah some specific instructions: he was to go back up North the same way he had come, to the desert of Damascus and after going there he was to anoint three men for the work they were to do: anoint Hazael as king of Aram; anoint Jehu as king of Israel and Elisha as Elijah's successor as prophet of the Lord. These three men, in their new position would complete the elimination of the Baal and Asherah priests (1 Kings 19:15–18).

THE CALL OF ELISHA

1 Kings 19:19–21; 2 Kings 2:1–9:3

Elisha, the son of Shaphat, was from Abel Mehobah.

He was plowing a field with oxen when Elijah found him. Elijah threw his cloak around him. Elisha then left his oxen and ran after Elijah, but Elijah told him to go back.

Elisha went back to his oxen, and then he slaughtered his ox team, broke up the plow equipment to use as firewood to cook the meat and gave it to the other people who were there.

Elisha then turned and began to follow Elijah becoming his attendant and soon his successor.

ELIJAH TAKEN UP TO HEAVEN

2 Kings 2:1–18

Elijah was taken up to heaven in a whirlwind as Elisha, his successor, watched. Elisha took the cloak that Elijah had left behind, hit the Jordan waters with it, and the waters divided as it had done earlier for Elijah.

Elisha now crossed over the Jordan with the waters divided to the right and to the left.

Elisha had received a double portion of the spirit that had rested on Elijah.

He now set forth to serve the Lord as directed by the Spirit.

Elisha's service as a prophet

A list of some of the miracles that God did through Elisha is the following:

He struck the Jordan waters and they divided; he walked through (2 Kings 2:13–14).

Some men from Jericho reported to Elisha that the water supply there was bad. Elisha asked for a bowl of salt. He threw the salt into the spring and the water became pure and useful from that day forward (2 Kings 2:19–22).

Being jeered by some youths, they calling him "baldhead" repeatedly, he called down a curse on them. Two bears came out of the woods and mauled forty-two of them (2 Kings 2:23–25).

Three kings—the king of Israel, the king of Judah and the king of Edom went to fight against Moab because the Moabites had broken an agreement they had made with Israel.

The three kings with their armies, having insufficient water, consulted Elisha. Elisha consulted the Lord and abundant water was supplied in a valley location for the men and all of their animals.

A widow's husband died with outstanding debts. All the food she owned in her house was a small amount of oil.

Elisha told her to send her sons out to borrow jars from all her neighbors. She did this. Then she poured a small amount of her oil into each jar.

Every jar ended up being full of oil. She went and sold the oil and paid all her debts and lived on that which was left over.

A well-to-do woman who lived in a town called Shunem, along with her husband, provided a room for the prophet Elisha to stay when he came for brief visits.

This woman and her husband also provided meals for Elisha whenever he was in need. The woman was childless and her husband was old, and there was little prospect that she would have a child unless

God intervened. The prophet called the woman and said she would have a son in about a year.

The woman soon became pregnant and in process of time she had a son.

But after a few years this same son became ill and died in his mother's arms. She told Elisha about her son's death. He took the young child, laid him on his bed, prayed to the Lord, then placing his body over the dead body of the boy two times, the child came to life once again, causing great joy to his mother (2 Kings 4:8–37).

DEATH IN THE POT

2 Kings 4:38–41

An unfamiliar herb was mixed in with some stew that was being cooked for a group of prophet-trainees. As the men began eating the stew they discovered it was poisoned.

Elisha told the men to place some flour in the pot. They did this and the stew was miraculously changed and was now edible. All now ate of it as the meal continued.

FEEDING OF A HUNDRED

2 Kings 4:42–44

Twenty loaves of barley loaves were brought with which to feed 100 men. It was not sufficient in size and amount to feed the 100 men.

But the Lord had told Elisha that there would be enough for all with some left over.

A miracle took place and after all 100 men had eaten, there was bread left over.

It was a miracle similar to that which Jesus later did in multiplying the five loaves and the two fishes in His public ministry.

NAAMAN HEALED OF LEPROSY

2 Kings 5

Naaman was the commander of the armies of the king of Aram, a country to the northeast of Israel.

Naaman was well regarded because of the many victories he had accomplished for the king. But Naaman had leprosy.

A young Hebrew girl, a servant in his household, suggested that he go see the prophet Elisha in Samaria and that he would be healed.

He finally went to Israel to the prophet. The prophet, through his servant Gehazi, told him to dip seven times in the Jordan River.

At first he rejected the instructions from the prophet. But then he reconsidered and went into the Jordan and immersed himself seven times in the water and was cured of his leprosy.

AN AXHEAD FLOATS

2 Kings 6:1–7

While the young prophet-trainees were cutting down trees by the Jordan River, intending to build a larger building for their use, the axhead of one of the young men fell off and into the water.

This young man immediately told Elisha what had happened. The prophet cut a small stick, threw it into the water, and the axhead floated to the surface.

The young man reached out his hand and took the axhead.

ELISHA TRAPS BLINDED ARAMEANS

2 Kings 6:8–23

With a plan to capture Elisha, Aram's men surrounded the town of Dothan where the prophet was living at the time. Elisha asked God to make the soldiers blind and the Lord did this. The prophet then led all the blinded men to Samaria and to the king of Israel.

Elisha told the king not to kill them but to feed all the men and send them back to their master. This was done and all the Arameans were returned to their master. After this event the Aram raids into Israel came to an end.

FAMINE IN BESIEGED SAMARIA

2 Kings 6:24–7:2

Ben Hadad, king of Aram, was besieging Samaria and the people were so out of food there they were eating their own children. But the Lord caused some sounds to occur of an approaching great army and all the Aramean soldiers hearing this, abandoned their camp and left all their tents and supplies behind them.

The prophet Elisha had predicted the lifting of this siege and the Lord had caused it to take place.

So the Lord had intervened and rescued the people of Samaria from the siege of Ben Hadad of Aram.

MICAIAH PROPHESIES AGAINST AHAB

1 Kings 22:1–25; 2 Chronicles 18:1–27

Micaiah was a true prophet of God. Ahab desired to retake Ramoth-Gilead from the king of Aram because it was a district owned by Israel.

Ahab asked his friend Jehoshaphat of Judah to go with him in attacking that area and retaking it.

But Jehosophat advised consulting the Lord first. After hearing from Ahab's false prophets, they called in Micaiah a true prophet of God. Micaiah predicted that Ahab would be killed in the battle and all Israel would be scattered like sheep without a shepherd.

The battle with the Arameans was soon engaged and that which Micaiah predicted came to pass. Ahab was killed and the Israelites were scattered on the hills as sheep without a shepherd. So as the Lord had said, "Let each one go home in peace," for Ahab, their shepherd, had been killed in the battle.

AHAZIAH—KING OF ISRAEL

1 Kings 22:51–53

Ahaziah reigned in Israel for two years and did evil in the eyes of the Lord. "He served and worshiped Baal and provoked the Lord, the God of Israel to anger, just as his father had done" (1 Kings 22:53).

JEHORAM—KING OF ISRAEL

(Joram)

Jehoram reigned eleven years in Samaria and walked in the evil ways of the kings of Israel, causing Israel to sin.

JEHU—KING OF ISRAEL

2 Kings 9–10

Jehu was anointed king of Israel and commissioned to kill all of Ahab's family line.

In a certain house, Jehu told two eunuchs to throw Jezebel down to the ground. They did this and dogs ate her body in fulfillment of Elijah's prophecy.

Jehu destroyed Baal worship in Israel and this pleased the Lord and earned him a promise from the Lord that his descendants would sit on Israel's throne to the fourth generation. But Jehu himself continued the sins of Jeroboam thus falling short of complete obedience to the Lord as Israel's king. He was not careful to keep the law of the Lord with all of his heart. He reigned twenty-eight years.

JEHOAHAZ—KING OF ISRAEL

2 Kings 13:1–9

Jehoahaz was the son of Jehu. He reigned seventeen years in Samaria. He did evil in the eyes of the Lord following the sins of Jeroboam the son of the Nebet (2 Kings 13:2).

For a time this king sought the Lord because of the severe oppression of Hazael, king of Aram. Yet the leaders and people refused to forsake the sins of Jeroboam. They continued the worship of the calf-idols and Asherah poles.

JEHOASH—KING OF ISRAEL
2 Kings 13:10–25

Jehoash, the son of Jehoaz, reigned sixteen years. He, as had all the kings of Israel, continued the idol worship first instituted by Jeroboam.

This king, visiting Elisha when Elisha was dying, was told by Elisha to open the east window and shoot an arrow; Jehoash did this. Then Elisha told him to strike the ground with some arrows. He stuck the ground three times only. Elisha told him if he had struck the ground five or six times he would have victory over Aram completely, but now he would defeat him only three times.

Then Elisha died.

JEROBOAM II—KING OF ISRAEL
2 Kings 14:23–29

Jeroboam reigned in Samaria forty-one years. He did evil in the eyes of the Lord and did not turn away from any of the sins of Jeroboam, son of Nebat, which he had caused Israel to commit (2 Kings 14:24).

He accomplished some military achievements for Israel, recovering Damascus and Hamath.

ZECHARIAH—KING OF ISRAEL
2 Kings 15:8–12

Zechariah reigned six months in Samaria and "He did evil in the eyes of the Lord as his father had done. He did not turn away from the sins of Jeroboam, son of Nebat, which he had caused Israel to commit" (2 Kings 15:9).

He was assassinated by Shallum, yet his enthronement was a fulfillment of God's prophecy to Jehu, which said, "Your descendants will sit on the throne of Israel to the fourth generation" (2 Kings 15:12).

SHALLUM—KING OF ISRAEL

2 Kings 15:13–16

Shallum reigned in Samaria one month and was assassinated by Menahem.

MENAHEM—KING OF ISRAEL

2 Kings 15:17–22

Menahem killed his predecessor and sacked the city of Tiphsah and ripped open the pregnant women; he reigned ten years in Samaria. He did evil in the eyes of the Lord as all his Israel predecessors had done. He paid off Pul, king of Assyria, not to invade the land, giving him 1,000 talents of silver.

PEKAHIAH—KING OF ISRAEL

2 Kings 15:23–26

Pekahiah reigned for two years in Samaria. He "did evil in the eyes of the Lord. He did not turn away from the sin of Jeroboam, son of Nebat, which he had caused Israel to commit" (2 Kings 15:24).

Pekah, one of his chief officers, conspired against him and assassinated him and took over his throne.

PEKAH—KING OF ISRAEL

2 Kings 15:27–31

As noted in the previous section, Pekah conspired against Pekahiah, his predecessor, and killed him. Then he took over his throne from which he reigned twenty years. "He did evil in the eyes of the Lord."

Tiglath Pilezer, king of Assyria, came and took away extensive lands from Israel and deported many Israelites during the reign of Pekah. Pekah was attacked and killed by Hoshea, who took his throne.

HOSHEA—KING OF ISRAEL

2 Kings 17

Hoshea was the last king of the nation of Israel. He reigned nine years in Samaria. "He did evil in the eyes of the Lord, but not like the kings of Israel who preceded him" (2 Kings 17:2).

In his ninth year Shalmanezer, king of Assyria, captured most of Israel's territory and took the people captive and placed them in the Assyrian cities of Halah, in Gozan on the Habor River and in the towns of the Medes (2 Kings 17:6).

Israel went into captivity because of their persistent sin and their unwillingness to obey the Lord's commands and covenant.

> "The king of Assyria deported Israel to Assyria and settled them in Halah, in Gozan on the Habor River and in the towns of the Medes. This happened because they had not obeyed the Lord their God, but had violated his covenant—all that Moses the servant of the Lord commanded. They neither listened to the commands nor carried them out."
>
> (1 Kings 18:11–12)

VI

Patterns from the

Kings of Judah

VI

Practical lessons to be learned from the lives and examples of the following Kings of Judah

Rehoboam—17 years
Abijah—3 years
Asa—41 years
Jehosaphat—25 years
Jehoram—8 years
Ahaziah—1 year
Athaliah—6 years
Joash—40 years
Amaziah—29 years
Azariah (Uzziah)—52 years

Jotham—16 years
Ahaz—16 years
Hezekiah—29 years
Manasseh—55 years
Amon—2 years
Josiah—31 years
Jehoahaz—3 months
Jehoiakim—11 years
Jehoiachin—3 months 10 days
Zedekiah—11 years

REHOBOAM—KING OF JUDAH

1 Kings 14:21–31

Soon after Rehoboam took the throne in Jerusalem from his father, Solomon, Rehoboam told the people that his rule would be more burdensome than that of his father. As a result all Israel except Judah and Benjamin rebelled against a future rule by the house of David.

The ten rebelling tribes chose Jeroboam the son of Nebat as their king.

This division of Israel into two parts was of the Lord and had been foretold by the prophet Ahijah to Jeroboam previously (1 Kings 11:29–39).

Rehoboam reigned in Jerusalem seventeen years. His mother's name was Naamah and was an Ammonite.

Judah did much evil after the first three years of Rehoboam's reign. They went deeply into idolatrous worship of all kinds, practicing many of the evils that had been followed by the Canaanites and others in the land before Israel had come.

There was continual war between Rehoboam and Jeroboam during his reign.

REHOBOAM FORTIFIES JUDAH

2 Chronicles 11:5–17

Rehoboam fortified fifteen cities in Judah and Benjamin, making their defenses strong.

Priests and Levites from the new apostate ten tribes came into Judah to worship and serve, along with many others who were seeking the Lord and wanted to sacrifice to the Lord in the traditional way. So Judah became very strong, as king and people walked in the ways of David and Solomon. This period of blessing and obedience to the Lord lasted for the first three years of Rehoboam's reign.

REHOBOAM'S FAMILY

2 Chronicles 11:18–23

Rehoboam had eighteen wives and sixty concubines. His favorite wife was Maachah, daughter of Absalom, who bore him four sons, one of whom was Abijah, who would become king after Rehoboam.

Rehoboam had twenty-eight sons and sixty daughters.

Shishak attacks Jerusalem

2 Chronicles 12:1–16

After Rehoboam had established himself as king and become strong, he and all Judah abandoned the Lord. This was after three good and blessed first years of his reign.

So God sent Shishak, the king of Egypt, who captured the fortified cities of Judah and later took many of the treasures of the temple and palace.

As a result of Shishak's coming, the king and the elders of Judah, upon hearing from the Lord through the prophet Shemiah, humbled themselves and acknowledged the Lord's glory and power. The Lord had said to them, "You have abandoned me; therefore, I now abandon you to Shishak" (2 Chron. 12:5).

Therefore the Lord spoke again through the same prophet saying he would soon give them deliverance from the king of Egypt. Yet he would leave them subject to him for a while so they would learn the difference between serving the Lord and serving the kings of other lands.

Because the king humbled himself, there remained some good in Jerusalem.

Rehoboam became king at forty-one and reigned in Jerusalem for seventeen years. "He did evil because he had not set his heart on seeking the Lord" (2 Chron. 12:14).

After he died his son Abijah succeeded him.

Practical lessons to be learned from the life and example of Rehoboam, King of Judah

Lesson No. 1

The attitude of one's heart of constantly seeking the Lord and obeying Him fully is a most basic ingredient in successful service to the Lord.

This basic and absolutely essential character attitude was absent from Rehoboam's life; hence, the tragic collapse of his public administration in the newly established nation of Judah.

His initial declaration of a planned increased harshness in his reign as Solomon's successor had frightened away ten of Israel's twelve tribes.

Now, despite a good three-year beginning, Rehoboam's failure to seek the Lord with all his heart resulted in his abandoning the law of the Lord and he and all Judah to become unfaithful to the Lord.

And because he and Judah abandoned the Lord, the Lord abandoned him and all of Judah. Abandonment of the Lord is hardly a recipe for success in God's kingdom.

So failure, not success, is what Judah experienced at this time.

There was only a partial recovery from the damage done when the king and the leaders humbled themselves before the Lord, a wholehearted commitment to the Lord from the very beginning to the ending of Rehoboam's seventeen year career would have assured a far more blessed reign.

Even though one has the best parentage and family background as Rehoboam had, two great and famous leaders, David and Solomon, and even though he made a good start for the first three years, these desirable factors were not sufficient to enable Rehoboam to continue on throughout his career as king of Judah in a successful manner. "He did evil because he had not set his heart on seeking the Lord" (2 Chron. 12:14).

There was missing in his life a most basic ingredient in successful service to the Lord. He needed to have a heart that is constantly seeking the Lord and obeying Him fully at all times.

And a wholehearted commitment and lifelong seeking and obeying the Lord by those who read these lines and by the one who is writing these lines will assure a blessed life for us as well.

A haphazard, lackadaisical, and hit-and-miss seeking of the Lord is not a good ingredient for success in God's service. Only wholehearted devotion, love, and willing, loving obedience to the Lord and His Word will bring the Lord's favor and power and blessing into one's life and calling and ministry. Anything less than this is a recipe for mediocrity or less.

Had Rehoboam sought the Lord with all his heart, he could have been a king of the stature of Asa, Jehosaphat, or a Hezekiah, rather than the mediocre lead ruler of the new nation of Judah.

ABIJAH—KING OF JUDAH
1 Kings 15:1–8; 2 Chronicles 13:1–14:1

Abijah was the son of Rehoboam and he reigned three years in Jerusalem; his mother was Maacha, the daughter of Absalom.

He committed all of the sins that his father had committed. These sins were committed because "his heart was not fully devoted to the Lord his God as the heart of David his forefather had been" (1 Kings 15:3).

Nevertheless God preserved him as king and gave him a godly son to succeed him. That son was Asa.

Notwithstanding the weakness of his commitment to the Lord, God gave him a great military victory over Jeroboam and his army. This victory was made possible because of the right stand that he and his people had taken with the Lord. "The men of Israel were subdued on that occasion, and the men of Judah were victorious because they relied on the Lord, the God of their fathers" (2 Chron. 13: 18).

God used Abijah's forces to subdue and punish Jeroboam and his forces. The Lord at this time struck down Jeroboam and he died.

PRACTICAL LESSONS TO BE LEARNED FROM THE LIFE AND EXAMPLE OF ABIJAH, KING OF JUDAH

Lesson

King Abijah had only a weak commitment to the Lord and he had committed all the sins his father Rehoboam had committed, yet notwithstanding these things, some unusually good things happened in his three year reign.

First of all, he and his wife had a fine son whom they named Asa. Asa became one of the best kings who ever occupied the throne in Jerusalem.

Secondly, in his battle with Jeroboam, an evil king of the northern nation of Israel, he and his men cried to the Lord when they realized their critical danger from Jeroboam's forces catching them with an ambush in behind Judah's forced, plus their expected force in their front.

King Abijah and his men relied on the Lord and cried to him and the Lord routed Jeroboam until they were fully subdued. Five hundred thousand of Jeroboam's men were killed, including Jeroboam himself. This was God's judgment on Jeroboam who had angered the Lord because of his idolatrous influence in the nation of Israel.

One wonders what greater things Abijah could have done had his heart been fully committed to the Lord?

The same question could be asked of us, his people today. How much more could we accomplish for the Lord if we gave our hearts fully to Him, purged all the sins from our lives and relied on the Lord when encountering serious threats and obstacles as we proceed in our service for the Lord?

ASA—KING OF JUDAH
1 Kings 9:15–24; 2 Chronicles 14–16

He reigned forty-one years in Jerusalem. His grandmother's name was Maacha, the daughter of Absalom.

Asa did what was right in the eyes of the Lord.

He commanded Judah to seek the Lord. He removed the foreign altars and high places "smashed the sacred stones and cut down the Asherah poles." He even deposed his grandmother Maacha from being queen mother because she had made a repulsive Asherah pole.

He cut the pole down and burned it in the Kidron Valley.

"Asa's heart was fully committed to the Lord all his life" (1 Kings 15:14).

He built up the defenses in the fortified cities. He and Judah had peace for ten years because they sought the Lord together and were keeping the Lord's commandments.

Zerah the Cushite came against Asa who had an army much smaller than Zerah had.

Yet Asa called on the Lord his God and God answered him and gave Judah a great victory. They killed many Cushite soldiers and chased away the others.

Much plunder was taken by the men of Judah and many villages around Gerar were destroyed, all features of a good and beneficial victory at that time.

Asa's reforms

2 Chronicles 15:1–19

After hearing the Lord's message through Azariah the prophet, Asa took courage and did the following:

a. He put away the idols from all of Judah's towns and the towns he had captured in the hills of Ephraim.
b. He repaired the altar.
c. He assembled all the people of Judah and Benjamin, Ephraim, and the others who had come from the other ten tribes, since they had heard that God was with Asa.
d. He offered many sacrifices to the Lord.
e. All those gathered in Jerusalem entered into a covenant to seek the Lord upon pain of death of those who would not seek Him.
f. The Lord was found by them all and the Lord "gave them rest on every side." And there was no more war until the thirty-fifth year of Asa's reign.

ASA'S LAST YEARS

2 Chronicles 16

Asa became angry when the Lord spoke to him through the prophet Hanani about his failure to rely on the Lord with the problem of Baasha, the king of Israel.

He had not relied on the Lord, but rather on the king of Aram. Asa could have destroyed Baasha's forces at that time—a force that later would threaten Judah's safety.

Somewhat later, when Asa had a disease in his feet, he relied on physicians rather than asking the Lord to heal him.

These latter developments were indications that Asa's faith in God was not as strong in his old age as it could have been, and as it had once been in his earlier years.

Asa died in his forty-first year of reigning as king of Judah.

He was buried in the tomb he had cut out for himself in the City of David.

They made a huge fire in his honor.

PRACTICAL LESSONS TO BE LEARNED FROM THE LIFE AND EXAMPLE OF ASA, KING OF JUDAH

Lesson No. 1

For a man to lead the people under his care in a certain direction, he must be going in that direction himself. King Asa of Judah was an example of a leader who was doing this.

From the very outset of his reign it was his desire to move the entire nation of Judah into a position where he and they would be a nation pleasing to the Lord.

During the first ten years of his reign he made some progress in what he was trying to do for Judah as God's man on the throne.

To be a king in Judah in those days was very much like a pastor of a large church in today's world, only on a larger scale. It was like an entire nation being a church congregation, and their king was their senior pastor-shepherd. If a godly king of Judah was able, he would move his entire population as close to God as he was able. That is what Asa was endeavoring to do.

So by personal example and also by the prerogatives of his authority as king and spiritual leader, he removed the foreign altars and high places and other idolatrous objects as nearly as he could from all the towns in Judah.

Then he commanded the people to seek the Lord.

In those days many of the people would take such an order from their king and do it, for they respected their king, especially one like Asa who they could see was living a holy and godly life.

Because the people of Judah were following Asa's lead and were putting away their idolatrous worship and following the Lord more favorably, God gave Judah ten years of peace with no war.

But after ten years, an overaggressive king from Cush in the south, whose military leader's name was Zerah, began a threatening move northward toward Judah.

King Asa had a sizable force, but still smaller in size than that of Zerah. He called on God, saying, "Help us, O Lord our God for we rely on you . . . do not let man prevail against you" (2 Chron. 14:11).

The Lord heard and answered Asa's call and struck down Judah's enemy and gave Judah a tremendous victory along with much spoil.

Lesson No. 2

One level of blessing from the Lord may be followed by a still higher level of blessing and revival from the Lord.

This was the experience of Asa and Judah.

Fresh from the great military triumph, which was due to the direct intervention of God himself, Asa and all Judah and Benjamin received further encouragement from the Lord through a godly prophet named Azariah.

The Lord promised that if Asa and Judah continued seeking the Lord they would find Him, and if they would not give up in working for him, their work would be rewarded.

This message from the Lord increased Asa's courage, so much so, that he now moved ahead for the Lord and Judah so as to move his people even closer to the Lord into a position where God would be even more pleased with them.

Asa removed still more idols from the land.

Asa repaired the altar of the Lord.

Asa called all Judah, Benjamin, and many from Israel's other tribes, and they all assembled in Jerusalem.

They made many animal sacrifices.

They made a joint covenant to seek the Lord.

They added a solemn oath to seek the Lord, strengthening still more the covenant they had made.

They blessed and praised the Lord with instruments, shouting, and acclamation.

"They sought the Lord eagerly and he was found by them. So the Lord gave them rest on every side" (2 Chron. 15:15).

This was in the fifteenth year of Asa's reign and the Lord now gave Judah peace for twenty years with no wars until the thirty-fifth year of Asa's reign.

These were years during which Judah could grow and prosper and serve the Lord with His peace and blessing.

Lesson No. 3

There is often a danger that a godly man may experience a decline in his faith during the zenith of his career or during old age.

This was true at one point for Moses; it was true for Solomon; it was true for Asa and later it was the case with king Uzziah who let pride be his downfall after many successful years of rulership.

In Asa's thirty-sixth year he looked to a foreign king for help against Baasha, king of Israel, instead of to the Lord for his help.

The Lord pointed out the failure of his faith in this regard, but it only angered Asa and so he imprisoned the man of God through whom the Lord had spoken to him. Also he brutally oppressed some of his people at this time.

Secondly, in his thirty-ninth year, Asa had a severe disease in his feet. Instead of asking the Lord to heal him he consulted the physicians.

Asa's action at this time is recorded as a weakening of his faith and commitment to the Lord.

Asa died in the forty-first year of his reign.

His overall life was pleasing to the Lord, however, and this is notwithstanding some weaknesses during his final years.

JEHOSAPHAT—KING OF JUDAH
1 Kings 22:41–50; 2 Chronicles 17:1–21:3

Jehosaphat was thirty-five years of age when he became king and he reigned twenty five years: His mother's name was Azuba, daughter of Shilhi.

"He did what was right in the eyes of the Lord."

He followed the Lord as his father Asa had done and did not depart from those good ways. He rid the land of the male shrine prostitutes that remained from Asa's reign. He was at peace with Ahab the king of Israel.

He walked in the ways of his forefather, David.

He sought the God of his father and followed His commands. He did not follow the evil practices of the kings of Israel. "His heart was devoted to the ways of the Lord." As another Bible version states it, "and his heart was lifted up in the ways of the Lord" (2 Chron. 17:6 KJV).

In the third year of his reign he sent some of his officials, along with Levites and priests, to all the towns of Judah, teaching the people from the Book of the Law of the Lord.

The fear of the Lord fell on all the kingdoms and lands surrounding Judah so they made no war with Jehosaphat.

The Philistines and Arabs even brought gifts to the king, gold and silver and large flocks of rams and goats.

He became very powerful. He fortified Judah's cities, and had men stationed in these cities. He stocked supplies in the towns and had large armies of fighting men in Jerusalem, over one million men ready to defend all of Judah.

He was allied with Ahab by marriage and during Jehosaphat's visit with Abab, Ahab asked him to join him in recovering Ramoth-Gilead. Jehosaphat agreed with the stipulation that a true prophet of the Lord be consulted first. As I have explained previously in this writing,

Micaiah spoke for the Lord and predicted the death of Ahab and the scattering of Israel's men as sheep without a shepherd. That which the prophet predicted took place (2 Chron. 18).

Returning to Jerusalem, Jehosaphat went out among the people of Beersheba in the south, to the hill country of Ephraim in the north and turned them back to the Lord (2 Chron. 19:4).

He then appointed judges in all of Judah's fortified cities, counseling them to render only just decisions.

He said, "Let the fear of the Lord be upon you. Judge carefully, for with the Lord our God there is not injustice or partiality or bribery" (2 Chron. 19:7).

In Jerusalem he appointed some of the Levites, priests and heads of the Israelite families to administer the law and settle disputes that would arise. He urged these appointees to urge the people not to sin against the Lord.

He set in place a chief priest and certain other men who were in charge of the king's matters.

Jehosaphat was doing all he could in Judah to promote righteous living, all this to avoid God's wrath from coming upon the people (2 Chron. 19:8–11).

JEHOSAPHAT DEFEATS MOAB AND AMMON

2 Chronicles 20

King Jehosaphat received a report that a large united force was planning to attack Judah, so he took immediate steps to plan a winning offensive against this massive army.

In order to defeat this threat of the Moabites, the Ammonites and the Edomites, he first called a national fast and addressed the Lord with a prayer for intervention.

God answered him through Jahaziel the prophet, assuring the king and the people that victory would be theirs.

Secondly, the Lord gave specific instructions as to when and where his army should go.

They obeyed the Lord's instructions as they proceeded into the battle; their march was accompanied by singers and many who were praising the Lord, and praising the Lord with musical instruments.

The Lord placed ambushes in behind all the armies of Moab, Ammon, and the Edomites.

Judah's enemies turned on one another and killed one another. The Moabites and Ammonites turned on the Edomites. The Edomites then turned on one another.

When Jehosaphat's men looked over the desert for their enemies, they all laid dead.

They then gathered up much plunder, taking three days to carry it away into Judah.

Then they returned to Jerusalem, rejoicing. They went into the temple with harps, lutes and other instruments and blessed and praised the Lord who had given them such a great victory.

Later Jehosaphat made an alliance with Ahaziah, a wicked king of Israel, an alliance to build a fleet of trading ships. The ships were built, but destroyed and never used for trading. This happened because Jehosaphat was doing close business with a wicked king and it displeased the Lord.

In retrospect, however, God gave Jehosaphat and Judah peace after they defeated their invading enemies at this time. This was as the Lord had done for his father Asa, after Asa defeated Zerah, the Cushite (2 Chron. 14:9–15).

Both of these kings, Asa and Jehosaphat, made full use of their high position in Judah to influence their people to serve the Lord, and God was pleased with them both, giving them great military victories and years of peace with their neighboring countries.

PRACTICAL LESSONS TO BE LEARNED FROM THE LIFE AND EXAMPLE OF JEHOSAPHAT, KING OF JUDAH

Lesson No. 1

Jehosaphat has left us a fine example in his wholehearted devotion to the Lord in which he persevered to the end of his life. We are told that he sought the Lord early and followed His commands. He was devoted to the ways of the Lord and did not depart from His ways.

He also believed in consulting the Lord before becoming involved in any major undertaking such as involvement in a military engagement. For example, when visiting with his friend, the king of Israel, Ahab, he asked Ahab to consult a godly prophet before agreeing to accompany him in going to recover Ramoth Gilead. This they did, consulting the Lord through Micaiah, a godly prophet.

Jehosaphat followed in the ways of his forefather David and sought the Lord as his father had done. As a result the Lord was with him from the very beginning of his reign.

Jehosaphat had seen how God blessed David in every way. He had seen how God blessed Asa his father in every way.

And that blessing and assistance from God was what he wanted for himself and for his people and that is what God gave him, for he made the God of Israel his Lord throughout his entire twenty-five years as Judah's king.

In the way he lived as a man in a prominent place, he has left a tremendous example for us as Christian believers to follow.

That the way he lived was pleasing to the Lord was amply shown by the many things God did for him and Judah while he occupied the throne in Jerusalem. And the Lord will do many great things for us, too, as we live our lives as Jehosaphat lived his.

Lesson No. 2

Jehosaphat set an example for us Christian leaders in his whole-hearted endeavors in using his position as king and spiritual-pastor-shepherd, to influence all his people to come as close to God as he could bring them.

How did he seek to accomplish this? In two ways:

First, he sent some of his officials, some priests and Levites to all the towns of Judah to teach from the Book of the Law of the Lord. God showed his approval of this by causing the fear of the Lord to fall on the kingdoms and lands surrounding Judah.

Secondly, returning to Jerusalem, after visiting Ahab, he went out among the people from Beersheba in the far south of Judah to the hills of Ephraim in the far north, and turned the people back to the Lord.

This latter effort was in keeping with his earlier efforts to turn people back to the Lord in the third year of his reign by sending out men to teach the Law of God in all of Judah's towns.

He also appointed judges in the fortified cities and charged them to render only decisions approved by the Lord (2 Chron. 19:7).

Lesson No. 3

In gaining a victory over Moab and Ammon, he acted wisely so the Lord would fight for Judah.

He first called a national fast and made a public prayer of intervention.

Secondly, he received specific battle instructions from the Lord, and then followed them fully.

Thirdly, his men proceeded to the battle with singing and instruments of praise. Then God went before them and set ambushes, and the victory came, ending with all dead bodies. Then much plunder. Judah's enemies killed one another because God had heard their prayers and seen their faith.

Returning to Jerusalem and entering the temple, they blessed and praised the Lord with songs and instruments.

Lesson No. 4

Great peace came to king Jehosaphat and all Judah after the military victories as it had come to Asa after his reforms and bringing his people back to God.

Great peace will come to us also as we seek the Lord, fight our battles with the Lord's assistance, and trust him from day to day, and month to month. We bless You for being our Lord and Master!

King Asa, Jehosaphat's father, had done well in commanding all Judah to seek the Lord, then later leading his people to enter into a public agreement to seek the Lord until he was found.

King Jehosaphat went even farther in that he sent out teachers with the book of the law among all the towns of Judah. Later, he himself went out among the people from Beersheba in the far south and as far north as the hills of Ephraim, and turned the people back to the Lord. This was Old Testament evangelism and spreading of the gospel.

Both men, father and son, were like-minded in their earnest desire to help their people to know the Lord and serve the Lord as they themselves were doing.

Two godly men, loving and serving their Lord and Master and doing all they could to influence others to do the same.

What a marvelous double example the Lord has given to encourage us to take the message of the cross of Christ and the new covenant to the precious men and women of our generation in these last days.

These two men loved the families and people of their nation, and being in a position to do something to help them, they did it. And with their efforts their Lord was pleased and many of their people were blessed and will be in heaven forever because of what they did. Lord, we bless Your Great Name!

JEHORAM—KING OF JUDAH

2 Kings 8:16–24; 2 Chronicles 21:4–20

Jehoram was thirty-two when he became king and he reigned eight years. He killed all his brothers and some of the princes of Judah after he became king.

He forsook the Lord and walked in the evil ways of the kings of Israel. He died of an incurable disease of his bowels in great pain.

He died to no one's regret and was buried with no great burning in his honor. He had disgraced his family and forefathers during his eight years in power.

During his time as king in Jerusalem, Edom, Libnah and the Philistines invaded Judah. They took Jehoram's goods, his wives and all his sons, except Ahaziah who became the next king in Judah.

AHAZIAH—KING OF JUDAH

2 Kings 8:25–29; 2 Chronicles 22:1–9

Ahaziah was twenty-seven when he began to reign and he reigned one year. His mother's name was Athaliah, a granddaughter of Omri of Israel. He walked in the ways of Ahab, doing evil in the eyes of the Lord. He was related by marriage to Ahab's family and so was influenced by Ahab's advisors. His mother encouraged him to do evil. He was later killed by Jehu along with Abab's family. He was a failure as a king.

ATHALIAH—QUEEN OF JUDAH
2 Kings 11:1–16; 2 Chronicles 22:10–23:15

Athaliah was the mother of Ahaziah, Ahaziah who had ruled as king of Judah for one year and had let himself be influenced by his mother, Athaliah.

After Ahaziah died, Athaliah took over the throne in Jerusalem herself and proceeded to kill all the other descendants of David. She succeeded in killing all of them except one child, little Joash. Joash, an infant at the time was hidden away by Johosheba, the daughter of king Jehoram and sister of Ahaziah; Ahaziah who had ruled Judah for one year and was now dead.

Wicked Athaliah ruled in Jerusalem for six years, all the time believing that all the other descendants of David's line were dead.

Satan, working through the evil actions and plans of the wicked woman Athaliah was obviously attempting to destroy the legitimate line of David's heirs to the throne of the Savior Jesus, The Messiah, who would be from David's family line and become the Savior of the world. Thank You, Lord, for bringing to naught the plans and attempts of Satan to prevent salvation from being brought to a needy human race.

The wicked queen Athaliah was finally executed and replaced by young Joash who became the legitimate ruler on the throne of Judah in Jerusalem. See 2 Kings 11:16 and 2 Chronicles 23:15.

PRACTICAL LESSONS TO BE LEARNED FROM THE LIVES AND EXAMPLES OF THE FOLLOWING KINGS OF JUDAH AND QUEEN ATHALIAH

Jehoram—8
Ahaziah—1
Athaliah—6

Lesson No. 1

The lives of these two men, and the female queen Athaliah, illustrate what not to do if you want to live with God's peace and blessing in your life and be an influence for good in the lives of others.

Jehoram, after being enthroned, killed all his brothers and some of the princes, then promptly forsook the Lord and walked in the evil ways of the kings of Israel. He died, after being king for eight years, of an incurable disease in his bowels.

Ahaziah reigned only one year and he walked in the ways of evil Ahab and did evil in the eyes of the Lord.

Athaliah, a wicked woman, and mother of Ahaziah had influenced her son to do evil while he was on the throne.

She murdered all the descendants of David with the exception of one—Joash, who was being hidden away by a godly and wise woman named Johosheba.

Lesson No. 2

The two kings, Jehoram and Ahaziah, were both in the line of David and were ruling in Jerusalem, and so had no rational or politically expedient reason to forsake the God of Israel and follow the idolatrous worship as the kings of Israel were continually doing. Yet forcible influence had come into their lives because both men had married one of Ahab's daughters and Ahaziah, Jehoram's son, was closely related to Ahab's family by marriage as well.

They both let themselves be influenced by this evil connection rather than by the good influence that could have come from their fathers and grandfathers, Jehoshaphat, and Asa.

The lives and careers of Jehoram and Ahaziah illustrate the dangers of marrying women from an evil and unbelieving family as both of these men did.

JOASH—KING OF JUDAH
2 Kings 11–12; 2 Chronicles 22:10–24:27

After Ahaziah the son of Athaliah had died, Athaliah began to kill all the royal line of David; she killed all except one—Joash.

Joash was hidden away by a godly woman named Jehosheba. Meanwhile Athaliah ruled Judah as a queen mother for six years, not knowing that Joash was alive and being raised in secret by his nurse.

Finally when Joash reached age seven, Jehoiada, the godly high priest, arranged for Joash's anointing as King of Judah.

Joash was anointed and installed as king under guard by groups of soldiers under Jehoiada's direction.

Athaliah was executed and put out of the way for the new young king to rule.

Joash now began to rule, although young, with Jehoiada's guidance and advice.

He reigned for forty years. He did what was right in the eyes of the Lord while Jehoiada was alive and guiding him. He undertook and accomplished needed repairs on the temple of the Lord. But after the strong leader and godly high priest, Jehoiada, passed away in death, the apostate officials of Judah came to the king and he listened to all their advice. It was advice which when followed, led Judah away from the temple worship, away from the God of Israel and into the worship of idols and Asherah poles.

It became quite obvious that Joash had no personal convictions or strength of character enough to stand up for what he knew was true and right.

He, rather, allowed himself to be led by those who were not the appropriate leaders. He, the leader, should have continued in the good paths that the godly Jehoiada had shown him, but he did not do this.

Soon, the Lord sent several prophets, urging him and the leaders of Judah to return to the Lord, but they would not listen. Finally, the Lord spoke through the prophet Zechariah, the son of Jehoiada saying, "This is what God says: 'Why do you disobey the Lord's commands? You will not prosper. Because you have forsaken the Lord, he has forsaken you'" (2 Chron. 24:20).

This prophecy so angered the leaders of Judah, and the king himself, that he ordered Zechariah to be killed. He was soon stoned to death.

In judgment against Joash and Judah who had now forsaken the Lord, God sent the army of the king of Aram into Judah. This army killed all the leaders of Judah, took much plunder and left king Joash seriously injured in his own bed because he had killed Zechariah the prophet.

Joash, therefore, because he forsook the Lord part way through his forty year reign, made shipwreck of his life and career as one of Judah's kings.

His life had provided a living link for the kings of David's line; he made some needed repairs in the temple of the Lord; he did good work while Jehoiada was with him to support and guide him, but the latter part of his forty years was a tragic failure. When he died he was buried in the city of David but not in the tombs of the kings. He did produce a son, Amaziah who succeeded him on the throne.

PRACTICAL LESSONS TO BE LEARNED FROM THE LIFE AND EXAMPLE OF JOASH, KING OF JUDAH

Lesson No. 1

Things went well for king Joash while he served the Lord. But when he departed from the Lord, things in his life and kingdom came under God's severe judgment and wrath. He departed from the Lord who had been so kind to him. Now he only brought God's wrath down on himself and his people.

The king line, descended from David, had been providentially pre-served by the wise actions of the husband and wife team of Jehoiada and his wife Jehosheba.

Jehosheba hid the infant Joash away in the temple for six years, with his nurse, in order to escape the murderous intentions of the wicked queen, Athaliah.

At age seven, under the priest Jehoiada's arrangements, Joash was crowned king and presented to the nation.

The wicked queen Athaliah was executed and Joash took the throne.

Joash had a forty-year reign and did well while Jehoiada was his advisor and helper.

But Jehoiada the priest failed to anticipate the forces that Joash would be up against after he departed in death.

Jehoiada must certainly have been aware of the mind-set of the officials who were surrounding the king. If only he had conferred with Joash and helped prepare him in his own character and resolve to be able to take a firm position regarding important issues of the kingdom, then the shipwreck of Joash's reign following Jehoiada's death may have been avoided.

But as it turned out, Joash lacked the personal character and strength to withstand the advice and influence of the officials around him.

Instead, he gave in to them, followed their evil advice and ended his forty-year reign in a flurry of wickedness and evil.

Together, he and his officials abandoned the temple, began worship-ing idols, Asherah poles and refused to listen to God's prophets who were attempting to bring them all back to the Lord and right-doing in the kingdom.

Finally, Joash ordered the death of one of God's prophets, Zechariah, the son of his long-time friend and mentor, Jehoiada the priest.

This prophet was killed by stoning.

To punish king Joash and his evil officials the Lord sent the king of Aram into Jerusalem and Judah. They killed all of Joash's officials and left Joash seriously injured. He was later killed in his own bed in reprisal because he had killed Zechariah the prophet who had reproved him for forsaking the Lord.

Hence the tragic ending of the life and reign of a man to whom the Lord had shown such great kindness from the very earliest days of his life.

The practical lesson to be learned from Joash's life?—faithful continuance in following and obeying our Lord will ensure his continued blessing and Presence. To depart from following Him, for whatever reasons, will result in tragedy and loss in his service and in his kingdom.

Joash learned his practical lesson from first-hand experience, but if we are wise we will not have to learn it in that way. We can profit from Joash's experience and avoid the type of tragic losses he experienced at the end of his life. We can thus go on to the end of our lives and service with peace, joy, and happiness, and receive the Lord's smile and commendation when we meet Him in heaven.

AMAZIAH—KING OF JUDAH

2 Kings 14:1–22; 2 Chronicles 25:1–28

Amaziah was twenty-five when he began to rule and he ruled twenty-nine years. He followed the example of his father Joash, but not as David had done. He did not serve the Lord wholeheartedly (2 Chron. 25:2).

He executed those who had killed his father.

Some men conspired against him and killed him and so he died a violent death. His son Uzziah was his successor.

PRACTICAL LESSONS TO BE LEARNED FROM THE LIFE AND EXAMPLE OF AMAZIAH, KING OF JUDAH

Lesson No. 1

We are told that Amaziah did what was right in the eyes of the Lord but not wholeheartedly.

Less than wholehearted serving of the Lord allows room for too many serious mistakes to come into a man's life and that was what happened in Amaziah's life and career.

Some examples of his mistakes in judgment were these:

1. He hired one hundred thousand troops from Israel as merce-
   naries to help him in a planned military engagement with the
   Edomites. But he was ignorant of the fact that the Lord would
   not be with him to bless an army made up with one hundred
   thousand men from Israel, a nation whose leaders and people
   had forsaken the Lord and were idol worshipers.

   A prophet told him about this factor and so he sent all these
   hired men back to Israel. But these men were now angry at
   Judah in later weeks invading Judean towns, killing three
   thousand people, and taking much plunder.

2. Amaziah fought against the Edomites, defeating them, but
   then he brought back with him the gods of Edom, bowed
   down to them, and burned sacrifices to them.

   This angered the Lord, yet Amaziah rejected the Lord's reproof
   through the prophet.

   Therefore, the Lord caused Jehoash, the king of Israel with his
   army, to confront Amaziah and defeat him in battle and this
   same king came into Jerusalem and did extensive damage to
   the city walls and took many valuables from the temple.

   Amaziah had forsaken the Lord. He lived for fifteen years
   following king Jehoash's invasion of Jerusalem and his defeat
   of Amaziah, but Amaziah was finally killed by conspirators
   in the city of Lachish.

   It seems that many of the major decisions and moves that
   Amaziah made turned out to be faulty decisions and faulty
   moves. This was clearly traced to his less than wholehearted
   serving of the Lord.

   In the course of his reign, therefore, he forsook the Lord and
   began to follow idols and so found the Lord to be his op-
   ponent rather than his helper. The Lord raised up an enemy
   army to pursue and defeat him and he finally died a violent
   death and he was buried in the city of Judah.

   King Amaziah has given us an excellent example of the way
   a man should not serve the Lord and those under his care.

This king clearly did some things right but many things wrong.

If we serve the Lord in a wholehearted manner He will bless us and give us success. If we serve Him in a lackadaisical, haphazard, and slipshod manner, our results will be disappointing to the Lord and disappointing to those under our care.

AZARIAH (UZZIAH)—KING OF JUDAH
2 Kings 15:1–12; 2 Chronicles 26:1–23

Uzziah was sixteen when he began to reign. He reigned fifty-two years. He did what was right in the eyes of the Lord. "He sought God during the days of Zechariah, who instructed him in the fear of God. As long as he sought the Lord, God gave him success" (2 Chron. 26:5).

Uzziah had a long list of successes during his reign and he became very powerful and famous. He conquered nearby nations. He tilled the soil. He built up his defenses; his men invented new and useful weapons. All things a good king should do.

God blessed him for he sought the Lord.

After he had become powerful, pride came in and he became unfaithful to the Lord. He entered the temple to burn incense, a service only priests were to do. He became angry when the priests spoke to him concerning this. In his anger toward the priests the Lord struck him with leprosy and he departed from the temple a leper for the rest of his life. He was required to live by himself, away from others. His son took over the king's duties until he died.

Pride became Uzziah's downfall, although he had previously become very successful, powerful, and famous doing a king's work, because he had followed the laws of the Lord and sought Him as a regular part of his daily life for many years. The Lord had helped him in all of his endeavors.

PRACTICAL LESSONS TO BE LEARNED FROM THE LIFE AND EXAMPLE OF UZZIAH, KING OF JUDAH

Lesson No. 1

King Uzziah's reign is a good example of how the Lord gives a man prosperity and success as long as he seeks the Lord.

This king counseled with Zechariah a man of God who taught him in the ways of the Lord.

Uzziah grasped his teaching, followed it, and began to seek the Lord on a regular basis and as a result he prospered in everything he did.

Uzziah had a long list of successes for several decades.

He had military successes; he built up his national defenses; he had a large trained army; he had success in agricultural endeavors. He had men who invented new and useful weapons that made his nation more secure. He became very famous and powerful.

These successes and his personal fame and power were due to his being diligent and greatly helped by the Lord in all his endeavors.

Lesson No. 2

Pride became Uzziah's downfall from his position of success, prosperity, and power.

Pride can also bring us down too from a position of success and fame, if we become careless.

King Uzziah allowed his great power lead to pride and pride led to his downfall.

He entered the temple sanctuary and began to offer incense on the altar there. This was an activity strictly prohibited to kings. Only ordained priests were authorized to do this.

When Azariah, a leading priest, along with eighty other priests, followed the king into the sanctuary and spoke to the king about what he was doing, the king became angry, not wanting to be interfered with. While expressing his resentment in angry tones to the priests, the Lord struck king Uzziah with leprosy. Immediately thereafter he was led out of the Lord's presence and he remained a leper for the remainder of his reign and life. He had to live in a house by himself for the remaining part of his life. His son Jotham took over his kingly duties until Uzziah died.

The lesson? It is this: Success is good and it will continue for us as long as we continue to obey the Lord. Serious disobedience to the Lord, as in Uzziah's case, will cause an end of success and prosperity.

A summary of lessons to be learned from king Uzziah's life, for his life has much to teach us:

1. There are great benefits in following the Lord's instructions through a godly man such as Zechariah the prophet.
2. Seeking the Lord brings great blessing and success.
3. The dangers of pride when one becomes well-known and powerful and successful.

Beware of the dangers that may come along with abundant success.

Uzziah's experience may remind us of Nebuchadnezzar's problem with pride: it required seven years of humbling to bring him to a place of humility (Dan. 4).

Note the following testimony concerning Uzziah and how the Lord had helped and blessed him:

1. "As long as he sought the Lord, God gave him success" (2 Chron. 26:5).
2. "God helped him against the Philistines . . . Meunites" (2 Chron. 26:7).
3. "His fame spread far and wide, for he was greatly helped until he became powerful" (2 Chron. 26:15c).

JOTHAM—KING OF JUDAH

2 Kings 15:32–38; 2 Chronicles 27:1–9

Jotham began to reign when he was twenty-five, and he reigned for sixteen years. "He did what was right in the eyes of the Lord, just as his father Uzziah had done, but unlike him he did not enter the temple of the Lord" (2 Chron. 27:2).

Jotham did much building as his father had done. He fought and conquered the Ammonites and became powerful like his father, "because he walked steadfastly before the Lord his God" (1 Chron. 27:6).

Jotham, therefore, was a very successful king in Judah although his reign lasted a much shorter time than did that of his father—sixteen years.

Jotham, wisely, did not repeat the mistake his father had made of entering the temple to offer incense, an activity only the priests were ordained to do.

PRACTICAL LESSONS TO BE LEARNED FROM THE LIFE AND EXAMPLE OF JOTHAM, KING OF JUDAH

Lesson No. 1

King Jotham did what was right in the eyes of the Lord and in doing this he has set a good example for us Christian believers today.

If we as Christian believers follow the Lord and do what is right in the eyes of the Lord, we shall please the Lord and be a blessing to others as Jotham was.

Jotham had both seen and learned of the success and prosperity that the Lord had given to his father, Uzziah. He knew that his father's success was because he had faithfully sought the Lord and had walked steadfastly with Him. His father had left a good example for his son, and now Jotham would serve in the king's office in the same way.

Lesson No. 2

Jotham had seen first-hand the mistake that his father made toward the end of his long career, by entering the temple to present incense, an action kings were forbidden to do. Jotham had been called into duty to undertake the administration of the entire kingdom because Uzziah was now a leper and so had to live separate from all others.

Jotham wisely learned from his father's mistake and never entered the temple sanctuary to burn incense as his father had done.

This was an advance on Jotham's part and we can also often learn from the mistakes made by our fathers or grandfathers or the mistakes made by other family members that have preceded us.

Lesson No. 3

Jotham, like his father, grew powerful because "he walked steadfastly before the Lord" but unlike his father, he did not allow pride to become his downfall. He kept his eyes upon the Lord, remained obedient to him and remained humble, and so completed his sixteen years on Judah's throne in peace and rested at death with his fathers in the City of David.

Thanks, Lord, for king Jotham's faithfulness and his perseverance in service as one of Judah's kings and men of God!

AHAZ—KING OF JUDAH

2 Kings 16; 2 Chronicles 28

Ahaz was twenty years old when he became king, and he reigned for sixteen years. "Unlike David his father, he did not do what was right in the eyes of the Lord! He walked in the ways of the kings of Israel and also made cast idols for worshiping the Baals . . ." (2 Chron. 28:2).

He had close personal ties with Tiglath-Pilezer, King of Assyria, and copied an altar this King had in Damascus.

He made extensive changes in the equipment and worship of the temple of the Lord in Jerusalem. Many of these changes were in deference to the Assyrian king, changes that were detrimental to the true and pure worship of the God of Israel.

Because Ahaz departed from the Lord and worshiped idols, even offering some of his sons on a pagan altar, he angered the Lord. The Lord thus caused the kings of both Aram and of Israel to send their armies against him. They both caused Ahaz much harm and they killed many of his people and brought about much trouble and loss to him.

PRACTICAL LESSONS TO BE LEARNED FROM THE LIFE AND EXAMPLE OF AHAZ, KING OF JUDAH

Lesson No. 1

The sixteen-year reign of Ahaz in Jerusalem illustrates what can happen to a king with a good father and a good grandfather, who rejects their faith and example and follows the path of evil.

Ahaz had a sixteen-year reign as did his father Jotham. Jotham followed the Lord, but Ahaz rejected the Lord and followed the Baals and other heathen gods. Ahaz even went so far as to "sacrifice his sons in the fire" to a heathen god that he was worshiping.

To reject the truth and follow an evil course as Ahaz did, will bring trouble and in the end judgment as it did to Ahaz.

The Lord sent two kings against Ahaz, the king of Aram and the king of Israel.

These two kings and their armies both defeated Ahaz. Many prisoners were taken from Judah and the king of Israel killed one hundred and twenty thousand of Judah's men. Also many high positioned leaders in Judah were killed, including the king's son Maaseiah, and Azrikam, the officer in charge of the palace and Elkanah, second to the king.

King Ahaz sent to the King of Assyria for help but received more trouble from him than help.

In his time of trouble king Ahaz, instead of turning to the Lord, "became even more unfaithful to the Lord" (2 Chron. 28:22).

Jotham, the father, with a sixteen-year reign, gives us a picture of a successful king.

Ahaz, the son, with a sixteen-year reign, gives us a picture of an unsuccessful king.

The reasons that made the difference between the two are instructive for all of us as Christian believers and servants of the same God of Israel.

HEZEKIAH—KING OF JUDAH

2 Kings 18–20; 2 Chronicles 29–32; Isaiah 36–39

Hezekiah was twenty-five when he became king and he reigned in Jerusalem twenty-nine years. He was a godly king doing what was right in the eyes of the Lord as David did. He removed the high places and other idolatrous objects of worship throughout Judah.

"Hezekiah trusted in the Lord, the God of Israel. There was no one like him among all the Kings of Judah, either before him or after him. He held fast to the commands the Lord had given Moses, and the Lord was with him; he was successful in whatever he undertook."

(2 Kings 18:5–7)

"He rebelled against the king of Assyria and did not serve him . . . he defeated the Philistines, as far as Gaza and its territory."

(2 Kings 18:7a–8)

HEZEKIAH PURIFIES THE TEMPLE AND RESTORES THE PURE WORSHIP OF THE LORD

From his earliest days of being enthroned as Judah's king, he took measures to restore the true worship of the God of Israel. He gave orders to open the doors of the temple and repair all that needed to be repaired.

He gave orders to cleanse the temple of all defilement and that the priests and Levites were to consecrate themselves for the Lord's service.

It was king Hezekiah's intention "to make a covenant with the Lord so that his fierce anger will turn away from us" (2 Chron. 29:10).

The men worked sixteen days purifying the temple, and then reported back to the king.

Afterwards, sacrifices were brought and offered to the Lord for all the people and a sin offering for "all Israel."

As the offerings were being made, trumpets and other musical instruments were played.

Later many more burnt offerings were made.

The king and the people knelt down and worshiped.

Fellowship offerings and drink offerings and burnt offerings were brought in abundance and so the pure worship of the Lord was restored in the temple.

The Levites helped the priests accomplish all the offerings and worship before the Lord.

After the temple was cleansed and the worship resumed, Hezekiah sent out a call to all of both Judah and Israel to come to Jerusalem to celebrate the Passover of the Lord, the God of Israel.

He sent his call by couriers throughout Israel and Judah, inviting them to the Passover. Many of the people greeted the invitations with scorn, but some humbled themselves and came from Zebulun, Asher, and Manasseh. A very large crowd assembled to keep the Passover.

Some of those who came from Israel were not ceremonially clean yet partook of the Passover feast.

Hezekiah prayed for these, asking God to forgive them, and the Lord heard Hezekiah's prayer, for these people were seeking the Lord, and the Lord healed them.

There was much singing and rejoicing by the priests and Levites and by all the people.

The assembly decided to extend the celebration another seven days and many additional animals were provided by the king and many also by his officials.

There was great joy in Jerusalem. Nothing this momentous had been seen since the days of Solomon.

"The priests and the Levites stood to bless the people, and God heard them, for their prayer reached heaven, his holy dwelling place" (2 Chron. 30:27).

This Passover celebration was especially unique because invitations had been sent out to all of Israel—to the people now divided into two separate nations, Israel and Judah—Israel made up of the northern ten tribes and Judah made up of the southern two tribes.

Many from Israel had come and taken an active part in the worship celebration.

When this joint celebration was ended, those who had come from Israel went out and smashed the idols, high places, and Asherah poles in Judah and also in Ephraim and Manasseh. Then they returned to their own homes.

CONTRIBUTIONS FOR WORSHIP

2 Chronicles 31:2–21

King Hezekiah organized the priests and Levites into divisions and assigned them to their appropriate duties to offer sacrifices and offer praise and worship to the Lord on a regular basis.

He also instructed the people to bring in the tithes needed to provide support for the priests and Levites.

The people began to bring gifts and tithes and there was a great abundance of provisions for that purpose.

Conaniah, a Levite, was placed in charge of storing the foodstuffs brought in and his brother, Shimei, was second in rank.

These two men supervised the storing of all the supplies. They had many helpers in this task.

Hezekiah organized all the peoples' service and activities carefully, assigning responsibilities to men by name (2 Chron. 31:14–21).

A summary statement of Hezekiah's service to the Lord and to Judah and Israel at this time is the following:

> "This is what Hezekiah did throughout Judah, doing what was good and right and faithful before the Lord his God. In everything that he undertook in the service of God's temple and in obedience to the law and commands, he sought his God and worked wholeheartedly. And so he prospered."
>
> (2 Chron. 31:20–21)

Sennacherib threatens Jerusalem and Judah

2 Kings 18:7–37; 2 Chronicles 32:1–23; Isaiah 36–39

"In the fourteenth year of king Hezekiah's reign, Sennacherib, king of Assyria, attacked all the fortified cities of Judah and captured them" (2 Kings 18:13).

After Sennacherib had captured all these key cities of Judah, king Hezekiah tried to buy him off so he would not come any farther and take over any more control of Judah. Hezekiah sent him great amounts of silver and gold, even stripping off the gold that had been used to cover the doors and doorposts of the temple. But these gifts and exactions did not satisfy the king of Assyria. He desired to take over the entire nation and people of Judah the way his predecessor had done to Israel, the northern ten tribes whose capital was Samaria.

So Sennacherib sent his high officials and military commander with a message to king Hezekiah. In this message was a question directed to Hezekiah: He asked how Judah's God could deliver Judah from his power if the gods of the other conquered nations could not deliver them?

Hezekiah took this message and sent word to Isaiah the prophet. Isaiah sent word to Hezekiah not to worry. The Lord would distract Sennacherib and that he would return to Nineveh and be killed (2 Kings 19:1–7).

Hezekiah then received a letter from the king of Assyria; he read it, then went into the temple and spread it before the Lord. Then he prayed this prayer,

"O Lord, God of Israel, enthroned between the cherubim, you alone are God over all the kingdoms of the earth, you have made heaven and earth. Give ear, O Lord, and hear; open your eyes, O Lord, and see; listen to the words Sennacherib has sent to insult the living God. . . . Now, O Lord our God, deliver us from his hand, so that all kingdoms on earth may know that you alone, O Lord, are God."

(2 Kings 19:15–19)

Isaiah, the prophet, sent a message to Hezekiah saying that the Lord had heard his prayer and then Isaiah gave an extended and complete message to Hezekiah concerning the pride and might of the Assyrian king and ended with the words,

"Therefore this is what the Lord says concerning the king of Assyria:

> He will not enter this city
> or shoot an arrow here.
> He will not come before it with shield
> or build a siege ramp against it.
> By the way that he came he will return;
> he will not enter this city
> declares the Lord.
> I will defend this city and save it,
> for my sake and for the sake of David my servant."
>
> (2 Kings 19:32–34)

That same night after Hezekiah had heard Isaiah's prophecy, the Angel of the Lord went out and killed one hundred and eighty-five thousand Assyrian troops.

In the morning there were only dead bodies to be found.

So Sennacherib broke camp and returned to Nineveh. A few days later he was worshiping in his pagan temple and two of his sons entered and killed him.

Thus Judah, Jerusalem, and Hezekiah were delivered from the threat of the mighty Sennacherib who had mocked the God of Israel.

HEZEKIAH'S PRIDE, SUCCESS AND DEATH

2 Chronicles 32:24–33

King Hezekiah became ill and was at the point of death. Word came from the prophet Isaiah that Hezekiah should put his house in order for he was going to die.

But Hezekiah turned his face to the wall and prayed, reminding the Lord that he had walked faithfully before the Lord all his life. Then he wept bitterly.

God heard his prayer and saw his tears, and a message came from Isaiah that Hezekiah would be healed and fifteen years added to his life.

A sign was given to him that he would be healed—the sun moved back fifteen degrees in the sundial.

He was healed and lived and reigned fifteen more years. After his healing he failed to thank the Lord for it. His failure to say thanks was due to his pride.

But soon he repented of his pride and avoided the Lord's wrath from coming upon him.

PRACTICAL LESSONS TO BE LEARNED FROM THE LIFE AND EXAMPLE OF HEZEKIAH, KING OF JUDAH

Lesson No. 1

King Hezekiah's overall approach to life and service to God and others is a superb example to all Christian believers in our service to God.

Some statements describing Hezekiah's life and service are the following:

"He did what was right in the eyes of the Lord, just as his father David had done" (2 Kings 18:3).

> "Hezekiah trusted in the Lord, the God of Israel. There was no one like him among all the Kings of Judah, either before or after him. He held fast to the Lord and did not cease to follow him; he kept the commands the Lord had given Moses."

> (2 Kings 18:5–6)

"This is what Hezekiah did throughout Judah, doing what was good and right and faithful before the Lord his God.

In everything that he undertook in the service of God's temple and in obedience to the law and the commands, he sought his God and worked wholeheartedly, and so he prospered."

(2 Chron. 31:20–21)

Hezekiah came to the throne in Jerusalem in the third year of Hoshea's nine-year reign. This fact is significant for it was during the reign of Hoshea of Israel that the nation of Israel was conquered by Assyria. Hoshea was the last king of the nation of Israel. The nation fell in 722 B.C. and this occurred in Hezekiah's sixth year as king of Judah.

King Hezekiah saw this happen to Israel, the sister nation of Judah. Samaria fell and all Israel fell at the hands of king Shalmaneser of Assyria, a predecessor of Sennacherib.

In the fourteenth year of Hezekiah's reign, eight years after the fall of Samaria and the nation of Israel, Sennacherib the new king of Assyria, began to show his intentions to capture all of Judah in the same way that Israel had been captured eight years earlier.

Hezekiah tried to buy him off by giving him great amounts of treasures from the temple, but this "buy-off" did not satisfy Sennacherib. He kept coming with threats against Jerusalem and all of Judah.

Sennacherib had said to Hezekiah, "Furthermore, have I come to attack and destroy this place without word from the Lord? the Lord himself told me to march against this country and destroy it" (2 Kings 18:25).

Being politically and spiritually astute, Hezekiah certainly was aware of the possibility of attack from Assyria even prior to his fourteenth year on the throne in Judah. But there was another factor that he believed made Judah more vulnerable to trouble and judgment than an aggressive foreign enemy. That factor was that the fathers of Judah were unfaithful and had done "evil in the eyes of the Lord." They shut the doors of the portico of the temple and "put out the lamps and did not burn incense or present any burnt offerings at the sanctuary to the God of Israel." "Therefore, the anger of the Lord had fallen on Judah and Jerusalem" (2 Chron. 29:6–8).

Hezekiah said further, "This is why our fathers have fallen by the sword and why our sons and daughters and our wives are in captivity. Now I intend to make a covenant with the Lord, the God of Israel, so that his fierce anger will turn away from us" (2 Chron. 29:9–10).

This was Hezekiah's outlook when he came to power and during his sixth year in power, and later in his reign:

> *He had seen the unfaithfulness of Ahaz* his father from the time he was a nine year old boy, an unfaithfulness that had lasted for sixteen years duration until he assumed the throne at the age of twenty-five.

> *He had witnessed the fall of Samaria* and the entire sister nation of Israel in his sixth year as king.

> *He knew Judah's capture was soon* on the agenda of Sennacherib's list, Sennacherib, who had communicated his interventions and plans clearly enough with the passage of time.

Lesson No. 2

Hezekiah came to the throne as a twenty-five-year-old young-and-godly king, with a strong plan and resolve to bring Judah back to the Lord and his protection and security. His plan would secure Judah's safety both from within and from without the borders of the land of Judah.

His resolve and intentions were expressed in these words, "Now I intend to make a covenant with the Lord, the God of Israel, so that his fierce anger will turn away from us" (2 Chron. 29:10).

The steps he took to work his plan were these:

> *Reform Judah's worship* by cleansing the temple.

Reorganize and reestablish the priests and Levites in their service to the people.

Have proper sacrifices made.

Have a Passover festival, all to be accompanied by singing, praise and instrumented music, all according to the laws of God and the customs established by David. By following these measures Hezekiah rebuilt the spiritual life of the nation. The people cooperated with their godly king and the Lord was with them throughout all these good endeavors.

"There was great joy in Jerusalem. . . . The priests and the Levites stood to bless the people, and God heard them, for their prayer reached heaven, his holy dwelling place" (2 Chron. 30:26–27).

We as Christian believers and leaders will do well to follow the wisdom of this king who believed, and rightly so, that a nation's basic security is best served by deepening its spiritual and moral roots, and taking measures that will bring it closer to God in its faith, holiness, and righteousness. He believed in the following: "Blessed is the nation whose God is the Lord" (Ps. 33:12) and, "Righteousness exalts a nation, but sin, is a disgrace to any people" (Prov. 14:34).

Lesson No. 3

In king Hezekiah's fourteenth year, with the spiritual foundations of Judah reestablished, and with the nation's communications with the Lord reconnected and idolatry abolished among the remnant and sin put away, the nation was now prepared to meet the crisis of Sennacherib's renewed threat to take over all of Judah.

In close contact with the prophet Isaiah and the backing of a newly revived spiritual people, the king kept the prophet informed concerning Sennacherib's threats and asked him to pray for Judah.

These two men next both sought the Lord when Sennacherib's threats continued and the Lord intervened and destroyed the Assyrian forces.

"King Hezekiah and the prophet Isaiah son of Amoz cried out in prayer to heaven about this. And the Lord sent an angel, who annihilated all the fighting men and the leaders and officers in the camp of the Assyrian king" (2 Chron. 32:20–21).

Judah's spiritual foundations had been reestablished, the Assyrian threat was past and Judah could continue as a nation for many more years.

God had worked through the man Hezekiah and his godly influence and leadership to extend Judah's life as a nation way beyond that of her sister nation of Israel.

Lesson No. 4

This account of Judah's deliverance from the Assyrian threat by means of God's supernatural intervention in the days of king Hezekiah and Isaiah the prophet may be a prelude to or at least a historical example of an event that is yet in the future of Israel's history. I refer to the invasion of Israel by Gog the chief prince of Meshech and Tubal.

This event is described and foretold in Ezekiel chapters thirty-eight and thirty-nine.

Many, many Bible scholars are on record as believing and teaching that this event, prophesied in Ezekiel, has never yet occurred and so is still in Israel's future.

Perhaps as intelligence begins to be gathered in future days by agencies in Israel and other places, and it begins to become clear that a massive invasion of Israel is imminent, Christian believers can have a part in praying and believing that the Lord will intervene in Israel's behalf in these last days, delivering them from the threat of the massive invasion that will involve many nations under the leadership of Gog, the chief prince of Meshech and Tubal.

Christian believers living in the city of Jerusalem and in other cities in Israel, including Messianic Jewish believers and others, would do well to be on the lookout for signs of this military invasion. They will be close to where the action will be and will be in a good position to have a part in the prayers and faith that God will use to bring about His great intervention on Israel's behalf.

Lesson No. 5

After king Hezekiah was healed and given fifteen more years of life, he allowed pride to enter his spirit and he failed to give thanks to the Lord for his healing. But soon afterwards this faithful man of God humbled himself and asked the Lord to forgive him.

The Lord forgave him and Hezekiah continued walking with the Lord for fifteen years, serving Him faithfully.

This experience of Hezekiah is both a reminder to us of the great importance of giving thanks to our Lord when He does good things for us. It also illustrates the serious dangers of allowing pride to enter our spirits. Also the king's experience is another example of the gracious forgiving mercy of our Lord and Savior.

MANASSEH—KING OF JUDAH

2 Chronicles 33:1–20

Manasseh was twelve years old when he became king and he reigned fifty-five years. He did evil in the eyes of the Lord, following the practices of the nations of Canaan before they had been driven out by Israel. He did the opposite of what his father Hezekiah had done. He built altars to the Baals; he worshiped the starry hosts, and he practiced sorcery and witchcraft. He also sacrificed his sons in the fire to a heathen god. In all these things he caused the Lord to be angry.

He led Judah and the people astray from the Lord into sin.

The Lord spoke to Manasseh and the people but they paid no attention, so God sent the Assyrian army commanders who took Manasseh prisoner. They bound him with brass shackles and imprisoned him in Babylon.

But in his distress, Manasseh humbled himself and prayed. The Lord heard his prayer and had him taken out of prison and restored to his throne in Jerusalem. He now knew that the Lord is God.

After his reenthronement he did many good things: He built up Judah's defenses; he began to throw out the idols; he restored the altar of the Lord and sacrificed offerings on it; he told the people to seek the Lord the God of Israel.

PRACTICAL LESSONS TO BE LEARNED FROM THE LIFE AND EXAMPLE OF MANASSEH, KING OF JUDAH

Lesson No. 1

Our heavenly Father will never turn away from one with a broken and contrite spirit.

That the Lord heard this king's humble entreaty while he was in prison, shackled as he was, illustrates the love and compassion of our wonderful God and Savior.

Although being an evil and wicked king for most of his career, when suffering imprisonment for his wickedness, he humbled himself before the Lord and prayed. He sought the Lord's favor.

God was "moved by his entreaty and listened to his plea." God brought him back to Jerusalem and to his throne. Now Manasseh knew that the Lord was God.

He began to do several good things that a good and godly king would do.

As we are told in Psalm fifty-one, "The sacrifices of God are a broken spirit, a broken and contrite heart O God, you will not despise" (Ps. 51:17).

Lesson No. 2

Notwithstanding the fact that Manasseh repented of his sins toward the end of his life, his wasted life illustrated the importance of one's seeking the Lord early in life.

During the course of his fifty-five year reign, most of his years were used to promote idolatry and evil among the people of Judah.

Regret for wasted and harmful years was the predominant feeling he undoubtedly carried with him in his years after coming back to the Lord.

Judah also never recovered from the extensive evil influence of king Manasseh's long evil reign over Judah.

He had been responsible for such extensive evils in Jerusalem and Judah that God had pronounced judgment on Judah during his reign—judgments which ultimately were executed upon the nation. Please see 2 Kings 23:26–27; 24:2–4 and Jeremiah 15:4.

Amon—King of Judah

2 Chronicles 33:21–25

Amon was twenty-two years old when he began to reign and he reigned two years. He did evil in the eyes of the Lord as his father Manasseh had done. But he never humbled himself as Manasseh had done. So his guilt only increased.

His officials plotted against him and assassinated him. Then the people of the land killed all of the officials who had assassinated him. His son Josiah became his successor on the throne.

Practical lessons to be learned from the life and example of Amon, King of Judah

Lesson

A wise man will learn from his father's mistakes, and a wise man will learn from his father's mistakes and evil life if his father turns from his mistakes and evil life and begins to live a godly and holy life.

Amon reigned two years and did evil in the eyes of the Lord as Manasseh had done, but he never humbled himself as his father had done.

Some sons learn from their father's mistakes as king Jotham did from Uzziah's mistakes. But Amon, sorrowfully, did not learn from Manasseh's conversion and godliness and so he did not follow the godly example that his father's conversion set before him, hence his guilt increased. "Amon's officials conspired against him and assassinated him in his palace" (2 Chron. 33:24).

Josiah—King of Judah

2 Chronicles 34; 36:1

Josiah was eight years old when he became king and he reigned thirty-one years. He did what was right in the eyes of the Lord, walking in the ways of his forefather David, not turning aside to the right hand or to the left.

In the eighth year of his reign, when he was sixteen, he began seeking the Lord, the God of David.

In the twelfth year of his reign he began to purge Judah and three tribal districts of Israel of all idols and heathen objects of worship. He went into cities of four districts outside of Judah—Ephraim, Manasseh, Naphtali, and Simeon. This was when he was twenty-years old.

In the eighteenth year of his reign he began to repair the temple. He used money that had been given by the remnant of Israel plus from the people of Judah and Jerusalem.

Two men, Jahath and Obadiah his assistant, were put in charge of all the temple repairs, also, other Levites were put in charge of other activities.

THE BOOK OF THE LAW FOUND

2 Chronicles 34:14

When the money was being brought out of the temple, Hilkiah the priest found the book of the law of the Lord that had been given through Moses.

This was told to the king and some of it was read to him. When the king heard it read, he tore is clothes, for he learned that the people were not obeying the things required of the Lord, so he sent Hilkiah and three others to inquire about this Book of the Law.

These men went to a godly prophetess, Hulda, who consulted the Lord concerning this Book of the Law and Judah's relationship to it.

The Lord's message to the king Josiah was that great judgment and punishment would be poured out on all Judah because of their neglect of God's covenant, but because Josiah had humbled himself, torn his robes and wept when he discovered the Book of the Law and Judah's disobedience to it, he would die in peace and not see the disastrous judgments that were to be poured out upon all of Judah (2 Chron. 34:19–28).

Upon receiving the message from the Lord through Hulda, the king called all Judah together to Jerusalem and he read from the Book of the Law that had been found in the temple.

He and all the people pledged themselves to walk in all the laws of the Lord. The people responded to his leadership and example and they followed the Lord the God of their fathers as long as Josiah ruled as their king (2 Chron. 344:29–33).

JOSIAH CELEBRATES THE PASSOVER

2 Chronicles 35:1–19

In the eighteenth year of his reign, Josiah and all Jerusalem and Judah and many from Israel celebrated the Passover. They endeavored to do everything according to the laws of Moses.

The Passover had not been so fully celebrated since the days of Samuel. "None of the kings of Israel had ever celebrated such a Passover as did Josiah, with the priests, the Levites and all Judah and Israel who were there with the people of Jerusalem" (2 Chron. 35:18).

THE DEATH OF JOSIAH

2 Chronicles 35:20–27

King Josiah interfered needlessly with Necho, the king of Egypt's military attack at Carchemish, in the east, near the Euphrates River. He was warned by the Egyptian king not to interfere, yet Josiah would not accept his warning. Hence, Josiah was soon shot with an arrow and was taken back to Jerusalem where he died.

He was buried in Jerusalem and all Judah and Jerusalem mourned for him.

His death and the shock and sorrow it brought to the people, became widely known and commemorated for years afterwards in traditional laments and songs sung by the people of Judah.

PRACTICAL LESSONS TO BE LEARNED FROM THE LIFE AND EXAMPLE OF JOSIAH, KING OF JUDAH

Lesson No. 1

Josiah at sixteen years of age began to seek the Lord, setting a good example for every young person today i.e. to begin seeking the Lord early in life.

This is something neither his father nor grandfather had done. Manasseh waited until he was past middle age to seek the Lord and Amon, his father, never did seek the Lord.

But Josiah apparently learned from the mistakes of his parent and grandparent and began to seek the Lord as a teenager of sixteen years.

He was following king Solomon's advice who said, "Remember your creator in the days of your youth" (Eccles. 12:1).

Lesson No. 2

Not only did Josiah begin to seek the Lord, but he also kept going in his following of the Lord after he began seeking Him.

We are told that "he did what was right in the eyes of the Lord and walked in the ways of his father David, not turning aside to the right or to the left" (2 Chron. 34:2).

Josiah went back in his history and chose a good model to follow—David.

Studying David's ways, he adopted them and made them his own. He wisely concluded that to be a success as a king he would choose and follow the basic approach of one of the best examples he could find.

This was a stroke of wisdom on Josiah's part.

Once he began following the Lord as David had done, he continued following steadfastly with daily discipline throughout all his life, not turning aside to the right or to the left i.e. he followed with dispatch and persevering determination.

He did what Solomon taught, "Make level paths for your feet and take only ways that are firm. Do not swerve to the right or to the left; keep your foot from evil" (Prov. 4:26–27).

And he did what the writer of Hebrews teaches us, ". . . let us run with perseverance the race marked out for us . . ." (Heb. 12:1).

And because Josiah made such a good and early beginning and then kept going, he pleased the Lord and succeeded as king.

What were some of the things he did as Judah's king?

Lesson No. 3

He began to take full advantage of his position as king and spiritual shepherd to bring his people away from idolatrous worship and back to the worship and service of the true God.

Some of the steps he took were these:

1. He read publicly all the words of the Book of the Covenant to Judah's elders, officials, priests, and Levites and others who gathered at the temple in Jerusalem.
2. He personally and publicly renewed his own covenant promise, in the presence of the Lord, to keep all the commands, regulations and decrees of the Lord, with all his heart and all his soul.
3. He asked all those present to renew their pledge of obedience to the laws and covenant of God, as he had done. The people followed his lead and did this.
4. He removed all the detestable idols from the territories of Jerusalem and Judah as he and the people were recommitting themselves to serve the God of Abraham, Isaac, and Jacob.
5. Arrangements were made to celebrate the Passover.

After this recommitment to the Lord, the people did not fail to follow the Lord as long as Josiah lived.

The Passover was soon celebrated by Josiah and all Judah, and many from Israel's territory joined in the celebration along with the people of Judah.

It was celebrated in the eighteenth year of Josiah's reign. It was an outstanding event and had not been so fully celebrated since the days of Samuel.

It was in the eighteenth year of Josiah's reign that the Book of the Law was rediscovered. The king and many of the people renewed their covenant with the Lord that same year that the Passover was celebrated in great fashion.

And during the years following these events we see a fully dedicated and consecrated young king come forth in Judah. His efforts were exemplary and pleasing to the Lord. Yet Judah's spiritual state before the Lord had declined so deeply during the years of her previous kings of Manasseh and Amon that Josiah's efforts were insufficient to bring her back into God's favor. God's anger against Judah still burned deeply and he had decided to remove Judah from His presence.

We read of this great and good king Josiah, "Neither before nor after Josiah was there a king like him who turned to the Lord as he did—with all his heart and with all his soul and with all his strength, in accordance with all the law of Moses.

"Nevertheless, the Lord did not turn away from the heat of his fierce anger, which burned against Judah because of all that Manasseh had done to provoke him to anger. So the Lord said, "I will remove Judah also from my presence as I removed Israel, and I will reject Jerusalem, the city I chose, and this temple, about which I said, 'There shall my name be'" (2 Kings 23:25:27).

This tells us that there are times when the best efforts of the best men are still insufficient to bring a nation back to God. This is when most of its people have allowed their hearts to become hardened and love their sinful ways more than the Lord's paths of obedience, peace, and holiness.

This was the attitude of the people in the days of king Josiah and the kings who followed him.

God had pronounced judgment upon them and they could not be recovered.

Jehoahaz—King of Judah
2 Chronicles 36:2–4

Jehoahaz was twenty-three years old when he became king of Judah. He was Josiah's son. He reigned three months and was dethroned by Necho, king of Egypt, Necho now appointed Eliakim, a brother of Jehoahaz as king in Jerusalem and he changed his name to Jehoiakim. Jehoahaz was carried off to Egypt.

Jehoiakim—King of Judah
2 Chronicles 36:5–8

Jehoiakim was twenty-five years old when he became king and he reigned in Jerusalem eleven years. He did evil in the eyes of the Lord, doing many detestable things.

Nebuchadnezzar attacked him and bound him in shackles and took him to Babylon along with valuable articles from the temple. He placed these articles in his temple in Babylon.

Jehoiachin—King of Judah
2 Chronicles 36:9–10

Jehoiachin was eighteen years old when he became king and he reigned three months and ten days. He did evil in the eyes of the Lord.

Nebuchadnezzar took him to Babylon along with valuable articles from the temple. He placed his uncle Zedekiah on the throne in Jerusalem.

Zedekiah—King of Judah
2 Chronicles 36:11–14

Zedekiah was twenty-one years old when he was made king in Jerusalem. He reigned eleven years and did evil in the eyes of the Lord and did not humble himself before the Lord after hearing the Lord's word spoken through Jeremiah. He became stiff-necked and hardened his heart, and would not turn to the Lord, the God of Israel. He also rebelled against king Nebuchadnezzar, who made him take an oath in God's name.

THE FALL OF JERUSALEM
2 Chronicles 36:15–23

The Lord had sent and spoken to the people of Judah many times, urging them to follow His laws and His paths, but the people would not listen.

They were warned to forsake their pagan idol worship. But again, the people only mocked and scoffed at the prophets who were speaking for the Lord.

Finally, there was no remedy!

God sent Nebuchadnezzar to punish Judah and to take many as prisoners to Babylon, also to kill many and ultimately to destroy and burn the temple of the Lord in Jerusalem, along with the palaces and other fine buildings there.

Judah became virtually uninhabited for seventy years while the people lived in Babylonian exile.

After seventy years, God roused Cyrus, the king of the newly empowered Medo-Persian Empire, to announce a restoration of the nation of Israel and a rebuilding of the temple of the Lord in Jerusalem.

Cyrus's proclamation was as follows, "This is what Cyrus king of Persia says: 'The Lord, the God of heaven, has given me all the kingdoms of the earth and he has appointed me to build a temple for him at Jerusalem in Judah. Anyone of his people among you—may the Lord his God be with him, and let him go up'" (2 Chron. 36:23).

PRACTICAL LESSON TO BE LEARNED FROM THE LIVES AND EXAMPLES OF THE FOLLOWING KINGS OF JUDAH

Lesson No. 1

The lives and reigns of these four men contributed to the final collapse of the nation of Judah. The evil influence of these men only served to continue and bring to a sad conclusion the evils that had accumulated in the reigns of Ahaz, Manasseh, and Amon.

These four kings presided over Judah during its final twenty-two-and-one-half-plus years. These were Judah's final declining years. They all did evil in the eyes of the Lord and would not listen to the Lord's messages given through his prophets.

Josiah, the last good king, had done his best to turn Judah away from her sins and to the Lord again but only a remnant responded to his efforts.

The previous reign of Manasseh, in particular, had influenced Judah more than any other to forsake the Lord and do evil and the people never recovered from the evils of that era.

As I have noted in the previous section on king Josiah, it was particularly due to Manasseh's evil leadership that turned the corner in Judah's spiritual decline from the Lord.

Note again the following scriptural assessment:

> Nevertheless, the Lord did not turn away from the heat of his fierce anger, which burned against Judah because of all that Manasseh had done to provoke him to anger. So the Lord said, "I will remove Judah also from my presence as I removed Israel, and I will reject Jerusalem, the city, I chose, and this temple, about which I said, 'There shall my name be.'"
>
> (2 Kings 23:25–27)

Judah had many good kings, such as Asa, Jehosaphat, Hezekiah, and others, but Judah had some evil kings also. The good kings always benefited and blessed the people, while the evil kings had the opposite effect of influencing the people to decline from the Lord, as a bad shepherd of sheep leads his sheep into much harm and loss.

The influence of Judah's good kings enabled the nation to outlast her sister nation of Israel by 136 years.

Lesson No. 2

Notwithstanding the final decline of both nations, the Lord was able to accomplish his vital purposes through the remnant of believers, godly kings, and prophets that remained true to the Lord despite the general spiritual decline that occurred in Israel's overall history.

The fall of Israel and its capital, Samaria was close to 722 B.C.

The fall of Judah and Jerusalem was approximately 586 B.C.

VII

Patterns from Those in Exile and the Return to Judah

VII

Patterns from Those in Exile

and the Return to Judah

EZRA

Ezra 1–10; Nehemiah 8–10

Seventy years passed after the fall of Jerusalem and all the land of Judah lay desolate while the exiles were living far away from their homeland.

After the seventy years had passed, the Lord moved upon Cyrus, the first king of the newly formed Medo-Persian Empire, to order a return of the Jewish exiles from Babylon and a rebuilding of the temple in Jerusalem.

The Lord moved upon many of the Jews there also to make the return to Judah and Jerusalem and begin to rebuild.

Cyrus provided finances and supplies for this rebuilding.

The rebuilding went well for a few years, but then ceased due to the opposition from the peoples living nearby Judah and Jerusalem.

Those who made up the opposition succeeded in persuading Cyrus's successor to order that the Jews cease building their temple. Consequently, for about fifteen years the building project in Jerusalem lay dormant.

Finally, after this long period of stoppage the Lord sent two prophets to the Jews in Judah telling them to begin the work again and to complete the rebuilding of the temple. The two prophets were Haggai and Zechariah.

After hearing from the Lord through the two prophets, the Jews began again to build, until opposition to their renewed efforts arose again.

The Jews were confronted again, but finally they wrote and sent a full explanatory letter to Darius of Persia, a letter in which they asked him to make a search for the original order decree of Cyrus. Darius ordered that such a search be made and Cyrus' original decree was found.

Then Darius wrote an order that, in accordance with Cyrus's decree, the Jews should resume their building and that no one should interfere with their work, and if they did interfere, severe penalties would follow.

Finally after much hard work and the help and encouragement of the two prophets, the work on the temple rebuilding was completed.

It was completed on the third day of the month of Adar in the sixth year of king Darius (Ezra 6:15).

All the people and their leaders celebrated the temple's completion with a solemn dedication ceremony along with many sacrifices and an installation of the priests and Levites in their worship duties.

Then the Passover was celebrated with great joy and thanksgiving.

After these things, during the reign of Arta-Xerxes, in the seventh year of his reign, Ezra came up from Babylon to Jerusalem to teach the laws of God to the people.

Ezra was a well-versed priest and teacher of the laws of the Lord.

Arta-Xerxes commissioned Ezra to go to Jerusalem to teach the people there the laws of God, to appoint magistrates and judges to administer justice to all the Jews.

He provided Ezra with all the money and other resources he would need to carry out this great task.

The hand of God was upon Ezra and the Lord had given Ezra favor and the backing of the great king and all of his high officials (Ezra 7:27–28).

A large number of Israelites and their families went with Ezra on their journey to Jerusalem from Babylon.

From the very beginning of their journey the hand of God was with Ezra and all those who journeyed with him. The Lord gave them protection from bandits along the way.

Before leaving on their journey to Jerusalem, Ezra proclaimed a fast, during which time they prayed for a safe journey for everyone including all their possessions.

God graciously answered their prayer at this time.

Before leaving Babylon Ezra took care to weigh out all the treasures of gold and silver that they were to give to those in Jerusalem; a careful and strict accounting of all these treasures was kept and delivered in Jerusalem (Ezra 8:28–34).

Soon after arriving in Judah, Ezra learned of the unfaithfulness of the leaders of the exile people. They had begun to intermarry with the peoples around Judah and Jerusalem. Therefore Ezra was humbled and prayed to the Lord a prayer of confession (Ezra 9).

While he was in a state of deep grief, discouragement, and bafflement, Shecaniah suggested to Ezra that there still was hope. He suggested that the people make a covenant with the Lord and send away all the foreign women who had been taken as wives by the Israelite men.

Ezra accepted this proposal and designated a certain number of days and selected family and division heads to talk to all who had married foreign women. Each case was dealt with separately and finally the entire problem was solved.

The officials put away their foreign wives and brought appropriate animal sacrifices to atone for the sins they had committed (Ezra 10).

NEHEMIAH

Nehemiah 1–13

Nehemiah was cupbearer to Arta-Xerxes, king of Persia. In the twentieth year of the king's reign, a Jewish brother came from Judah, along with some others. These men reported concerning the situation of the exiles who had returned to Jerusalem and Judah.

They said the walls were still in disrepair, the gates were still in a burned condition.

Upon hearing this report, Nehemiah wept and mourned and fasted for several days.

Then he prayed to the Lord, confessing Israel's sins and reminding the Lord of his conditional promise given through Moses, that if his people would repent and pray when they were scattered in some distant land, that God would hear their prayer and bring them back to their own land again.

Nehemiah also prayed for favor as he planned to go before the king and request some time away from his duties so he could go to Jerusalem and help the returnees with the rebuilding. Also he asked for letters to give to the governors of TransEuphrates and letters for timber supplies.

The king granted all of Nehemiah's requests, for the gracious hand of his God was upon him.

Nehemiah was first with the Heavenly King in prayer, and then he was second before the earthly king. Then he was third before his fellow Jews, for he was a starter of a great project.

After arriving at Jerusalem he inspected the walls at night without having yet told any of the officials there what he planned to do. It was in his heart to help with the rebuilding of all of Jerusalem's walls.

After his inspection tour Nehemiah spoke to the Jews there, exhorting them to begin rebuilding the walls. They agreed saying, "Let us start rebuilding" (Neh. 2:18).

So the work was started. Various groups of men took the lead in rebuilding the gates and wall sections.

The names of these leaders were recorded by Nehemiah and the names of the gates and wall sections that each group of men worked on were named by Nehemiah.

The listing of the names of these leaders and their fathers' names were along with a name or description of the wall section or gate name each group was rebuilding is significant. It was better to give their names and work descriptions than to merely say "A lot of Jews were repairing the wall." What Nehemiah did in using the men's names, dignified their tasks and added useful incentives and motivation to their work. It elevated its importance for their sake and for the sake of history.

OPPOSITION TO THE REBUILDING OF THE WALLS

Nehemiah 4

Opposition to the rebuilding of the walls of Jerusalem came from Sanballet the Horonite, from Tobiah the Ammonite, and from Geshom the Arab.

Plots by these enemies were afoot to fight against the Jews.

These enemies were also making insults against the work the Jews were doing. They did not want the work of the Jews to succeed.

Nehemiah, therefore, organized guards with weapons to protect the workers during the days, and took other security steps to protect against possible attacks by these enemies.

Some other serious problems arose among the people from wealthier Jews who were demanding the people take out mortgages on their homes, vineyards, and lands in order to buy grain and other foods for their families and these men were charging usury for their loans.

Nehemiah denounced these practices as wrong. The offenders promised to give back the properties they had taken plus the usury money.

To ensure compliance, Nehemiah, their governor, caused these of-fending men to give an oath to the priests that these wrongs would be corrected. The people thus kept their promises (Neh. 5:13).

As the governor of the Jews, Nehemiah did not make burdensome financial demands of the people as their previous governors had done. Nehemiah and his men did not eat the food allotted to them or endeavor to acquire land or money from the people because of their services there.

They rather helped with the wall rebuilding and were like St. Paul and his fellow apostles who in the New Testament era did not require financial support for their apostolic labors among the churches which they founded (Neh. 5:14–19).

Nehemiah and his men followed the above-mentioned policies during the twelve years he was their governor.

FURTHER OPPOSITION TO THE REBUILDING

Nehemiah 6

After the walls had been fully repaired, except for the doors that still needed to be set in the gate spaces, two of Nehemiah's enemies, Sanballet and Geshem, began sending invitations to him to come and meet with them in an agreed-upon village. But Nehemiah turned down their invitations, knowing their motive was to harm him.

At the fifth invitation a messenger came with an unsealed letter and a lying report within.

Nehemiah sent a reply saying he was on to them and all their false charges were "rubbish" so to speak.

Further attempts to oppose Nehemiah were made by hiring Jewish prophets and prophetesses to prophecy lies about him, so as to intimidate him and disturb his confidence.

But Nehemiah remained committed to the Lord and continued trusting Him and would not allow himself to be deceived or upset by his enemies.

After the doors had been set in all the gate areas, Nehemiah placed his brother Hanani in charge of Jerusalem, with Hananiah appointed as the commander of the citadel. Also he gave instructions concerning the opening of the gates and posting of guards by each of the gates and near some of the resident houses.

Next, the Lord put it in his heart to assemble the officials, nobles and common people for registration of everyone by families. The total number of people was about fifty-thousand, plus numerous animals—horses, mules, camels, and donkeys (Neh. 7:66–69).

EZRA READS THE LAW

Nehemiah 8

After the people had assembled from all the towns, Ezra began to read from the Book of the Law. He stood on a high wooden platform built especially for the purpose. Thirteen men stood with him atop this platform, some standing on his right hand and some standing on his left.

Upon hearing the law read, the people first wept, then later became quieter and began to experience great joy as they heard and understood the law of the Lord.

Later, the people brought tree branches and built for themselves booths and lived in them for several days in celebration of the Lord and reminders of their history and experiences with the Lord from earlier times.

THE ISRAELITES CONFESS THEIR SINS

Nehemiah 9

The people being together confessed their sins and the sins of their forefathers; they read from the Book of the Law and worshiped the Lord.

Many Levites were present with the people and prayer was made on behalf of all the people, a prayer that traced Israel's full history and noted God's great patience and forgiving compassion toward Israel even up to their present return to Judah again.

THE AGREEMENT OF THE PEOPLE

Nehemiah 10

After their time of confession, worship, and the joint prayer of all the people, they made a solemn agreement that they would keep the Lord's requirements and laws.

They made a binding agreement and put it in writing. The leaders and people placed their seal or signature to the written agreement and carefully listed the specific measures of the pact that was being agreed upon—to keep the laws and regulations that were given to Israel.

The officials of Judah lived in the city of Jerusalem and one of every ten of the population living in the other towns of Judah, by lot, was brought also to live in Jerusalem, so its population would be representatives of the cities of Judah. Also a general description of the population of all of Judah's towns is given i.e. families descended from Judah and Benjamin.

Also the genealogical lists of Judah's priests and Levites and gatekeepers who were organized to serve the nation at the temple in Jerusalem were made.

A list of the priests and Levites who had returned with Zerubbabel and Joshua was given.

Special note must be given to the careful recording of names of families and the names of those who were assigned positions of leadership and each leader had an assistant leader. This assured the smooth carrying out of responsibilities throughout the activities of the nation of Judah and smooth administering of services to the people. Also it provided harmony in all that was done.

There was a full and complete public dedication of the walls with two large choirs of singers and instruments marching atop the walls, praising the Lord. There was great joy and praise given to the Lord. "The women and children also rejoiced. The sound in Jerusalem could be heard far away" (Neh. 12:43b).

NEHEMIAH'S REFORMS

Nehemiah 13:1–31

1. During a reading from the Book of the Law of Moses, it was learned that no Ammonites or Moabites were allowed in the temple. Then it was discovered that Eliashib the priest had provided a large room for Tobiah the Ammonite.

When Nehemiah learned of this he was angry and cleared Tobiah's household things out of this room and brought in the provisions for the priests and Levites.

2. Provisions for the priests and Levites were not given to them. And Nehemiah rebuked the officials for this. He asked, "Why is the house of God neglected?" (Neh. 13:1). To correct this fault he assigned three men and an assistant to be responsible for maintaining the supply rooms for the priests and Levites. He chose these four men "because these men were considered trustworthy" (Neh. 13:13). See 7:2.

Nehemiah was obviously studying the characters of all the men of Judah, as he had opportunity to do so, and making an assessment of the men's trustworthiness.

3. He took steps to stop desecrating the Sabbath—men bringing merchandise into the city and selling it on the Sabbath.
4. Nehemiah rebuked some who were marrying foreign women—women from Ashdod, Ammon, and Moab.

He reminded these men of king Solomon's practice in this regard and how it had caused him to forsake the Lord. Solomon had married many foreign women (Neh. 13:23–27).

One of the sons of Joiada, the son of Eliashib, the high priest, was son-in-law to Sanballet the Horonite, was there. Nehemiah drove him away (Neh. 13:28).

From the first time we learned about Nehemiah, he was seen as a true reformer. He was aware of the mistakes and sins of Judah's past and now that they were making a new start as a nation, he was determined that all things should be done according to the book of Moses. He was determined that no former mistakes should be repeated. He did not want more wrath to be stirred up against Israel (Neh. 13:18).

Nehemiah was in many ways an Old Testament "Martin Luther."

Both Ezra and Nehemiah were reform-minded leaders. They both desired to see Israel reestablished as a holy, godly, and obedient nation again.

Together, they were working from the blueprint of God's holy law and covenant to see Israel living in all the will of God again, steering clear of the mistakes of their past.

Their goals were the same as those of some of the earlier godly kings of Israel and Judah such as David, Asa, Jehosaphat, Hezekiah, Josiah, and some others, men who used all their high position to influence their people to come as completely into God's place of blessing and favor as possible.

PRACTICAL LESSONS TO BE LEARNED FROM THE LIVES AND EXAMPLES OF EZRA AND NEHEMIAH

Lesson No. 1

God often communicates with heads of nations.

He revealed future events by dreams to Pharaoh in the days of Joseph. He revealed future events by dreams to Nebuchadnezzar in the days of Daniel.

He spoke often by His prophets to the kings of united Israel, Judah and the northern kingdom of Israel.

Now in the days of the Jewish exiles, God, "moved the heart of Cyrus" to the intent that the God of heaven desired him to build a temple for him in Jerusalem.

In the book of the prophet Isaiah, the Lord spoke to Cyrus as follows: "He is my shepherd and will accomplish all that I please, he will say of Jerusalem, 'Let it be rebuilt,' and of the temple, 'Let its foundations be laid'" (Isa. 44:28).

God took the initiative in the return of the Jewish exiles to Jerusalem and Judah.

This initiative had been predicted by the Lord through the prophet Jeremiah, and so Jeremiah's prophecy could be fulfilled, the Lord moved upon Cyrus, the founder of the Medo-Persian Empire to cause the exiled Jews to return again to Jerusalem and Judah and to determine that the temple should be rebuilt.

Along with Cyrus, the Lord moved upon the hearts of some of the Jewish exiles to return to Judah and begin the rebuilding.

Some of the leaders in the early days were Zerubbabel and Jeshua. Much later, God raised up Ezra and Nehemiah to strengthen the Jews in their efforts to make a new beginning as God's chosen people and nation.

Zerubbabel and Jeshua took the lead of the first group of exiles that returned to Jerusalem. After they had arrived there, they first built an altar and immediately began offering sacrifices on it to the Lord.

This was their first step. Soon afterward the people began rebuilding the foundations of the temple as Cyrus had authorized them to do. When the foundation was completed there was a great celebration and praise to the Lord by everyone.

But after some progress in the temple rebuilding, the work was stopped by their opposition. This opposition resulted in a fifteen-year delay in the work.

But after the Lord sent the two prophets, Haggai and Zechariah, the building was started again and finally completed.

It was about sixty years later that Ezra came from Babylon with a full and generous commission from Arta-Xerxes to teach the Jews there the laws of the God of Israel.

Ezra was a priest and teacher and a descendant of Aaron. He was well versed in the laws of Moses and well known to the king of Persia. The king had great confidence in his knowledge and ability. The hand of God was on Ezra and so the king commissioned him and provided everything he needed to make the journey to Jerusalem to teach the Jews. About fifty thousand men returned along with him.

He arrived in Jerusalem in the seventh year of Arta-Xerxes.

This generous provision of all Ezra's needs was a clear evidence that the Lord's hand was indeed with him.

The king's assistance to Ezra and those with him also included written orders to all the officials in TransEuphrates to assist him and the Jews who were rebuilding in Jerusalem and Judah with any needs they would make known to them.

Lesson No. 2

Nehemiah has set a good example for us in his use of prayer and fasting in a time of great concern.

He made use of prayer and fasting because of the urgency of his concern for the exiles in Jerusalem (Neh. 1:4–11).

Lesson No. 3

There may be times when we as men of God in advantageous positions in society or in government may use these positions to help the cause of God's people and kingdom. Nehemiah had a position in the Persian government as cupbearer of the king and he made use of his position to gain support and help for his fellow Jews.

He was a godly man who knew the Lord and was living in fellowship with Him.

Lesson No. 4

A basic qualification for the Lord to be able to use us is that we be men of character and godliness as Ezra and Nehemiah were, ready and willing to respond to any work he would call us to do.

Ezra and Nehemiah were acquainted with the laws of Moses and were committed to obeying these laws.

Ezra had gone before king Arta-Xerxes in the seventh year of his reign and the king had agreed to all Ezra asked him for and provided a decree of permission and pledge of provision of all his needs, including permission to have men travel with him to Jerusalem.

Nehemiah, in the twentieth year of Arta-Xerxes, was given permission, after he asked for it, to go to Jerusalem to help rebuild the walls and help the Israelites.

He prayed for favor with the king and obtained it along with letters that he requested.

Favor with this king, Arta-Xerxes, was granted to both men because they asked God for it and because the hand of God was on them both as they proceeded to help the returned Jews.

To accomplish the things they had in mind for the returnees, they needed the large support and authorization that only a powerful government leader could provide.

The movement concerning a restored Israel and Judah, began first with Cyrus, was helped forward by Darius, and later by Arta-Xerxes.

Lesson No. 5

In Ezra and Nehemiah the Lord has set before us a dual example of the great results that can come when godly men approach first the Heavenly King, our Lord, in believing prayer for favor with a powerful earthly king, or a comparable ruler.

Both men envisioned doing a great work for God's people, but a work for which they needed extensive authorizations and resources.

Both men went to the king of Persia who possessed everything they needed to accomplish their tasks.

Because the hand of God was upon them, both men obtained the king's full favor and everything they asked for—full authorization and all the resources they needed for their respective tasks. See Ezra 7:1–28 and Nehemiah 1:11; 2:1–8.

What God did for Ezra and Nehemiah He will do for believing men of God today who have been called to great tasks for which they need large authorizations and resources.

Without the earthly king's help these two men could not have accomplished their tasks, but with it they were able.

But their heavenly King, their God, had been petitioned first and because of His effectively disposing the mind and heart of the earthly king, all their needs were supplied and their assigned tasks were completed.

In American society today we cannot expect our federal government to do for us what the king of Persia did for Ezra and Nehemiah, but there are other sources of supplies to which we may go for personnel and resources in a large task the Lord has called us to undertake.

These are resources available and as we go to our Heavenly King with our petitions, he will provide for us all we need from sources known to him—sources he will make known to us.

An overall summary of the restoration of the exiled
Jews being formed into a viable nation again in their homeland,
after their seventy years of exile
presents the following elements:

1. God sovereignly spoke to Cyrus the founder of the Medo-Persian Empire to build a temple for the Lord in Jerusalem.

2. Zerubbabel, Jeshua and nine other men took the lead along with a large number of the exiles, and returned to Jerusalem and began to rebuild the temple.

   After some initial progress, there were delays due to opposition, but finally the temple was completed in 516 B.C.

3. About fifty-nine years later in 457 B.C. Ezra came to Jerusalem to teach the laws of Moses to the people.

   About fifty-thousand men came with him. His teaching and influence helped bring all those of the newly formed Jewish nation more in keeping with the laws of God.

4. Twelve years after Ezra's visit, Nehemiah came to Jerusalem in 445 B.C. He helped rebuild the walls and served as governor there for several years, finally to return to the Persian king for a brief time.

After being away from Jerusalem for a brief time, Nehemiah returned for a second visit (Neh. 13:6–7).

During all of Nehemiah's visits and service among the returned Jewish exiles, he encouraged the Jews and sought to bring the entire nation in line with every facet of the will of God for their lives.

He, like Ezra, was committed to the laws of Moses for all of the Jews. Both Nehemiah and Ezra knew that obedience to the laws of God in every part of the nation's life was the place where God's full blessing, his peace and prosperity and safety would be found. They both were eager to avoid the serious mistakes of Israel's past history.

Lesson. No. 6

In Ezra and Nehemiah the Lord has set before us another dual example of the great results that can come when godly men work from the blueprint of the Word of God in their endeavor to advance God's kingdom.

For Ezra and Nehemiah, it was the only "way to go" correctly with God's will and it is the "way to go" in present-day church planting among the unsaved or building up believers to a mature faith in an already planted, young and growing congregation.

Ezra and Nehemiah both followed God's blueprint of the Word of God and found success and so shall we today as we follow their example.

Both of these men, Ezra and Nehemiah, were strong men, completely committed to the inspiration and authority and importance of the laws of God as given to Moses.

Both men had obtained unusual favor and access to the Persian king of their day. This was clearly because the hand of God was upon them both. Also, God had worked wonders in the attitudes of Cyrus, Darius and Arta-Xerxes to help the Jews make a new beginning as a nation.

And he worked in the life of a fourth king named, Xerxes, in an entirely different setting, to help preserve the Jews from destruction in the same era in the case relating to Esther and Mordecai. This story is told us in the book of Esther.

Both Ezra and Nehemiah were men of great faith in God as well as a superb faith in God's written word and both had a desire to serve God fully.

Lesson No. 7

In Nehemiah's seeing through to its completion the rebuilding of the city walls of Jerusalem, we have a good example of perseverance, attention to personal detail, single-mindedness in supervising a difficult task that was beset with much opposition and danger. He refused to allow himself to be tricked or deceived by his enemies. The men worked with a trowel in one hand and a sword nearby for instant use in the other hand, if it were needed. Most all of the men did a superlative job of building until the wall was completed. Praise God!

ESTHER

Esther 1–10

Xerxes, one of the kings of the Medo-Persian Empire, arranged an elaborate display of his kingdom and glory for 180 days, concluded by a seven day banquet for all his officials. This was in the third year of his reign.

Toward the end of the banquet he called for his wife Vashti to come in and display her beauty, but she refused to come, so she was deposed of her queenship. Having been deposed, she in time was replaced by a beautiful Jewish girl named Esther.

Esther now was the king's favorite wife and queen.

Mordecai had raised Esther and was her guardian; very few if any were aware that Esther was Jewish except she and Mordecai.

Soon after Esther was chosen as queen of the empire Mordecai uncovered a plot by two of the king's officers to assassinate the king. The names of the two men involved in the plot were Bigthana and Teresh.

Mordecai reported the plot to Esther and she told the king about it, with credit for the tip off being given to Mordecai.

Upon investigation the truth of the plot was verified and the king had the two men hanged on a gallows.

Somewhat later the king promoted Haman, an Amalekite, to be second in the kingdom and the king commanded all his officials to bow to him as they would to the king himself, with a great posture of worship and reverence.

But Mordecai, who had a position in the kingdom, refused to bow to Haman. The reasons for his refusal to bow were religious, it being equivalent to idolatry—and perhaps also because Haman was an Amalekite, a member of an accursed people in Israel's history.

Haman, learning of Mordecai's refusal to bow, was angered and planned to kill not only Mordecai but all the Jews in all 127 provinces of the empire, perhaps surmising that all the Jews would adopt the same attitude toward him that Mordecai, the Jew, had adopted.

Haman obtained the king's approval for his plot to kill all the Jews.

Mordecai soon learned of Haman's plot and that a date had been set for its being carried out. So he conferred with Esther and asked her to go before the king and intercede for the Jews deliverance.

She agreed to do this, asking that Mordecai and others fast with her for three days prior to her going before the king.

On the third day she, dressed in her royal robes, and was invited by the king to come forward with her request.

Esther's first request was for the king and Haman to come to a banquet she had prepared.

Her second request was that the king and Haman come to a second banquet.

Haman was delighted at the attention he was receiving with now a second invitation to dine in the company of the king and the queen again. Yet he was still chagrined that Mordecai would not give honor to him when the two would meet.

Haman's wife suggested to him that he have a high gallows built and hang Mordecai on it.

Haman liked this idea very much so he ordered such a gallows to be built immediately.

That night the king could not sleep so he asked that the chronicles of his reign be brought in and reading these, he happened to read of Mordecai's discovering and report of the intended plot by the two doorman officers to assassinate the king.

Learning that Mordecai had never been rewarded for what he had done, he asked Haman for recommendations for rewarding "the man whom the king delights to honor."

Haman, believing the king had himself in mind, listed many glowing recommendations for such a man.

But the man who the king had in mind was Mordecai and not Haman.

After Haman had completed his glowing list of recommendations, the king ordered Haman to carry out all his recommendations for the Jew Mordecai and not for himself.

Haman left and did all he was told and had recommended—but now on Mordecai's behalf, and then he returned to his home with his head covered in grief. His wife and advisors said to him that since it was before Mordecai, of Jewish origin that his fall was beginning to take place, he would soon come to ruin.

Haman soon went to the second banquet that Esther had arranged for the king and for himself. At the banquet Esther made her third request of the king, that she and her people, the Jews, be spared from execution.

The king now discovered that Haman was the instigator of this massive crime, although the king himself had originally authorized it.

Nonetheless, Haman's fate was now decided. Although Haman begged Esther for mercy, the king soon ordered that Haman be hanged on the same seventy-five-foot-high gallows that Haman had planned for Mordecai.

Soon Haman was hanged on this gallows.

The Jews who were dispersed and scattered throughout the Medo-Persian Empire were in danger of being destroyed at this time, but this evil deed was never carried out.

Thank you, Lord, for providentially intervening and preventing this tragedy.

THE KING'S EDICT IN BEHALF OF THE JEWS

Esther 8

The thirteenth day of the twelfth month, the month Adar, was the day the king's edict was to be carried out. It gave the Jews the right to assemble and to defend themselves, to kill and destroy any armed force that would come against them intending to harm the Jews and their families, and also a right to plunder the properties of their enemies.

The thirteenth day of Adar, Purim and the fourteenth day, became days to commemorate in all succeeding generations of the Jewish people.

In all 127 provinces and in Susa, the Capital, the Jews destroyed their enemies.

In Susa 800 were killed, including Haman's ten sons, who were hanged on gallows.

In the other provinces 75,000 of the Jews enemies were killed, for a total of 75,800 killed.

This story shows how widespread the Jews had become in this far-flung empire—extending from India to the upper Nile area. It shows certainly and most prominently, the sovereign and providential hand of God in rescuing the Jewish people from an evil destruction.

Mordecai became very prominent in Susa and throughout the empire after these events. He became second to the king in position and power. He did much for the Jews and spoke up for their welfare (Esther 10:1–3).

PRACTICAL LESSONS TO BE LEARNED FROM THE LIVES AND EXAMPLES OF ESTHER AND MORDECAI

In the book of Esther we are shown the interconnectedness of a series of events, any one of which when viewed by itself may not have appeared very significant. But when the whole story was told we were able to see how each event fit into the whole. Then we saw how in the end the lives of thousands of Jews were saved from destruction.

First, Vashti the queen of the Persian Empire refused to go before the banqueters to show off her beauty and so was replaced by a beautiful girl who happened to be Jewish. Mordecai, her caretaker, had raised her from childhood.

Secondly, Mordecai, also Jewish, refused to bow to Haman for religious reasons and so an evil plot was made by Haman to kill not only Mordecai, the Jew, but all the Jews in the entire empire of 127 provinces.

Haman was obviously an evil-hearted man, but nonetheless, had been promoted to a position of tremendous influence in the kingdom, being next in power to the king himself.

Thirdly, and still providentially, Mordecai had learned of an assassination plot against the king and had reported it to Esther and she then had passed on this information to the king.

Fourthly. Later, the king could not sleep one night and reading the empire chronicles he learned what Mordecai had done in saving the king's life, and decided to reward him greatly for what he had done.

Later, Haman's evil intentions were brought to the attention of the king by Esther the queen, now in high position. Ultimately the planned destruction of the Jews was thwarted. Rather, those who hated the Jews in the empire were themselves put to death.

Jew hate has been present among the nations from the earliest days of Israel's nationhood because they are God's chosen people and satanic hatred manifests itself through nations that do not recognize the divine call of the Jewish people.

Although the Jews were a scattered people because of their unbelief and disobedience to the Lord, God still loved them and had not abandoned them. He saved their lives from destruction.

In the book of Esther we have a testimony and sharing of an example of God's love and care for the Jewish people.

We as Christian believers will do well to follow this example of our Lord and God, and love the Jewish people as he does and always let our attitudes and action show the same love and regard for God's chosen people as He has always had for them—a love and care which is dearly demonstrated in the book of Esther.

The Lord said to Abraham "I will bless those who bless you, and whoever curses you I will curse" (Gen. 12:3). This declaration concerning Abraham and his descendants applies in every age and to all people.

By working to save the lives of the Jews, Esther and Mordecai were blessing the Jews. They both had done a good work and God was pleased with what they had done, as God will be pleased with us, too, if we can help the Jews find salvation or we can help the Jews in other ways, as well, as Esther and Mordecai did.

Fifthly, since Esther was queen and thus close to the king, she told him of the close connection between herself and Mordecai—that he had been her caretaker and the one who had raised her from childhood.

The king thus promoted Mordecai to the position of being second to the king in power and authority. He became known throughout the empire and always spoke up in behalf of his people the Jews.

He had a position comparable to that of his fellow Jew, Daniel in the earlier Babylonian empire, and Joseph still earlier in the nation of Egypt, alongside Pharaoh.

In the story of Esther we see how clearly the Lord, first ordered a series of providential events to save the Jews from destruction and, second providentially prepared individuals—a beautiful Jewess and a committed and God-fearing Jewish man, Mordecai, who worked with the Lord to accomplish His purposes.

VIII

Patterns from the Life of Job

VIII

Job

Job 1–42; Ezekiel 14:14, 20; James 5:11

Job lived in an eastern land called Uz. Uz was thought to be a land between north Arabia and the Euphrates River. What was the probable era when Job lived? Most likely it was during the time of the patriarchs, the time of Isaac specifically. Job lived about two-hundred years.

We are told that Job was blameless and upright; "he feared God and shunned evil" (Job 1:1).

He and his wife had ten children, seven sons and three daughters.

He was very wealthy and was the greatest man in his district.

He had immense flocks of sheep, three thousand camels, 500 yokes of oxen, 500 donkeys and many servants.

Job's seven sons would take turns hosting feasts in their homes. They would invite the three sisters to these feasts and they would eat and drink.

After each time of feasting Job would send and have his sons and daughters purified and he would sacrifice a burnt offering for each of his ten children. He did this as a regular custom, as a precaution in case his children had sinned and cursed God in their hearts during their feasting and socializing together.

JOB'S FIRST TEST

Satan came into the presence of the Lord and the Lord asked if he had observed the godly life Job was living? Satan said to the Lord, "Does Job fear God for nothing . . . he is greatly blessed but stretch out your hand and strike everything he has, and he will surely curse you to your face" (Job 1:9–11).

The Lord then gave Satan permission to strike everything Job possessed but he was not allowed to touch his body.

Soon thereafter a series of messengers began coming to Job, reporting that first his oxen and donkeys and some of his servants were attacked by the Sabeans and carried off.

Next, he learned that fire had fallen from the sky and burned up his sheep and servants.

Then, three Chaldean raiding parties had come and taken his camels and killed more of his servants.

Lastly, he was told that a mighty wind had come in from the desert and the house of his oldest son was blown down while all his sons and daughters were feasting within and all were killed.

Upon hearing all these reports from the surviving messengers, we are told that Job,

> ". . . got up and tore his robe and shaved his head. Then he fell to the ground in worship and said: Naked I came from my mother's womb, and naked I will depart. The Lord gave and the Lord has taken away; may the name of the Lord be praised. In all this, Job did not sin by charging God with wrongdoing."
>
> (Job 1:20–22)

JOB'S SECOND TEST

Satan came before the Lord again and the Lord asked Satan if he had considered His servant Job? How he had maintained his integrity even though Satan had incited the Lord against him to ruin him without any reason?

Satan replied, "Skin for skin!" "A man will give all he has for his own life. But stretch out your hand and strike his flesh and bones, and he will surely curse you to your face."

The Lord said to Satan, "Very well, then, he is in your hands; but you must spare his life" (Job 2:4–6).

So Satan departed from the Lord's presence and afflicted Job with painful sores on his body from the soles of his feet to the top of his head. This affliction was perhaps elephantitus, a severe type of leprosy.

Now Job scraped himself with a piece of broken pottery and sat among some ashes.

His wife seeing him suggested that he curse God and die, but Job said to her, "You are talking like a foolish woman. Shall we accept good from God, and not trouble?" (Job 2:10).

In response to this second test also Job did not sin in what he said.

Godly Job was holding to his integrity through all these severe tests of his faith. He was vindicating the Lord's overwhelming pleasure and pride in His servant Job.

JOB'S THREE FRIENDS

Job 2:11–31
Eliphaz, Bildad, and Zophar

These three friends of Job were all older men and each man would soon speak in an effort to explain why he believed Job's family losses, his business losses and personal physical afflictions had come upon him.

Each friend speaks and in response to each speech Job makes his reply in course to each one.

These speeches or discourses between Job and his three friends occurred in three cycles. The first friend would speak and Job would make his reply. Then the second man would speak and Job would make his reply. Then the third friend would speak and Job would reply to the third friend, and so on. This cycle of speeches occurred three times.

After the three cycles of speeches were finished, Job gave a general reply to all three men. Afterwards a fourth friend, Elihu, spoke. Elihu was a much younger man than were the first three friends who spoke. That was the reason for his being the last friend to speak—his youth. But although he was the last friend to speak, he had been present from the very beginning of the discourses with Job. He had been closely listening to all that was said.

I. First cycle of speeches—Job 4:1–14:22

Job's opening statement

Job 3:1–24

Before any of the speeches of Job's friends were made, they sat silently around him for seven full days out of respect for Job and out of deference to the extreme suffering they saw he was going through. Nor did they even then speak, first but waited until finally Job himself made an opening statement.

Job's first utterance was to curse the day of his birth. "Why did I not perish at birth and die as I came from the womb?" (Job 3:11). If he had died at birth, Job said, "I would be asleep and at rest with kings and counselors of the earth . . ." (Job 3:13–14). He is miserable. He says, "I have no peace, no quietness; I have not rest, but only turmoil" (Job 3:26).

The speeches of Job's three friends begin after Job's opening statement. A brief summary of the three cycles of speeches are as follows:

First cycle of speeches Job 4:1–14:22

ELIPHAZ'S FIRST SPEECH

Job 4:1–5:27

He advises Job, "But if it were I, I would appeal to God. I would lay my cause before him" (Job 5:8). And he says, "Blessed is the man whom God corrects; so do not despise the discipline of the almighty" (Job 5:17). He lists seven calamities from which God will rescue Job. He says in a conclusion, "We have examined this and it is true. So hear it and apply it to yourself" (Job 5:27).

Eliphaz's discussion implies that Job is suffering because of his guilt. He "assumes that material prosperity will follow those who are upright and adversity will come upon evil doers."[4]

He hints that Job must have done some great sin to bring such suffering on himself (Job 4:1–12).

He suggests that it would be wise for Job to seek the Lord.

Then Job makes his reply to Eliphaz (Job 6–7).

BILDAD'S FIRST SPEECH

Job 8:1–22

Bildad believes the death of Job's children is a divine judgment, Job 8:4, and he urges Job to repent.

Then Job makes his reply to Bildad (Job 9–10).[5]

ZOPHAR'S FIRST SPEECH

Job 11:1–20

Zophar condemns Job's multitude of words and he calls him to task for holding to a position of integrity. He criticizes Job for believing and saying to God "My beliefs are flawless and I am pure in your sight" (Job 11:14), and he says of Job, "Know this: God has even forgotten some of your sins" (Job 11:6). And he says further,

---

[4]Young, *Introduction to the Old Testament*, p. 315
[5]Ibid.

"Yet if you devote your heart to him."

". . . and stretch out you hands to him, if you put away the sin that is in your hand and allow no evil to dwell in your tent, then you will lift up your face without shame; you will stand firm and without fear" (Job 11:13–15).

Then Job replies to Zophar (Job 12–14).

Job says, "Doubtless you are the people, and wisdom will die with you!" (Job 12:1).

"I have become a laughingstock to my friends, though I called upon God and he answered—a mere laughingstock, though righteous and blameless!" (Job 12:4).

And "My offenses will be sealed up in a bag; you will cover over my sin" (Job 14:17).

II. Second cycle of speeches—Job 15:1–21:34

Eliphaz's second speech
Job 15:1– 21:34

Eliphaz repeats his first platitudes and appeals to the wise and ancients as his authorities.

Job replies, "I have heard many things like these; miserable comforters are you all! Will your long-winded speeches never end? What ails you that you keep on arguing?" (Job 16:1–3).

"My spirit is broken, my days are cut short, the grave awaits me. Surely mockers surround me; my eyes must dwell on their hostility" (Job 17:1–2).

Bildad's second speech
Job 18:1–21

Bildad reproaches Job and continues with the basic pagan philosophy with which he began.

He says, "When will you end these speeches? Be sensible, and then we can talk. Why are we regarded as cattle and considered stupid in your sight?" (Job 18:1–3).

Job says in reply to Bildad and to the others also,

> "Have pity on me, my friends, have pity, for the hand of God has struck me. Why do you pursue me as God does? Will you never get enough of my flesh? . . . I know that my Redeemer lives, and that in the end he will stand upon the earth. And after my skin has been destroyed, yet in my flesh I will see God; I myself will see him. With my own eyes—I, and not another. How my heart yearns within me!"
>
> (Job 19:21–27)

III. THE THIRD CYCLE OF SPEECHES—JOB 22:1–31:40

ELIPHAZ'S THIRD SPEECH

Job 22:1–30

Eliphaz in this his third and final speech reaches a height of blasphemy he had not reached before. He urges Job to repent. He says, "Submit to God and be at peace with him; in this way prosperity will come to you. Accept instruction from his mouth and lay up his words in your heart. If you return to the almighty, you will be restored . . ." (Job 22:21–23a).

He says earlier in this third speech to Job, "Will you keep to the old path that evil men have trod? They were carried off before their time, their foundations washed away by a flood" (Job 22:15–16).

Here Eliphaz is placing Job in the same category as the wicked generation that was washed away by the flood in Noah's day.

In Job's reply to Eliphaz he refers to his frustration in not being able to go to God himself to state his case and defense before the Lord. He says, "I would state my case before him and fill my mouth with arguments" (Job 23:4).

Job is holding firmly to his integrity and innocence before the Lord. He says further, "But he knows the way I take; when he has tested me, I will come forth as gold" (Job 23:10).

BILDAD'S THIRD SPEECH

Job 25:1–6

Bildad has little or no argument against Job at this time. Perhaps he is giving here a mere protest. Its brevity may indicate he has exhausted his argument.[6]

ZOPHAR

Zophar has no reply at this time, but all of Job's three friends believe that he is self-righteous.

JOB'S FINAL REPLY TO HIS THREE FRIENDS

Job 26–31

Job now gives a final reply to his three friends. He says of them, "I will never admit you are in the right; till I die, I will not deny my integrity. I will maintain my righteousness and never let go of it; my conscience will not reproach me as long as I live" (Job 27:5–6).

Later Job asks, "But where can wisdom be found? Where does understanding dwell?" (Job 28:12).

He replies, "and he said to man, The fear of the Lord—that is wisdom, and to shun evil is understanding" (Job 28:28).

Job recalls his earlier days when he was in his prime and God blessed his household.

He was highly respected as a leader in his district. He fed the hungry, helped the orphans and widows. He "broke the fangs of the wicked." He comforted the mourners.

---

[6]See Young, *Introduction to the Old Testament*, p. 318.

He contrasts his former days with the attitudes of men toward him in his pitiable, afflicted state now. The lowest of persons mock him and sing songs of disdain about him. All his family and friends have turned against him.

In chapter thirty-one he lists over twenty sins he believes he is innocent of, beginning with a covenant he made to not look lustfully at a girl to breaking the spirit of his land tenants.

He believes he is innocent of all these sins.

The complete list comprises the defense of his integrity before God.

He says, "Oh, that I had someone to hear me! I sign now my defense—let the almighty answer me; let my accuser put his indictment in writing. Surely I would wear it on my shoulder, I would put it on like a crown" (Job 31:35–36).

Elihu's speech

Job 32:37

Up to this point Elihu has refrained from speaking out of deference to the ages of the first three friends of Job.

Elihu says, "I too will have my say; . . . reply (Job 32:17–20):

Elihu now speaks and a "boiled down" version of what he says is this:

He believes Job's three older friends have not answered his arguments thus Job still believes he is righteous in his own eyes. But Elihu, although young, believes he has understanding enough to refute Job and show a side of his case that has not been shown as yet.

Of Job he says, "To his sin he adds rebellion; scornfully he claps his hands among us and multiplies his words against God" (Job 34:37).

And he also says of Job, "So Job opens his mouth with empty talk; without knowledge he multiplies words" (Job 35:16).

According to Elihu's view, God is just even though he afflicts his people, since he is God. God will never do an injustice to anyone.

Job acquiesces; it would seem, to Elihu's views since he does not answer him. Also Elihu is not reprimanded by God in the end as Job's three other friends are.[7]

Elihu's speech seems to show some misunderstanding of Job's case but is not based upon as blatantly wrong philosophy as were the speeches of the three.

He maintains God's complete justice in bringing discipline on Job and believes it may bring about greater moral character after the discipline.

He does not assume Job has committed great evils as the other three friends did.

There is no reply by Job to Elihu.

THE LORD SPEAKS

Job 38:41; 42:1–17

The Lord addresses Job and soon begins to ask Job eighty-five to eighty-six questions about the processes of creation, about the snow, the hail, the rain, and about many of the animals and their habits.

Job is flabbergasted by these many questions.

He says, "My ears had heard of you but now my eyes have seen you. Therefore I despise myself and repent in dust and ashes" (Job 42:5–6).

---

[7]James, Fausset and Brown *Commentary on the Whole Bible* p. 309.

Job finally learns that God's infinite wisdom and purposes are behind the testings that come into the lives of godly persons. He learns that "all things work together for good to those that love God, to them that are called according to his purpose" (Rom. 8:28).

God affirms Job's integrity and Job has been humbled and his pride brought down.

Job's understanding of God is much broadened and he repents of the narrowness of his earlier understanding of God. He now knows that God is sovereign in his life even though his understanding of those purposes is still incomplete.

But now all is well.

God instructs the three friends to take sacrifices to Job and ask him to pray for them. This is further vindication of Job's innocence.

One of the purposes of the book of Job is to show Job's integrity and innocence.

GOD'S ESTIMATE OF JOB'S FRIENDS:

They had not spoken "what was right" concerning God as Job had done and that, had made God very angry with the three. They were to take the appropriate sacrifices to Job so their sins could be forgiven (Job 42:7–10).

PRACTICAL LESSONS TO BE LEARNED FROM THE LIFE AND EXAMPLE OF JOB

Lesson No. 1

Job's losses and physical sufferings were not due to God's punishment for some heinous sins he had committed.

Job's three elderly friends were close to being unanimous in their opinion that Job's own actions were the cause of his trouble. But Job, through all the discussions, maintained his integrity and innocence—an innocence and integrity that was in the end affirmed by the Lord Himself.

But the eighty-five to eighty-six questions asked Job by the Lord in chapters thirty-eight to forty-one left Job baffled and without strength. God had used Job's sufferings to broaden his understanding of the Lord and deepen his faith and spiritual life. They accomplished many, many good things in his life and made Job an example for all subsequent sufferers in the history of God's people.

In God's wisdom the Lord was accomplishing purposes in Job's life and character that Job could not understand but were necessary in God's sight.

The Lord accomplishes holy and necessary things in our lives, too, by the sufferings He often calls us to go through.

Some passages in the New Testament that speak to Christian believers on this subject are the following: Acts 14:22; Romans 5:3–5; 8:17–18; 1 Corinthians 4:17–18; 12:9–10; James 1:2–4; 5:10–11; Hebrews 12:9–11; 1 Peter 4:12–19.

From all these related passages I will quote one in particular that has been a special source of comfort and blessing to me personally throughout the years of my Christian walk.

But even though I quote only one of the passages listed, they all inform us of our expectation of suffering in the Christian life and its sanctifying purposes for us in the eyes of our gracious Lord and Savior.

The passage I shall quote is as follows:

> "For our light affliction, which is but for a moment, worketh for us a far more exceeding and eternal weight of glory; while we look not at the things which are seen: for the things which are seen are temporal; but the things which are not seen are eternal."
>
> (2 Cor. 4:17–18, KJV)

It is as if the Lord and our afflictions are in the back room of our house working and working for us, for weeks and months on end and they are still working:

Philippians 1:6 says, "Being confident of this very thing, that He which hath begun a good work in you will perform it until the day of Jesus Christ" (KJV).

We can be confident that any work the Lord begins He will continue with it until it is finished. That is just the way the Lord does things! He will not quit until the task that he began in our lives is finished. He will finish that which he began. "Bless you, Lord!"

"It took God seven days to make the heavens and the earth, the sun, the moon and the stars, Jupiter and Mars, but He's still working on me," is part of a song we sometimes hear and sing.

Lesson No. 2

Job, through all his sufferings, was patient as were the godly prophets who suffered through verbal and physical abuse as they delivered the messages God gave them to deliver to a people who were very often rebellious and unreceptive.

Job is held forth as one who was patient in the face of extreme suffering that those around him could not correctly explain or understand the reasons for. But though Job suffered severely, he refused to sin or deny the Lord as long as it lasted.

He finally was vindicated by the Lord and came forth with a deepened spiritual life and faith and a much better understanding of God than he had prior to his suffering (Ja. 5:10–11).

To order additional copies of this title call:
1-877-421-READ (7323)
or please visit our web site at
www.winepressbooks.com

If you enjoyed this quality custom published book,
drop by our web site for more books and information.

www.winepressgroup.com
"Your partner in custom publishing."

Bibliography

BOOKS, COMMENTARIES AND CHART

1. Jamieson, Fausset, Brown
   A Commentary on the Old and New Testaments Vol. I and II
   Zondervan Publishing House, Grand Rapids, Michigan.

2. Meyer, F.B.
   Great Men of the Bible Vol. II   Zondervan Publishing House,
   Grand Rapids, Michigan c. 1982. The Zondervan Corp. Meyer
   F. B. 1847–1929.

3. Young, Edward J.
   An Introduction to the Old Testament
   WMB. Eerdmans Publishing Co. Grand Rapids, Michigan.
   1954, c. 1939 Fifth Printing, 1954.

4. Chart: *The Prophets and Kings of Israel and Judah and the
   Restoration*
   Used by permission of Ray Ludwigson former
   professor of Bible at Wheaton College Wheaton, Ill.

Endorsements

In today's world of "role models", this book is an important antidote to worldly "hero worship." If ever we needed some clear examples of how to pattern and order our lives, it is today. The world presses in through music, TV, books, movies and the internet with all kinds of compelling voices calling for our allegiance and imitation.

For the Christian, this book can serve as a spiritual compass. It gives clear instruction regarding Godly perspective on life. These Biblical biographies clearly present living models and patterns for life, even in the 21st Century.

I highly recommend this book to all who are serious about knowing God and doing His will. I am convinced that Paul Ireland's book, Patterns for Living, read together with the bible, will assist every serious God seeker and follower to have what is needed "for life and godliness through our knowledge of Him." (II Peter 1:3)

Dr. Edward Neteland, Executive Director
Christian Association of Senior Adult Ministries (CASA)

"In a short, pithy, and clear style, Paul Ireland highlights the lives of Old Testament personalities and draws practical lessons from their struggles and lives. Sunday school teachers and others will find in its content a useful resource of information and rich applications for spiritual growth."

Dr. Peter Hintzoglou
Professor, Fuller Theological Seminary
Pasadena, California

The author presents practical lessons with principals for living life purposefully, extracted from the lives of those biblical persons as they lived their stories under the direct instructions of God. As the author writes he creates an atmosphere of free-flowing prose in context of biblical exposition highlighted by portable, understandable, interesting and discoverable truths for living life purposefully.

This is a must read book for all who desire to live an attractive, authorative life that reaches its highest potential, brings good to others, and glory to God!

There is definite help for the serious student. More so than that, these lessons help us discover the purpose for which we were created, as well as awaken a hunger in the soul to be all that God intended.

Rev. William Hemphill
Senior Pastor, Concord Baptist Church
Los Angeles, California